Turbo C®++ Programming

An Object-Oriented Approach

Turbo C®++ Programming

An Object-Oriented Approach

Ben Ezzell

Addison-Wesley Publishing Company, Inc.
Reading, Massachusetts Menlo Park, California New York
Don Mills, Ontario Wokingham, England Amsterdam Bonn Sydney
Singapore Tokyo Madrid San Juan

Copyright © 1990 by Ben Ezzell
ISBN 0-201-55023-7

Cover Design: Doliber Skeffington
Production Editor: Amorette Pedersen
Set in 11.5-point Times by Benchmark Productions

ABCDEFGHIJ-MW-943210
First Printing, July 1990

To Peter—who has been a good student in programming and an excellent *ahjahn* (teacher) in the language and customs of Thailand, where I have been residing while writing this book.

Also, to the people of ChiangMai (Thailand) who have been both kind and tolerant of a new *farahng* (foreigner) as he has struggled with unfamiliar language and customs. And to the many friends I have found here—all of whom have made me feel very welcome and very much at home in a fascinating land.

And last, but far from least, to Jack—who persuaded me to come (though only a minimum of persuasion was required).

TABLE OF CONTENTS

INTRODUCTION   xi

CHAPTER 1
AN INTRODUCTION TO OBJECTS   **1**
    Object-Oriented Practices   1
    Inheritance   2
    OOPTest1: Using Records   4
    OOPTest2: Using Objects   6
    Public, Protected, and Private Access   8
    Creating Methods   9
    Encapsulation   10
    Implementing Methods   12
    Program Organization   14
    OOPTest4: Using Polymorphism   16
    Summary   19

CHAPTER 2
CONSTRUCTOR AND DESTRUCTOR METHODS   **29**
    Introducing Constructor and Destructor Methods   29
    Defining a Constructor Method   32
    Implementing Constructor Methods   34

Declaring Object Instances with Constructors   35
From Theory to Practice   36
Where the Action Is   43
Summary   47

CHAPTER 3
VARIATIONS IN INHERITANCE   **63**
Base and Derived Class Access   63
Overriding Derived Access   65
Qualified Names   66
Multiple Inheritance   66
Friends of Classes   71
The this Reference   72
Summary   72

CHAPTER 4
AN OBJECT-ORIENTED MOUSE   **87**
The Case of the Bashful Mouse   87
Using an Object Include File   88
The Object Definitions   90
Method Implementations   92
The GMouse Method Implementations   99
The TMouse Methods   101
The Mouse Pointer Utility   104
Conventional Style Button Operations   105
Summary   108

CHAPTER 5
OBJECT BUTTON CONTROLS   **141**
Graphics and Text Button Operations   141
The TBoxes Unit   144
The Button Object   150
The Button Test Program   156
Summary   156

CHAPTER 6
EXTENDING OBJECTS IN C++   **183**
Object Data Abstraction   183
Extending Objects   185
Global Variables   190

Compiler Operations for Static Methods 191
Static Versus Virtual Methods 193
Summary 194

CHAPTER 7
VIRTUAL OBJECT METHODS **201**
The Virtual Method Table 201
Creating Virtual Methods 207
Summary 209

CHAPTER 8
SCROLLBARS AND OBJECT EXTENSIBILITY **215**
Object Extensibility 215
Programming for Extensibility 216
The ScrollBar Object 217
The ScrlTest Demo 230
Omissions 230
A Text-Mode ScrollBar 232
Summary 233

CHAPTER 9
DYNAMIC OBJECT INSTANCES **261**
Advantages of Dynamic Objects 261
Pointers to Objects 262
Allocation and Initialization 262
Disposing of Dynamic Objects 263
The Destructor Keyword 264
The Destructor Method 265
Destructor Tasks 266
Summary 268

CHAPTER 10
DYNAMIC OBJECTS AND LINKED LISTS **275**
A Brief Explanation of Pointers 276
Sorting Lists 277
The Precede Utility 281
The PHONE1 Demo Program 282
The PHONE2 Demo Program 290
The List Methods 291
Summary 295

CHAPTER 11
BINARY TREE OBJECTS   **315**
   Binary Tree Structures   315
   A Binary Tree Application   318
   Implementing a Binary Tree Object   321
   Building the Tree   322
   Disposing of the Tree   324
   Printing the Tree   326
   Binary Searches, Insertions, and Deletions   327
   Removing an Item From the Tree   330
   The RemoveLink Method   333
   Other Methods   337
   Summary   340

CHAPTER 12
MULTIPLE SEARCHES ON BINARY TREES   **357**
   Creating a Search Index   358
   Other Considerations   364

APPENDIX A
LINKED LISTS AND MIXED OBJECTS   **375**
   How Not To Do It   375
   Solutions and Suggestions   377
   A Trio of Demo Programs   378

APPENDIX B
OOP TERMINOLOGY   **401**

APPENDIX C
THE OBJECT MOUSE UTILITY   **409**
   General Mouse Procedures and Functions   410
   The Text Mouse Object   415
   The Graphics Mouse Object   415

INDEX   **417**

INTRODUCTION

Some things just keep getting better and better.

From the beginning, Turbo C 1.0 provided us with an excellent compiler and an integrated development environment. Later, version 2.0 added the graphics interface unit, graphics drivers, character sets and a host of support for all types of graphic applications. Now, Turbo C ++ provides new conveniences and power with the appearance of objects, programming elements that are capable of autonomous actions and decisions.

Object-oriented programming is far more than simply a catch-phrase or advertising gimmick. It is a genuine departure from previous programming methods, offering new capabilities and new conveniences that were lacking in all except a few specialized languages.

More importantly, for most programmers object-oriented programming is the realization of a dream—the actualization of what we have always felt, suspected, and wished programming should really be.

Now it is!

All This and More

Object-oriented programming capabilities are not all that Turbo C++ has to offer. AT&T's version 2.0 of C++ is the most important of the new features, but Turbo C++ also provides: a full implementation of the latest ANSI C standard, a new integrated development environment (IDE) complete with mouse support, multiple, overlapping windows and a multi-file editor (demonstrated by an on-line Tour program), a Virtual Run-time Object-Oriented Memory Manager (VROOMM), on-line hypertext help complete with cut-and-paste program examples, and a host of new library functions including heap checking and BCD math functions.

Topics and Contents

While Borland has provided a plethora of new features, this book will not attempt to provide a complete guide to everything in Turbo C++. The principal subject of this book is object-oriented programming as implemented by Turbo C++.

In order to demonstrate the capabilities of C++, the examples used in this book will begin with a few simple object implementations and then expand into more complex objects showing additional features and capabilities inherent in the object-programming concept. In this fashion, instead of having to wade through a completely new example for each new concept introduced, the basic program concepts will remain constant through several subsequent examples.

The disk accompanying this volume contains a variety of additional object-oriented program examples that provide further suggestions or illustrations or may simply be used as starting points for your own object-oriented implementations.

Enough introductions. Let the fun begin!

CHAPTER 1

AN INTRODUCTION TO OBJECTS

In common parlance, an object is anything at all—a rock, a shadow, a tree or even an abstract concept or thought. Programming objects possess both characteristic *attributes* and *behaviors*. A shadow possesses the attribute of being dark and the behavior of always appearing opposite to a light source. Programming objects also possess attributes that are unique to the object (for example, data) and possess specific responses to environmental changes (functions for example).

Given this extension of the traditional C lexicon of combining data structures and programming responses to create objects, objects become autonomous entities which possess both information and responses. They provide us with programming tools that have a new scope of capabilities. However, objects also possess other characteristics that are important to understand, both in theory and in practice.

Object-Oriented Practices

In this chapter, several example programs will be used to demonstrate the basic elements of object-oriented programming without using any overly complex tasks. At the same time, the precepts governing object-oriented programming will be explained and illustrated, together with possible problems and pitfalls.

First, here is an overview of the three principal properties which dominate object-oriented programming: inheritance, encapsulation, and polymorphism.

- *Inheritance* is a property of objects, allowing the creation of a hierarchy of objects with descendants inheriting access to their ancestors' code and data structures.
- *Encapsulation* is modularity applied to data, combining record structures with procedures and functions, called *methods*, which manipulate the record data, forming a new data type called an *object*.
- *Polymorphism* is the property of sharing a single action (and action name) throughout an object hierarchy. Using polymorphism, each object in the hierarchy implements the action in a manner appropriate to its specific requirements.

Inheritance

Much of science is concerned with hierarchies and relationships (or artificial relationships) between objects. Fossil archaeologists look for relationships between extinct species and historians record events and dynasties and seek to understand relationships between causes and events. Biologists classify insects, plants, and animals by taxonomy; genealogists draw and study family trees; and stock market analysts study price fluctuations. All of these are studies of relationships between individual events, studies that may provide predictive information.

All of these charts, however, are based on the concept that objects lower in the hierarchy are influenced by, inherit characteristics from, or are descended from those above them in the chart.

Figure 1-1 shows a classification hierarchy for objects of type *vehicle*. On the top level, we find the object "vehicles." In the first generation of descendants, the vehicles object is broken down into four very different operating mediums: water, land, air, and space, which seem to have little in common.

Objects in each of these second-generation categories have inherited one principal characteristic from their parent object; each has the characteristic defined as "vehicle" and, therefore, has inherited a property (powered mobility) which separates a vehicle from other devices such as computers, furniture, or houses.

Figure 1-1: A Vehicular Family Tree

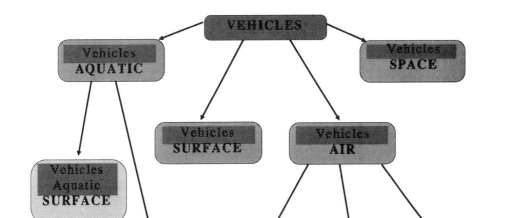

In the third generation, objects of the class "surface" and "submarine" appear below "aquatic," but both have inherited the characteristics "vehicle" and "aquatic" from their parent generation. This classification tree can be carried further and in each case a specific object inherits all of the characteristics that defined its parent object and its parent's parent.

Object Inheritance by Declaration

As an example of how object inheritance operates, four variable types have been declared in Table 1-1. On the left they are declared as struct (record) types and on the right, as object types.

Table 1-1: Record Declarations versus Object Declarations

RECORD DECLARATION	OBJECT DECLARATION
`struct { int x,` `        int y;`	`class location` `        {  int x, y;   }`

RECORD DECLARATION	OBJECT DECLARATION

```
        } location;

struct { location where;        class point : public location
         int color;                    { int color;  };
       } point;

struct { point  pixel;          class rect : public point
         int sx, sy;                  {  int  sx, sy;  };
       } rect;
struct { point  pixel;          class circl : public point
         int rx;                      {  int rx;  };
       } circl;
struct { point  pixel;          class ellip : public circl
         int rx, ry;                  {  int ry;  };
       } ellip;
```

In Figure 1-2, the four object variables appear in a tree relationship. As you can see, these four variable types can be declared either as records or as objects. The advantage of declaring them as objects is not because the source code is slightly shorter (the .EXE code will be slightly longer); instead, look at the two source code listings for OOP-Test1 and OOPTest2.

OOPTest1: Using Records

In the first example, the variables are declared as record types similar to the examples in the left column of Table 1-1, and in the second example, as object types similar to the examples in the right column of Table 1-1.

```
//============================//
//  OOPTest1 Program Listing  //
//  using record structures   //
//============================//
```

```
#include <iostream.h>
#include <conio.h>
#include <stdio.h>
```

```
typedef   struct  {   int x;
                      int y;   } location;
typedef   struct  {   location  pixel;
                      int color;           } point;
typedef   struct  {   point    place;
                      int      radius;     } circle;

main()
{
   location   testpt;
   circle     acircle;

   testpt.x = 10;
   testpt.y = 20;
```

Figure 1-2: An Object Hierarchy with Inheritance

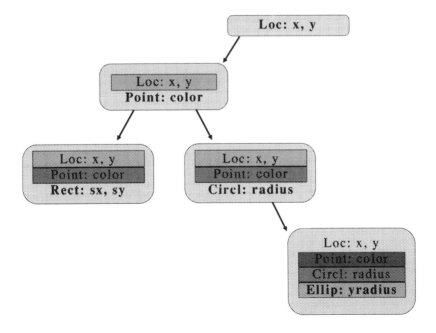

Assigning values to the TestPt variable is simple (and it should also be a familiar practice), but the values for the variable ACircle are not so easily referenced. For example:

```
acircle.x = 30;
acircle.color   = 50;
```

where the instructions attempt to reference the field elements x and color, will produce errors informing you that these elements are not part of the structure. Instead, for the structured variable, the entire genealogy of the record structure has to be explicitly referenced both to assign values:

```
acircle.place.pixel.x = 30;
acircle.place.pixel.y = 40;
acircle.place.color   = 50;
acircle.radius        = 60;
```

and to subsequently access the assigned values:

```
clrscr();
printf( "acircle.place.pixel.x is %d\n",
        acircle.place.pixel.x );
printf( "acircle.place.pixel.y is %d\n",
        acircle.place.pixel.y );
printf( "acircle.place.color   is %d\n",
        acircle.place.color );
printf( "acircle.radius        is %d\n",
        acircle.radius );
printf( "testpt.x              is %d\n", testpt.x );
printf( "testpt.y              is %d\n", testpt.y );
getch();
}
```

OOPTest2: Using Objects

In this second example, the same record structures and variables are created, but this time the variables are defined as classes (objects).

```
//================================//
//    OOPTest2 Program Listing    //
//    from records to objects     //
//================================//
```

```cpp
#include <iostream.h>
#include <conio.h>
#include <stdio.h>

class location {  int x;
                  int y;            };
class point : public location
              {  int   color;    };
class circle : public point
              {  int   radius;   };
```

Notice that class point and class circle are followed by a colon and the name of an ancestor class, identifying each as a descendant of a specific ancestor object class; location in the first case and point in the second. Unlike humans, objects normally have only one immediate ancestor though multiple inheritance is permitted in C++ (and will be discussed later).

At this point, the object type circle has inherited the same equivalent data fields as if it had been declared as:

```cpp
typedef struct {  int x, y, color, radius;  } circle;
```

In this simple example equivalence is easy, but as the object types become less simple, equivalence will be less apparent and less real. For the moment, however, let's continue with the example:

```cpp
main()
{
    location   testpt;
    circle     acircle;

    testpt.x = 10;
    testpt.y = 20;
    acircle.place.pixel.x = 30;
    acircle.place.pixel.y = 40;
```

```
acircle.place.color    = 50;
acircle.radius         = 60;
```

At this point, the analogy to a record structure no longer holds valid and OOPTest2.CPP will compile with multiple error messages informing you, in most cases, that the referenced fields are not members of the class referenced.

What's happening here?

Public, Protected, and Private Access

If you are familiar with object-oriented programming in Turbo Pascal, you are probably aware that dot-referencing of object data fields is permitted even though it is not considered sound programming. In Turbo C++, however, the concepts of public, protected, and private, control access to object fields and to object methods.

Private means, quite simply, that the data elements are directly accessible only within an object and in order for values to be assigned to or read from an object's data fields, methods must be defined to explicitly access these data elements. By default, object data fields are always private. Both data and methods may be explicitly declared private using the keyword private: or may simply be private by default if no other level of access has been assigned.

Protected is a second level of access, less restrictive than private, and allows derived classes (descendant classes) to make direct access to the private data elements of a base class (ancestor class). The keyword protected: is used to set this level of access.

Public is the third level of access and is normally used just for methods. Data elements may also be given public scope, making them accessible—by dot-referencing—outside of the object itself. For such general access, the keyword public: is required and is also commonly used in declaring the ancestor of a descendant object class.

Remember, unless protected or public access is specified, data elements and methods are private by default. However, each access specification may appear one or more times and in any order.

In OOPTest2, the data elements are private by default and inaccessible since no methods have yet been created. These methods will be introduced momentarily.

Object Inheritance Terminology

In the example OOPTest2, the record type Loc was declared as an object type (class) and the variables testpt and acircle became object variables or instances of objects.

The object class location is the ancestor of the object class point, while the object class circle is the descendant of point, which is the descendant of location.

In Figure 1-2 both circl and rect are descendants of point. Normally, sibling relationships are irrelevant and only descendants and ancestry and the inheritance from ancestor to descendant are important, though there are exceptions and they will be discussed later.

Creating Methods

In object-oriented programming, *methods* or *object methods* are the equivalent of functions in conventional programming and consist of functions similar to the conventional and familiar, but which work in a new way. As with all programming, using methods requires recognition of their capacities and limitations.

In their simplest form, methods provide the means by which you assign and access object data elements. In OOPTest2 the data elements within the several objects were not accessible; therefore, in OOPTest3 methods will be provided to access these data elements, both to assign values to them and to retrieve current values:

```
//==============================//
//    OOPTest3 Program Listing   //
//    adding Method definitions  //
//==============================//

#include <iostream.h>
#include <conio.h>
#include <stdio.h>

class location {  int x;
                  int y;
   public: void  set_x( int xval );
           void  set_y( int yval );
           int   get_x();
           int   get_y();                };
```

In this version, class location is provided with four method declarations to permit access to the x and y data elements. Note that only the method declaration appears in the definition of the object—the implementation for each method will appear separately.

Also, pay special attention to the statement public: which declares that these methods are accessible outside of the object; for example, they can be called by other procedures as well as methods belonging to this specific object. Later, other objects will be created with methods that are either private or protected and can only be accessed within the object (or the object's descendants) by other methods.

Encapsulation

Encapsulation refers to the process of combining both code and data into an object, as demonstrated by the examples in OOPTest3.

Some object-oriented languages, such as Turbo Pascal 5.5, do not enforce encapsulation while others, such as Smalltalk or Turbo C++, enforce strict encapsulation. Where encapsulation is enforced, data elements belonging to an object are only accessible through the methods provided with the object. If no method is provided to read or write an object's data element from outside the object, then the data cannot be directly accessed by the programmer.

In object-oriented programming (in theory) it should be unnecessary to ever access an object's internal data fields directly. The programmer should always provide methods to access objects' internal data fields. With C++, this is enforced and direct access-prevented.

Object-oriented programming has the ability to create libraries that extend C's inherent capabilities and these libraries can be distributed for use by other programmers. As a result, it is doubly important for proper access methods to be provided and for these methods to be documented. Because encapsulation is enforced, it is also important that each object provide at least minimal methods for access for each data element.

Otherwise, if a method is provided to set a data element but no method is provided to later retrieve that element, the resulting object may work, but only up to the point where a subsequent descendant object finds it necessary to access some data element where no method has been provided.

Also, even though encapsulation is enforced, it may also be helpful for the data fields belonging to objects (and their identifiers) to be documented.

Distributing object libraries is a topic of its own and will be covered later in more detail. For the moment, keep in mind that any object-oriented library can be distributed and, even if you develop objects only for your own use and never distribute the "raw" object libraries, the demands of proper encapsulation and proper methods should still be observed. A few examples of the possible pitfalls in object-oriented programming will be shown in later examples.

Scope and Limitation

In Turbo C++, data elements within an object are private and can only be accessed from outside the object via public methods. At the same time, all data elements and all methods within an object are accessible to all methods within the object or its descendants (subject to inheritance declarations of public or private). Methods belonging to an object may also be private and therefore, can only be accessed by other methods within the object but not by external reference.

Again, setting the scope of a method is done using the declaration public:.

```
class point : public location
{   int   color;
    public: void   set_color( int cval );
            int    get_color();                  };
```

In the second object definition, class point is defined as a descendant of class location but adds a new data element called int color, and two new methods to assign and access the value of color. Remember, as a descendant of location, point automatically inherits the x and y data elements and all of location's methods accessing these data elements.

```
class circle : public point
{   int   radius;
    public: void   set_radius( int rval );
            int    get_radius();                 };
```

In a similar fashion, class circle is defined as a descendant of point, and adds a new data element, radius, and two methods to access radius but also inherits from point and location.

Implementing Methods

After methods have been declared, it is also necessary to provide an implementation for each method—a definition of how a specific method accomplishes its intended task.

```
                              // methods for location class //
void location::set_x( int xval )  { x = xval; }
void location::set_y( int yval )  { y = yval; }
int  location::get_x()  {  return( x );  }
int  location::get_y()  {  return( y );  }
```

The preceding method implementations are similar to conventional function definitions, with one important difference: each method is explicitly linked to its object using the name of the object and the scope access (or resolution) operator ::.

```
                              // methods for point class //
void  point::set_color( int cval )  { color = cval; }
int   point::get_color()  {  return( color );  }
```

In similar fashion, the method implementations for point, (above) and circle (below) define how each method operates and each is explicitly linked to its appropriate object class.

```
                              // methods for circle class //
void  circle::set_radius( int rval ) { radius = rval; }
int   circle::get_radius()  {  return( radius );  }
                              // end of methods //
```

After defining the method implementations, OOPTest3 duplicates the exercise begun in OOPTest1, now using dot-references to the object methods instead of using extended dot-referencing to access the data record fields.

```
main()
{
   location  testpt;
   circle    acircle;

   testpt.set_x( 10 );
```

```
    testpt.set_y( 20 );
    acircle.set_x( 30 );
    acircle.set_y( 40 );
    acircle.set_color( 50 );
    acircle.set_radius( 60 );
    clrscr();
    printf( "acircle.x      is %d\n", acircle.get_x() );
    printf( "acircle.y      is %d\n", acircle.get_y() );
    printf( "acircle.color  is %d\n",
                                acircle.get_color() );
    printf( "acircle.radius is %d\n",
                                acircle.get_radius() );
    printf( "testpt.x       is %d\n",  testpt.get_x() );
    printf( "testpt.y       is %d\n",  testpt.get_y() );
    getch();
}
```

Notice that acircle.get_y() and testpt.get_y() return separate values even though the same method name is called in both cases and the only method implementation defined for get_y() belongs to location. However, acircle and testpt are separate instances of objects and each has its own data records. Precisely the same thing is true if I created several instances of a single object type; each instance has its own data records even though the method implementation is shared between the several instances. This is also true between instances of different object types.

In Pascal, a shorthand reference format is often used where instead of saying:

```
    testpt.set_x( 10 );
    testpt.set_y( 20 );
```

the with statement would be used as:

```
with testpt do
begin
    set_x( 10 );
    set_y( 20 );
end;
```

Since the with statement is not supported in C, each method call must be explicitly dot-referenced with the object name.

Even lacking the with statement, the explicit references did work. However, using separate and specific statements to assign values to each data field is a tedious and repetitive process at best and in real programming practices, can quickly become an annoyance. Alternatives such as employing the characteristic of *polymorphism* will be demonstrated shortly.

Program Organization

A variant program organization is being used for the demo programs in this book; primarily for purposes of explanation and not because object-oriented programming requires any special variation in style. A general program structure appears in Figure 1-3.

Notice that the type declaration for each object is followed immediately by the object's method definitions, however, the method implementations themselves appear later and are grouped together. Only after all of the objects have been defined are the global variables, the non-object procedures, and the functions listed.

There is no firm rule requiring this organization of the program listing. The program's global variables could appear at the beginning and then the object declarations could be grouped together with the method definitions following, or the global variables could follow the type declarations. The overall structure is generally unimportant and the organization shown is intended to group elements for your convenience in reference.

There is a secondary reason for this organization. When defining methods for objects, the programmer should be particularly careful to ensure that all variables are local to the method (that is, local to the procedure or function), with the exception of those variables that belong specifically to the object.

For several reasons, global variables should never be referenced by an object's methods. First, it's difficult to ensure that a global variable is not incompatible with the object's use. Second, using a global variable directly or indirectly circumvents the concept of encapsulation. Third, any object using a global variable is not cleanly transportable (as with the Mouse and Button objects which will be created in Chapter 2, but transported for use in subsequent programs).

One method of ensuring that global variables are not accidentally utilized by methods is to have a program's global variable declarations follow the object and method definitions. Exceptions will occur if for any reason this organization or any of these guidelines prove impractical.

Figure 1-3: Demo Program Organization

Program header,
  include references, etc.

class location
    data elements
    method definitions

class point : public location
    data elements
    method definitions

class circle : public point
    data elements
    method definitions

implementation for object methods
    location
    point
    circle

global variables,
typedefs, etc.

other procedures, functions
  main procedure

C and C++ Conventions

So far, and continuing through out this chapter, several conventions of C and C++ programming have been deliberately ignored in order to make the examples used here as clear as possible. These conventions are: object definitions are normally placed in a separate header file using the .h extension; the implementation for an object's methods are commonly found in a separate file using the .CPP extension and; the program

using the defined objects also appears as a separate source file using the
.cpp extension.

In addition to following standard C practices and customs, these
conventions also provide certain advantages. Following conventional
usage, the .h header files are available for reference as #include
"xxxx.h" in the main programs using the defined objects. At the same
time, compile times and program source sizes are reduced since the
objects can be precompiled separately from the main programs.

As a further advantage—and also one of the principal strengths of
object-oriented programming—objects created in this way are reusable
and can be called on by several programs without requiring recompila-
tion for each. (In Turbo Pascal, objects are treated in a similar manner
by compiling as units, .TPU files, rather than .OBJ files.)

These first example programs are intended to demonstrate the basic
principals of object-oriented programming and are certainly not designed for reusability. Therefore, they have been created using single,
rather than multiple, source code files. In later examples, programs will
be created and presented using the conventional C/C++ multiple file
sources.

Having exhausted this explanation, I'll return to the real business at
hand: object-oriented programming.

OOPTest4: Using Polymorphism

The term *polymorphism* is taken from Greek, meaning "many shaped."
It is a method of giving an action a single name that is shared throughout
an object hierarchy, but accomplishes the named action in different
fashions (as appropriate to the specific object referenced by the action).

In OOPTest3, three objects were created that used multiple methods
to reference individual data elements—a practice which is both necessary and desirable since you may wish to set or access only specific data
elements. However, having to call each method individually for each
data element is not always desirable, nor is individual access always
necessary. More often, and particularly when an object is first created
or used, you'll want to set all of an object's data elements (or most of
an object's data elements) at one time.

The obvious alternative is to create a procedure (method) containing
generalized assignment statements and to pass data assignments to
objects as parameter lists rather than using individual method calls to
initialize each data variable within an object. Therefore, in OOPTest4,
three new methods are created.

```
//==============================//
//   OOPTest4 Program Listing   //
//     new method definitions   //
//==============================//

                              ... as per OOPTest3 ...

class location
{
   protected:  int x;
               int y;
      public:  void  create( int xval, int yval );
                       ... remaining methods per OOPTest3 ...
};

class point : public location
{
   protected: int   color;
      public: void create( int xval, int yval, int cval);
                       ... remaining methods per OOPTest3 ...
};

class circle : public point
{
   protected: int   radius;
      public: void create( int xval, int yval,
                           int cval, int rval );
                       ... remaining methods per OOPTest3 ...
};

// methods for location class //

void location::create( int xval, int yval )
{
   x = xval;
   y = yval;
}
                       ... remaining methods per OOPTest3 ...
```

Providing location with a single method called with two parameters is not particularly different from similar practices in conventional C programming and, as in other circumstances, default values can also be supplied.

```
// methods for point class //

void point::create( int xval, int yval, int cval )
{
   location::create( xval, yval );
   color = cval;
}
                              ... remaining methods per OOPTest3 ...
```

For the point object, the same method name, create, is repeated without conflict (through polymorphism) because each instance of create belongs to a different object (class). However, rather than having point::create set the values for x and y, location::create is called with these values and only the remaining argument is handled directly.

```
// methods for circle class //

void circle::create( int xval, int yval,
                     int cval, int rval )
{
   point::create( xval, yval, cval );
   radius = rval;
}
                              ... remaining methods per OOPTest3 ...
```

In a similar fashion, circle::create handles the rval parameter directly, passing the remaining arguments to point::create which, in turn, passes two of the arguments to location::create, and all is accomplished quite neatly.

```
main()
{
   location   testpt;
   circle     acircle;
```

```
testpt.create( 10, 20 );
acircle.create( 30, 40, 50, 60 );
```
... see OOPTest3 ...
```
}
```

The original six instructions required in OOPTest3 are replaced by two instructions accomplishing the same tasks, while the remainder of the OOPTest4 demo program (not shown here) is essentially the same as OOPTest3.

The redeclaration of the create method is an example of polymorphism; the name of the method and its general function are inherited, but the specific implementation for each method version has been redefined for the new object. In future examples, polymorphism will be used extensively to carry a method name forward though several generations of objects while defining new specifics for each. (See the "Virtual Methods" section in Chapter 5.)

In other cases, methods such as get_color and set_color will not be redefined for descendant objects but will simply be inherited without revision when the essential function does not require adaptations.

Summary

You've been introduced to the basics of object-oriented programming and shown how static objects are defined and simple methods are implemented.

In Chapter 2, two new types of methods, constructor and destructor methods, which are used to initialize objects and to deallocate objects when they are no longer needed, will be introduced. At the same time, the previously theoretically-oriented demo programs will be revised to provide a more practically-oriented example of object capabilities.

In Chapter 3, variations on method and data element inheritance will be demonstrated.

Following are the complete source codes for the principal demo programs used in this chapter. These may also be found on the disk accompanying this volume.

```
//==============================//
//   OOPTest1 Program Listing   //
//   using record structures    //
//==============================//
```

```
#include <iostream.h>

#include <conio.h>

#include <stdio.h>

typedef  struct {  int x;

                   int y;   } location;
typedef  struct {  location  pixel;

                   int color;          } point;
typedef  struct {  point   place;

                   int     radius;    } circle;

main()
{
    location   testpt;
    circle     acircle;

    testpt.x = 10;
    testpt.y = 20;
    acircle.place.pixel.x = 30;
    acircle.place.pixel.y = 40;
    acircle.place.color   = 50;
    acircle.radius        = 60;
    clrscr();
    printf( "acircle.place.pixel.x is %d\n",
        acircle.place.pixel.x );
    printf( "acircle.place.pixel.y is %d\n",
```

```
        acircle.place.pixel.y );
    printf( "acircle.place.color    is %d\n",
        acircle.place.color );
    printf( "acircle.radius         is %d\n",
        acircle.radius );
    printf( "testpt.x               is %d\n", testpt.x );
    printf( "testpt.y               is %d\n", testpt.y );
    getch();
}


            //=============================//
            //   OOPTest2 Program Listing   //
            //   from records to objects    //
            //=============================//
#include <iostream.h>

#include <conio.h>

#include <stdio.h>

class location {  int x;

                  int y;  };       // notice that no methods //
class point :                      // are yet defined for    //
   public location                 // any of these objects   //
          {  int  color;  };       // therefore, this code    //
class circle : public point        // will produce a total    //
          {  int  radius; };       // of twelve errors ...     //
```

```
main()

{

    location   testpt;

    circle     acircle;

    testpt.x = 10;

    testpt.y = 20;

    acircle.place.pixel.x = 30;

    acircle.place.pixel.y = 40;

    acircle.place.color   = 50;

    acircle.radius         = 60;

    clrscr();

    printf( "acircle.place.pixel.x is %d\n",

        acircle.place.pixel.x );

    printf( "acircle.place.pixel.y is %d\n",

        acircle.place.pixel.y );

    printf( "acircle.place.color   is %d\n",

        acircle.place.color );

    printf( "acircle.radius        is %d\n",

        acircle.radius );

    printf( "testpt.x              is %d\n", testpt.x );

    printf( "testpt.y              is %d\n", testpt.y );

    getch();

}
```

```
//==============================//
//   OOPTest3 Program Listing   //
//   adding Method definitions  //
//==============================//

#include <iostream.h>

#include <conio.h>

#include <stdio.h>

class location {  int x;

                  int y;

     public: void  put_x( int xval );

             void  put_y( int yval );

             int   get_x();

             int   get_y();                };
class point : public location

             {  int  color;

     public:    void  put_color( int cval );

               int   get_color();             };
class circle : public point

             {  int      radius;

     public:     void  put_radius( int rval );

               int   get_radius();            };

             // methods for location class //
void location::put_x( int xval )   { x = xval; }

void location::put_y( int yval )   { y = yval; }
```

```
int  location::get_x()  {  return( x );  }

int  location::get_y()  {  return( y );  }

                // methods for point class //
void  point::put_color( int cval )  { color = cval; }

int   point::get_color()  {  return( color );  }

                // methods for circle class //
void  circle::put_radius( int rval ) { radius = rval; }

int   circle::get_radius()  {  return( radius );  }

                // end of methods //

main()

{

   location   testpt;

   circle      acircle;

   testpt.put_x( 10 );

   testpt.put_y( 20 );

   acircle.put_x( 30 );

   acircle.put_y( 40 );

   acircle.put_color( 50 );

   acircle.put_radius( 60 );

   clrscr();

   printf("acircle.x      is %d\n", acircle.get_x() );

   printf("acircle.y      is %d\n", acircle.get_y() );

   printf("acircle.color  is %d\n", acircle.get_color());
```

```
    printf("acircle.radius is %d\n",

                            acircle.get_radius() );

    printf( "testpt.x      is %d\n", testpt.get_x() );

    printf( "testpt.y      is %d\n", testpt.get_y() );

    getch();

}


                //==============================//
                //    OOPTest4 Program Listing   //
                //   adding polymorphic methods  //
                //==============================//

#include <iostream.h>

#include <conio.h>

#include <stdio.h>

class location

{

    protected:

        int x;

        int y;

    public:

        void  create( int xval, int yval );

        void  set_x( int xval );

        void  set_y( int yval );

        int   get_x();

        int   get_y();
```

```
};

class point : public location
{
   protected:
      int   color;
   public:
      void   create( int xval, int yval, int cval );
      void   set_color( int cval );
      int    get_color();
};

class circle : public point
{
   protected:
      int   size;
   public:
      void   create( int xval, int yval,
                        int cval, int rval );
      void   set_size( int rval );
      int    get_size();
};

                // methods for location class //
void location::create( int xval, int yval )
   {   x = xval;   y = yval;   }
```

```
void location::set_x( int xval )  {  x = xval;  }

void location::set_y( int yval )  {  y = yval;  }

int  location::get_x()  {  return( x );  }

int  location::get_y()  {  return( y );  }

               // methods for point class //
void point::create( int xval, int yval, int cval )

{

   location::create( xval, yval );

   color = cval;

}

void point::set_color( int cval )  {  color = cval;  }

int  point::get_color()  {  return( color );  }

               // methods for circle class //
void circle::create( int xval, int yval,
                     int cval, int rval )

{

   point::create( xval, yval, cval );

   size = rval;

}

void circle::set_size( int rval )  {  size = rval;  }

int  circle::get_size()  {  return( size );  }
```

```
                    // end of methods //

main()

{

    location   testpt;

    circle     acircle;

    testpt.create( 10, 20 );

    acircle.create( 30, 40, 50, 60 );

    clrscr();

    printf( "acircle.x     is %d\n", acircle.get_x() );

    printf( "acircle.y     is %d\n", acircle.get_y() );

    printf( "acircle.color is %d\n", acircle.get_color());

    printf( "acircle.size  is %d\n", acircle.get_size() );

    printf( "testpt.x      is %d\n", testpt.get_x() );

    printf( "testpt.y      is %d\n", testpt.get_y() );

    getch();

}
```

CHAPTER 2

CONSTRUCTOR AND DESTRUCTOR METHODS

In addition to data elements and methods, which are analagous to conventional records and procedures as shown in Chapter 1, objects usually possess special methods called *constructor* and *destructor* methods. These methods are essential for initializing and disposing of virtual objects and, in the case of constructor methods, are also valid for static object instances.

In this chapter, these method types and virtual object instances will be introduced and explained. Also, a final version of OOPTest will be created in order to use the object types in a practical rather than theoretical application.

Introducing Constructor and Destructor Methods

The objects illustrated so far have been implicitly static; that is, memory is permanently allocated for each object instance when the program is compiled and remains allocated until the program terminates, just as is done for static variables.

Frequently, distinct advantages lie in creating dynamic objects; allocating memory for each object instance only so long as the object is needed and then, after the object's usefulness is past, freeing the allocated memory for reuse.

The principal reason for having constructor and destructor methods is to provide a convenient and practical means of allocating and deallocating memory for dynamic objects and of initializing an object or (through the destructor method) of cleaning up after an object.

C++ imposes a few constraints on objects that possess constructor methods. (For static objects, destructor methods are optional, but recommended.) If a class has a constructor, the constructor is always used to initialize instances of the object when they are created or declared.

The constructor method name is the same as the name of the object class. Destructor method names are also the same as the object class except that these are prefaced by the tilde character (~). Hence, the destructor method is the compliment of the constructor method. (In object-oriented Pascal, constructor and destructor methods may have any name, but are generally titled Init and Done.)

While constructor methods can be defined as private (but should not be), destructor methods must *never* be defined private; they must always be public.

Constructor and destructor methods do not return any type of value, not even void. While this violates conventional C wisdom and standards, it is necessary in C++ practices. It is only true for constructor and destructor methods—all other methods follow the standard practice of returning some sort of value.

If an object possesses a constructor method, static declarations of object instances or arrays of object instances must be explicitly initialized when declared (see OOPTest5). For arrays of objects, they must be explicitly declared static with a default initialization (see OOPTest6).

Constructor methods can be called with arguments to initialize individual object instances, but for arrays of object instances, alternate constructor methods may be required to supply default arguments (see "Overloading Constructors").

It is recommended that object constructors reference ancestor constructor methods rather than setting inherited values directly.

While constructor methods may be called either explicitly or implicitly, destructor methods can only be called implicitly. (For more details, see Chapter 8.)

Constructors and destructors share the characteristics of other object method types, but have certain unique features:

- Constructors and destructors do not return values and do not have return value declaration.

- Constructors and destructors cannot be inherited although descendant (derived) classes can call ancestor (base) class constructors and destructor methods.
- Constructors may have multiple definitions.
- Constructors may possess default arguments, may call object initialization methods, or both.
- Constructor methods cannot be virtual methods.
- Destructor methods may be declared as virtual, but all destructor methods for classes derived from ancestors with virtual destructor methods are implicitly virtual.
- When constructor and destructor methods have not been explicitly defined, they may be generated implicitly by the compiler. When implicitly generated, constructor and destructor methods are always public.
- Addresses for constructor and destructor methods cannot be taken.
- Constructor and destructor methods may be implicitly invoked when declaring or destroying an object instance. This will occur without any explicit references within a program.
- Constructors are invoked when local or temporary object instances are created. If the object class has one or more constructor methods defined, one of these will be invoked; otherwise, a constructor will be implicitly created by the compiler.
- The constructor method creates and initializes the object instance.
- Constructor methods will, when allocation is required, make implicit calls to the new operator.
- Destructors are invoked when object instances go out of scope.
- The destructor method reverses the constructor process by destroying the created object instance.
- Destructor methods will, when deallocation is required, make implicit calls to the delete operator.
- When pointers to object instances go out of scope, destructor methods are not implicitly called. Instead, the delete operator must be called explicitly to destroy the object instance.
- Objects with constructor or destructor methods cannot be members of a union.
- When exit is called within a program, destructors for local elements within the current scope are not called. Global elements are destroyed in their normal sequence.

- When abort is called within a program, no destructors are called.
- Destructor methods may be explicitly invoked indirectly through a call to delete, or directly by using the destructor's full, qualified name.
- The delete operator is used to destroy object instances which have been allocated using new. But explicit calls to the destructor method are required for object instances allocated specific addresses through calls to new.
- The declaration for location follows previous examples except, instead of declaring the method create, two constructor methods are declared, both named location, but with different calling parameters. This is a practice known as *overloading*.

Defining a Constructor Method

The demo program OOPTest5 shows one form of defining and using constructor methods, beginning with the object location declaration:

```
class location
{
    protected:
        int x;
        int y;
    public:
        location() { x = 0; y = 0; }
        location( int xval, int yval );
        void    set_x( int xval );
        void    set_y( int yval );
        int     get_x();
        int     get_y();
};
```

Overloading Functions

Overloading is a practice allowing the same function name to be used in different implementations as long as the implementations can be distinguished by the type or number of calling parameters. In this fashion, a single function name can be called to perform some abstract operation using different types of operands rather than having to create distinct function names for each version.

This practice is particularly useful in C++, where multiple constructor methods may be necessary. However, as previously stated, constructor methods must be given the same name as the object class.

Thus, if location() is called, either implicitly or explicitly, the first constructor method is used and default values assigned. If location(...) is called with specific parameters, the second constructor method is called to assign those parameters.

In Turbo C++, an explicit overload declaration is not required though other versions of C and C++ may require specification.

Inline Functions

The default constructor, location(), also provides an example of an inline function definition:

```
location () { x = 0; y = 0; }
```

Since the implementation of the function is brief, instead of providing a separate implementation definition, the necessary instructions are given immediately following the declaration.

Another example of an inline function definition appears in the declaration of the point object as:

```
point ()   { x = 0; y = 0; color = 0; }
```

but could also be written as:

```
point ()  : location (), { color = 0; }
```

In this second form, location() is referenced to handle the default assignments for x and y and only color is implemented within the method declaration. Notice, however, the comma following location(). Also note that the direct assignment of values to x and y in the first point constructor is only possible because these object elements were defined as protected, rather than being private by default. If these object elements were private then the second form of the constructor would be mandatory.

As with the overload specifier, Turbo C++ does not require an explicit inline specification, though other versions of C and C++ may behave in a different fashion.

Inline Disadvantages

While any function may be defined inline and inline expansion does not change the semantics of the function call, the optimization of the function call depends on the capabilities of the compiler and how the call is made. However, an inline function can be used only in the file where it is defined since the definition must be visible at the point of call. For inline functions to be used across files, they should be included in a header file.

Implementing Constructor Methods

In OOPTest5, all of the constructor methods have been overloaded. Two versions of each, each with the same function name, have been declared, but one version of each has been implemented by inline definition. This leaves the remaining versions to be implemented in accordance with the usual practices:

```
location::location( int xval, int yval )
{
    x = xval;
    y = yval;
}

point::point( int xval, int yval, int cval ) :
    location( xval, yval )
{
    color = cval;
}
```

This second point constructor follows the practice of referencing the location constructor to set the x and y values. In like fashion, the circle constructor references the point constructor, passing back the arguments for xval, yval, and cval, but setting the size value directly:

```
circle::circle( int xval, int yval, int cval, int rval )
    : point( xval, yval, cval )
{
    size = rval;
}
```

Since the various object elements were all declared as protected, these assignments could have been made directly in all cases but it is probably better practice to make such assignments indirectly, via ancestor methods and constructor references.

Notice also that none of these constructors, neither here in the implementation nor in the preceding declarations, are prefaced with a return value type—not even void—because *constructor and destructor methods do not return any type of value.*

The remaining method definitions are essentially the same as for previous examples.

Declaring Object Instances with Constructors

I stated previously that if a class has a constructor, the constructor is *always* used to initialize instances of the object when they are created or declared. This initialization, however, is usually implicit rather than explicit, as shown in the main procedure in OOPTest5:

```
main()
{
    location   testpt( 10, 20 );
    circle     acircle( 30, 40, 50, 60 );
```

Two object instances are declared here—testpt, which is object type location, and acircle, which is object type circle—and each is declared with a parameter list, initializing the object's data fields.

These are examples of implicit initialization since the methods location::location and circle::circle are never called explicitly, but are implied by the declaration of object instances. There are also some special hazards in such implicit initialization. These hazards, and ways to avoid them, will be shown in a moment.

First, the objects testpt and acircle could also have been declared using the empty constructor:

```
main()
{
    location   testpt();
    circle     acircle();
```

initializing the object fields as zero (the default values in this case), and then having other values assigned in subsequent instructions. And this is essentially what will be done in OOPTest6.

From Theory to Practice

The object examples used so far have been treated as if they were little more than data records. This is fine for demonstrating various idiosyncracies and requirements in handling objects; objects per se can be much more than data records, and are far more useful and interesting.

Therefore, in OOPTest6, the mundane will be discarded in favor of the interesting and colorful and, while objects are hardly limited to graphics applications, graphics are an excellent medium for demonstrating object capabilities.

In the previous examples, however, very little has been done to give the objects in question any real graphics capabilities. In OOPTest6, new methods will have to be defined to provide these features:

```
class Location
{
   protected:
      int x;
      int y;
   public:
      Location() { x = 0; y = 0; }
      Location( int xval, int yval );
      void   create( int xval, int yval );
      void   set_x( int xval );
      void   set_y( int yval );
      int    get_x();
      int    get_y();
};
```

The declaration of object class Location remains pretty much the same but with the addition of one new method, create, and the change in the name itself from location to Location—which will be explained in the section "Subtle Errors: #1." Of course, the two constructor methods have also been renamed to correspond to the capitalization of the object class title.

The object class Point is also carried forward from previous examples, but like Location is now capitalized and has acquired three new methods: create, draw, and erase. These methods will provide the foundations for screen image capabilities.

```
class Point : public Location
{
    protected:
        int   color;
    public:
        Point() { x = 0; y = 0; color = 0; }
        Point( int xval, int yval, int cval )
            : Location( xval, yval ), { color = cval; }
        void   create( int xval, int yval, int cval );
        void   draw();
        void   erase();
        void   move( int ptx, int pty );
        void   set_color( int cval );
        int    get_color();
};
```

In this version, both constructor methods have been defined using inline code and, therefore, do not appear in the method implementation section where the remaining methods are given their functional capabilities.

The object class Circle inherits Point's methods but redefines the create, draw, erase, and set_color methods before adding its own set_size and get_size methods.

```
class Circle : public Point
{
    protected:
        int   size;
    public:
        Circle() { x = 0; y = 0; color = 0; size = 0; }
        Circle( int xval, int yval, int cval, int rval );
        void   create( int xval, int yval,
                       int cval, int rval );
```

```
        void   draw();
        void   erase();
        void   set_color( int cval );
        void   set_size( int rval );
        int    get_size();
};
```

Several methods are duplicated here for descendant object types because each is required to handle similar tasks in slightly different fashions. This duplication will also occur in the Square object, following. However, in object-oriented programming, reusability rather than duplication is the custom and the current duplication of effort is temporary. In Chapter 5, virtual methods will be introduced which can be used to rewrite OOPTest6 without these redundancies. Virtual methods, while simple to use, are not simple to explain and will be discussed later.

```
class Square : public Point
{
   protected:
      int   size;
   public:
      Square() { x = 0; y = 0; color = 0; size = 0; }
      Square( int xval, int yval, int cval, int rval );
      void   create( int xval, int yval,
                        int cval, int rval );
      void   draw();
      void   erase();
      void   set_color( int cval );
      void   set_size( int rval );
      int    get_size();
};
```

Subtle Error #1: Name Conflicts

The objects location, point, and circle, are now being renamed as Location, Point, and Circle to avoid a conflict. For Location and Point, the change is simply to maintain consistency because it is the Circle object where the conflict appears.

In earlier examples, since the graphics.h header was not used, circle was perfectly acceptable as an object name. Now, since the graphics.h file must be called on to provide the appropriate screen functions, a conflict occurs between the name circle for an object and the name circle as a graphics function.

In object-oriented Pascal, this conflict would be done away with by simply allowing the object definition of circle to override the graphics function circle and then reaching the latter function from within an instance of object circle by dot-referencing the graphic function as graphics.circle(...).

The C++ compiler, however, does not permit such overrides and distinctions but it does differentiate between upper- and lowercase identifiers. By capitalizing the object names, the conflict is removed, both for circle vs Circle and for square vs Square. Capitalize object types and method names as a means of preventing conflicts with existing function names (which are always lowercase).

Method Implementations, Continued

Having declared the several object types and their appropriate methods, method implementations must also be supplied for each. As you should recall, two constructor methods have been defined using overloading, for each object and several of these constructor methods were further implemented by inline code and do not appear in the implementation section. One of the Location constructors still requires implementation:

```
Location::Location( int xval, int yval )
{
    create( xval, yval );
}
```

Instead of setting x and y directly, the xval and yval parameters are passed to another object method: create ... why? Does this sound a bit round-about?

In a sense, the Location constructor does take the long way around to accomplish an otherwise simple task because the create method is implemented as

```
void Location::create( int xval, int yval )
{
    x = xval;
```

```
    y = yval;
}
```

which more than slightly resembles the location constructor method in
OOPTest5 and earlier.

However, the create method will be essential in its own right for later
operations and, since it has to exist, it can be used instead of duplicating
the same code in the Location method. In this case, there is really very
little code to duplicate. Remember, this will not always be the situation.

The reason the create method is necessary is slightly convoluted. It
does duplicate the principal function previously handled by the constructor function but it is also necessary—for the object to act in an
appropriate and desired fashion—to be able to assign an object's value
parameters at some time other than when the object initiated. At other
times, it is desirable to be able to assign these values during initiation
(as done in OOPTest5).

However, a constructor method cannot be called at will. It is normally
called when an object instance is declared and then it is called implicitly.
This second access method, create, provides a means of setting the
object's characteristics which can be called at any time and repeatedly
if need be. Since the create method is necessary, it simply saves repeated
coding to have the constructor method, Location, act by calling the
create method.

This same practice will be carried forward for the other objects
descended from Location. Point's create method calls Location's create
method and Circle and Rectangle call Point.

```
void Point::create( int xval, int yval, int cval )
{
    Location::create( xval, yval );
    color = cval;
}
```

Point's draw method is quite simple, as are the erase and move
methods:

```
void Point::draw()
{
    putpixel( x, y, color );
}
```

```
void Point::erase()
{
    putpixel( x, y, getbkcolor() );
}

void Point::move( int ptx, int pty )
{
    erase();
    x = ptx;
    y = pty;
    putpixel( x, y, color );
}
```

As you can imagine, these methods are specific to the Point object and would not implement the Circle or Square objects well at all. This situation will change when virtual methods are introduced in a later chapter.

The Point::set_color method is also specific to the Point object even though it may not appear so at first glance. However, set_color calls the draw method which is specific to Point and unsuitable for other object types.

```
void Point::set_color( int cval )
{
    color = cval;
    draw();
}
```

The Point::get_color method, on the other hand, simply returns a value and is compatible with all descendant objects and, therefore, is not repeated.

```
int  Point::get_color()
{
    return( color );
}
```

The Circle object method implementation begins with the constructor method, Circle::Circle, which calls Point, just as Point called Location.

```
Circle::Circle( int xval, int yval, int cval, int rval )
   : Point( xval, yval, cval )
{
   size = rval;
}

void Circle::create( int xval, int yval,
                     int cval, int rval )
{
   size = rval;
   Point::create( xval, yval, cval );
}
```

The Circle::create method, in like fashion, calls Point::create. But there's also a subtle flaw here. Notice that neither Point::create nor Circle::create call their respective draw methods; neither actually creates an image on the screen. Why?

The answer is because Circle::create (and Square::create) call Point::create and, if Point::create called draw, it would be Point's draw which would be executed rather than Circle's or Square's, which would not be the desired image.

Later, using virtual methods, Point::create will be able to include a draw command which will serve to create the correct images for Circle and Square as well as any other descendant objects.

For the moment, however, it is necessary to implement several duplicate methods for each object, thus Color::set_color parallels Point::set_color.

```
void Circle::set_color( int cval )
{
   color = cval;
   draw();
}
```

The Circle::draw method, except in name, is not a parallel of any earlier method but is a specific implementation for the Circle object and calls the circle function in the graphics.h header.

```
void Circle::draw()
{
```

```
    setcolor( color );
    circle( x, y, size );
}

void Circle::erase()
{
    int temp = color;

    color = getbkcolor();
    draw();
    color = temp;
}
```

The Circle::erase method temporarily resets the object instance's color to the background color before calling the draw method to erase the screen image. Circle's remaining methods are carried forward from previous examples without any particular changes.

The Square object class duplicates all of Circle's methods with the exception of the specific implementation of the draw method. This duplication is necessary because both Square and Circle are descendants of Point and only share inherited methods, not those methods defined by each other. Square::draw provides instructions specific to drawing squares rather than circles, while the rest of the methods are identical to those implemented for Circle.

```
void Square::draw()
{
    setcolor( color );
    rectangle( x - ( size / 2 ), y - ( size / 2 ),
               x + ( size / 2 ), y + ( size / 2 ) );
}
```

Where the Action Is

As with C programs, the principal action in a C++ program (or, at least, the genesis of the action) is found in main. In this case, since the rest of the program consists of object definitions and methods, main is certainly the center of the action, beginning by declaring two arrays of objects:

```
main()
{
   static Circle acircle[32];
   static Square asquare[32];
```

The two arrays of acircle and asquare are implicitly initialized at the same time that they are declared. However, because the Circle and Square object classes possess constructor methods, the explicit reference as static object instances is required. Since no parameters are provided at this point, the default constructors (Circle::Circle() and Square::Square()) are used, initiating the x, y, color, and size elements as zero (though other values could be specified as defaults).

A second static instance of the Square object class is also declared but, since it is not an array element, it can be declared with a parameter list:

```
Square bsquare( 300, 150, 7, 250 );
```

You may also note that size appears as a local variable in main. You should also remember that object fields are isolated by encapsulation; therefore, there is no conflict between the object's size variable and main's size variable.

```
int graphdriver = DETECT, graphmode, grapherror;
int i, j, maxx, maxy, maxc, Cnt;
int cx, cy, size, testcolor;

clrscr();
initgraph( &graphdriver, &graphmode, "C:..\\BGI" );
grapherror = graphresult();
if ( grapherror )
{
   cout << "Graphics error: "
      << grapherrormsg( grapherror ) << "\n";
   cout << "Program aborted ...\n";
   exit( 1 );
}
```

Cout, Cin, and <<

C++ provides two new streams: cin, which is connected to the standard input and cout, which is connected to the standard output. Both can process all standard data types and, in C++, cout is flushed automatically when cin is called. The cout stream is used in place of the more familiar printf directive but it executes essentially the same task.

The << or *put to* operator is used to send data on its right to the stream on its left. While using the same symbol, it is distinguished from the shift-left operator by context. This is another example of overloading.

After initializing the graphics (assuming no error has occurred), the current screen resolution is determined before a background of random dots is created.

```
maxx = getmaxx();
maxy = getmaxy();
maxc = getmaxcolor();

cleardevice();
for( i=1; i<=1000; i++ )
   putpixel( random(maxx)+1, random(maxy)+1,
             random(maxc)+1 );
```

The Point object type could have been used for the screen background but it seems unnecessary to devote so much overhead to create 1,000 objects which will simply sit there. The simpler, non-object-oriented, approach is used.

For the next step, there is a distinct advantage in using objects which, once created, can remember their position, size, and current colors.

```
cx = getmaxx() / 2;
cy = size = getmaxy() / 2;
Cnt = size / 8;
for( i=1; i<=Cnt; i++ )
{
   acircle[i].create( cx, cy, i, size );
   acircle[i].draw();
   size -= 8;
   cx -= 10;
```

```
        cy -= 4;
    }
```

After calling the create method to set individual values for the object instances in the acircle array, a second loop repeats while waiting for a key stroke and instructs each of the objects to change color, sending waves of color changes down the array of circles on the screen.

```
while( !kbhit() )
    for( i=1; i<=Cnt; i++ )
    {
        j = acircle[i].get_color();
        if( j > 1 ) j--; else j = 15;
        acircle[i].set_color( j );
    }
getch();
```

Last, the array of objects are also able to remove themselves from the screen.

```
for( i=1; i<=Cnt; i++ ) acircle[i].erase();
```

Since each object instance knows its coordinates and size as well as its current color, each individual object instance is able to respond appropriately to commands to change color or to erase themselves.

And the array of Square objects performs in a similar fashion.

```
cx = 2 * getmaxx() / 3;
cy = size = getmaxy() / 2;
Cnt = size / 6;
for( i=1; i<=Cnt; i++ )
{
    asquare[i].create( cx, cy, i, size );
    asquare[i].draw();
    size -= 6;
    cx -= 10;
    cy -= 4;
};
while( !kbhit() )
```

```
    for( i=1; i<=Cnt; i++ )
    {
        j = asquare[i].get_color();
        if( j > 1 ) j-; else j = 15;
        asquare[i].set_color( j );
    }
getch();
bsquare.draw();
for( i=1; i<=Cnt; i++, delay(100) )
    asquare[i].erase();
bsquare.erase();
getch();
}
```

There is one difference in the performance of bsquare, aside from the shape of the objects. The object bsquare does not belong to the array and acts independent of the rest of the objects. It also erases itself.

Summary

You've been introduced to the basics of object-oriented programming and have seen how static objects are defined and constructed and how their methods are implemented, ending with a simple demonstration of how two arrays of graphic objects are capable of simple actions. Chapter 3 will cover other aspects of inheritance, referencing methods and other special topics.

In Chapter 4, a more complex object will be created to provide a mouse interface which will be used in subsequent chapters for several purposes.

Following are the complete source codes for the principal demo programs used in this chapter. These may also be found on the disk accompanying this volume.

```
//==============================//
//    OOPTest5 Program Listing  //
//        constructor methods   //
//==============================//
```

```
#include <iostream.h>
```

```
#include <conio.h>

#include <stdio.h>

class location

{

   protected:

      int x;

      int y;

   public:

      location() { x = 0; y = 0; }

      location( int xval, int yval );

      void  put_x( int xval );

      void  put_y( int yval );

      int    get_x();

      int    get_y();

};

class point : public location

{

   protected:

      int  color;

   public:

      point()  { x = 0; y = 0; color = 0; }

      point( int xval, int yval, int cval );

      void  put_color( int cval );
```

```
    int    get_color();
};

class circle : public point
{
   protected:
      int   size;
   public:
      circle() { x = 0; y = 0; color = 0; size = 0; }
      circle( int xval, int yval, int cval, int rval );
      void  set_size( int rval );
      int   get_size();
};

            // methods for location class //
location::location( int xval, int yval )
   { x = xval;  y = yval;  }
void location::put_x( int xval )  { x = xval;  }
void location::put_y( int yval )  { y = yval;  }
int  location::get_x()  { return( x );  }
int  location::get_y()  { return( y );  }

            // methods for point class //
point::point( int xval, int yval, int cval )
   : location( xval, yval )  { color = cval;  }
void point::put_color( int cval )  { color = cval;  }
```

```
int  point::get_color()  {  return( color );  }

                // methods for circle class //
circle::circle( int xval, int yval, int cval, int rval )

   : point( xval, yval, cval )  {  size = rval;  }

void circle::set_size( int rval )  {  size = rval;  }

int  circle::get_size()  {  return( size );  }

                // end of methods //

main()

{

   location  testpt( 10, 20 );

   circle    acircle( 30, 40, 50, 60 );

   clrscr();

   printf( "acircle.x     is %d\n", acircle.get_x() );

   printf( "acircle.y     is %d\n", acircle.get_y() );

   printf( "acircle.color is %d\n", acircle.get_color());

   printf( "acircle.size  is %d\n", acircle.get_size() );

   printf( "testpt.x      is %d\n", testpt.get_x() );

   printf( "testpt.y      is %d\n", testpt.get_y() );

   getch();

}
```

```
//=============================//
//   OOPTest6 Program Listing  //
//   a graphic demonstration   //
//=============================//

#include <iostream.h>

#include <stdlib.h>

#include <conio.h>

#include <stdio.h>

#include <graphics.h>

#include <dos.h>

class Location
{
    protected:
        int x;

        int y;

    public:
        Location() { x = 0; y = 0; }

        Location( int xval, int yval );

        void   create( int xval, int yval );

        void   set_x( int xval );

        void   set_y( int yval );

        int    get_x();

        int    get_y();

};
```

```
class Point : public Location

{

    protected:

        int  color;

    public:

        Point() { x = 0; y = 0; color = 0; }

        Point( int xval, int yval, int cval )

            : Location( xval, yval ), { color = cval; }

        void  create( int xval, int yval, int cval );

        void  draw();

        void  erase();

        void  move( int ptx, int pty );

        void  set_color( int cval );

        int   get_color();

};

class Circle : public Point

{

    protected:

        int  size;

    public:

        Circle() { x = 0; y = 0; color = 0; size = 0; }

        Circle( int xval, int yval, int cval, int rval );

        void  create( int xval, int yval,
```

```
                         int cval, int rval );

        void   draw();

        void   erase();

        void   set_color( int cval );

        void   set_size( int rval );

        int    get_size();

};


class Square : public Point

{

    protected:

        int   size;

    public:

        Square() { x = 0; y = 0; color = 0; size = 0; }

        Square( int xval, int yval, int cval, int rval );

        void   create( int xval, int yval,

                        int cval, int rval );

        void   draw();

        void   erase();

        void   set_color( int cval );

        void   set_size( int rval );

        int    get_size();

};
```

```
                // methods for Location class //
Location::Location( int xval, int yval )

   {   create( xval, yval );   }

void Location::create( int xval, int yval )

   {   x = xval;   y = yval;   }

void Location::set_x( int xval )   {   x = xval;   }

void Location::set_y( int yval )   {   y = yval;   }

int  Location::get_x()   {   return( x );   }

int  Location::get_y()   {   return( y );   }

                // methods for Point class //
void Point::create( int xval, int yval, int cval )
{

   Location::create( xval, yval );

   color = cval;

}

void Point::draw()   {   putpixel( x, y, color );   }

void Point::erase() {   putpixel( x, y, getbkcolor() );   }

void Point::move( int ptx, int pty )
{

   erase();

   x = ptx;
```

```
    y = pty;

    putpixel( x, y, color );

}

void Point::set_color( int cval )

{

    color = cval;

    draw();

}

int  Point::get_color()  {  return( color );  }

                // methods for Circle class //

Circle::Circle( int xval, int yval, int cval, int rval )

   : Point( xval, yval, cval )  {  size = rval;  }

void Circle::create( int xval, int yval,

                    int cval, int rval )

{

    size = rval;

    Point::create( xval, yval, cval );

}

void Circle::draw()

{

    setcolor( color );

    circle( x, y, size );
```

```
}

void Circle::erase()

{

    int temp = color;

    color = getbkcolor();

    draw();

    color = temp;

}

void Circle::set_color( int cval )

{

    color = cval;

    draw();

}

void Circle::set_size( int rval )  {  size = rval;  }

int  Circle::get_size()  {  return( size );  }

                // methods for Square class //

Square::Square( int xval, int yval, int cval, int rval )

    : Point( xval, yval, cval )  {  size = rval;  }

void Square::create( int xval, int yval,
                     int cval, int rval )

{
```

```
   size = rval;

   Point::create( xval, yval, cval );
}

void Square::draw()

{
   setcolor( color );

   rectangle( x - ( size / 2 ), y - ( size / 2 ),

              x + ( size / 2 ), y + ( size / 2 ) );
}

void Square::erase()

{
   int  temp = color;


   color = getbkcolor();

   draw();

   color = temp;
}

void Square::set_color( int cval )

{
   color = cval;

   draw();
}
```

```
void Square::set_size( int rval )  {  size = rval;  }

int  Square::get_size()  {   return( size );  }

                    // end of methods //

main()
{
   static Circle acircle[32];
   static Square asquare[32];
         Square bsquare( 300, 150, 7, 250 );
   int graphdriver = DETECT, graphmode, grapherror;
   int i, j, maxx, maxy, maxc, Cnt;
   int cx, cy, size, testcolor;

   clrscr();
   initgraph( &graphdriver, &graphmode, "C:..\\BGI" );
   grapherror = graphresult();
   if ( grapherror )
   {
      cout << "Graphics error: " <<
         grapherrormsg( grapherror ) << "\n";
      cout << "Program aborted ...\n";
      exit( 1 );
   }
   maxx = getmaxx();
   maxy = getmaxy();
```

```
maxc = getmaxcolor();

                                        // create a background //
cleardevice();

for( i=1; i<=1000; i++ )

   putpixel( random(maxx)+1, random(maxy)+1,

             random(maxc)+1 );

                                        // draw receding circles //
cx = getmaxx() / 2;

cy = size = getmaxy() / 2;

Cnt = size / 8;

for( i=1; i<=Cnt; i++ )

{

   acircle[i].create( cx, cy, i, size );

   acircle[i].draw();

   size -= 8;

   cx -= 10;

   cy -= 4;

}

while( !kbhit() )

   for( i=1; i<=Cnt; i++ )

   {

      j = acircle[i].get_color();

      if( j > 1 ) j - -; else j = 15;

      acircle[i].set_color( j );
```

```
      }

   getch();

   for( i=1; i<=Cnt; i++ ) acircle[i].erase();


                                    // draw receding squares //
   cx = 2 * getmaxx() / 3;

   cy = size = getmaxy() / 2;

   Cnt = size / 8;

   for( i=1; i<=Cnt; i++ )

   {

      asquare[i].create( cx, cy, i, size );

      asquare[i].draw();

      size -= 6;

      cx -= 10;

      cy -= 4;

   };

   while( !kbhit() )

      for( i=1; i<=Cnt; i++ )

      {

         j = asquare[i].get_color();

         if( j > 1 ) j - -; else j = 15;

         asquare[i].set_color( j );

      }

   getch();

   bsquare.draw();
```

```
    for( i=1; i<=Cnt; i++, delay(100) )

        asquare[i].erase();

    bsquare.erase();

    getch();

}
```

CHAPTER 3

VARIATIONS IN INHERITANCE

In the first two chapters, object inheritance and ancestor method references were shown using the "conventional" or usual forms. There are, however, a number of variations in object declarations and references to suit special circumstances or to provide for special constructions.

This chapter includes discussions on these topics, including *derived class access, overriding derived access, qualified names, multiple inheritance, friend classes,* and the keyword *this.*

Previously, the keywords private, protected, and public were used to control access to object data fields and methods both by descendant object types and by applications. But two of these access keys, private and public, are used in another context as well.

Base and Derived Class Access

The reserved words, public and private apply to access of methods inherited from ancestor classes as well as access of methods outside an object class. The reserved word protected is not applied to class inheritance.

Previously, all examples of object inheritance used the public keyword. Try going back to any of the preceding examples and removing the public declaration, making inheritance private by default, and observe the results when the program is compiled.

For example, Circle not only has the ancestor class Point, but access is also declared as public. This means that Point's methods are accessible—not only by Circle's methods but also as if these same methods had been defined as belonging to Circle.

On the other hand, if public inheritance access had not been specified, access would default as private and, while Circle's methods could still access Point's methods, they could not be accessed directly as if they were methods belonging to Circle.

Derived class inheritance is governed in the following ways:

- For a public inherited ancestor (base) class:

    Public members, both methods and data elements, of the ancestor class are treated as public members of the descendant class.
    Protected members of the ancestor class are protected members of the descendant class.
    Private members of the ancestor class are private to the descendant class.

- For a private inherited ancestor class (by default if public not specified):

    Public, protected, and private members, both methods and data elements, of the ancestor class are treated as private members of the descendant class.

For instance, with class Circle : Point, methods belonging to Point can be accessed by methods belong to Circle as:

```
int Circle::get_circle_color()
{
    return( get_color() );
}
```

The get_circle_color method can be called to return the color value of the object:

```
NColor = aCircle::get_circle_color();
```

But the get_color method cannot be called directly because the inherited methods are private to the descendant object and:

```
NColor = aCircle::get_color();
```

will report that the Point::get_color() method is not accessible.

Likewise, with class Circle : public Point, methods belonging to Point can be accessed by methods belong to Circle and as if these same methods also belonged to Circle:

```
int Circle::get_color()
{
    return( Point::get_color() );
}
```

In this case, there is no need to define the get_circle_color method because get_color is directly accessible:

```
NColor = aCircle::get_color();
```

In most cases, and in most of the examples in this book, the public identifier is used for object class inheritance. However, the effects of private typed inheritance can be conveniently explored in any of these examples—an area of experimentation I strongly suggest.

Overriding Derived Access

The effects of derived access can be adjusted or overridden by using a *qualified-name* within the declaration of the derived object class:

```
class XObj
{
    int A;                          // private by default    //
  public:
    int B, C;
    void XFunc();
}
```

In XObj, A is private by default; B, C, and XFunc() are public by declaration.

```
class YObj : private XObj
{
    int D;
```

At this point in YObj, A is not accessible; B, C and XFunc() are private by derived access and D is private by default.

```
public:
    XObj::B;
    int YFunc();
}
```

Also, at this point in XObj, C and D remain private but B is now public. XFunc() is also still private but may be accessed by YFunc() or any other methods within YObj or YObj's descendants. XFunc cannot be accessed externally as a method belonging to YObj or descendants.

Qualified Names

Qualified method names provide a means of resolving ambiguous references (see also "Multiple Inheritance," following) and of explicitly identifying object instances in method references or functions.

In brief, a qualified name consists of class identifier, the scope resolution operator (::), and the method or element name.

Thus, the Circle::get_color method, uses a qualified name to resolve the circular conflict which would otherwise occur and, at the same time, to identify which ancestor object's method is being specifically referenced.

```
int Circle::get_color()
{
    return( Point::get_color() );
}
```

Without the qualified method name, the preceding method would be a circular reference, calling itself recursively and repeatedly until a stack overload caused the program to crash.

In the following section, qualified names will be used to resolve ambiguous references.

Multiple Inheritance

Most object classes have only one immediate parent (ancestor) class and, in object-oriented Pascal, objects are permitted only one immediate ancestor. In C++, however, multiple ancestors are permitted. An object class can inherit data and method elements from any number of ancestors or, with special provisions, may even inherit more than once from a single ancestor.

OOPTest7 provides an example of two object classes used interactively; information from one object type instance is used to provide parameters for a second object type instance. This type of interaction is common in object-oriented programming but, in this case, is used simply as a preview before the same task is implemented by an object type with multiple ancestors in OOPTest8 and OOPTest9.

In OOPTest7, a new object class, Label, is defined and used with the previous object types, Circle and Square, to create a series of circles and squares with labels centered inside. While the results are not very complex, it will serve to demonstrate more object capabilities.

After static arrays of object instances aLabel, aCircle, and aSquare have been declared, the OOPTest7 demonstration begins as the Label object instance, aLabel[i], is given a random position and the arbitrary label, "Circle."

```
aLabel[i].SetLabel( random(2*maxx/3)+maxx/6,
                    random(2*maxy/3)+maxy/6,
                    "Circle" );
```

Next, aCircle[i] asks aLabel[i] for the position coordinates and the width of the text label before drawing the screen circle.

```
aCircle[i].Create( aLabel[i].get_x(),
                   aLabel[i].get_y(),
                   i+9,
                   aLabel[i].get_width()/2+10 );
```

Finally, because the Circle object controls the screen color settings, the Label object's Write method is called to put the text label on the screen.

```
aLabel[i].Write();
```

The same steps are carried out using Square object instances.

These are very minimal interactions that serve to show how such situations can be simplified by creating new object types that are descended from both Label and Circle (or from Label and Square).

OOPTest8 begins with the object types in OOPTest7 but introduces two descendant object types, LabelCircle and LableSquare, each of which has two immediate ancestors in Label and Circle and Label and Square, respectively.

```
class LabelCircle : public Circle, Label
```

Notice that only one public declaration is required here. It is also perfectly acceptable to say

```
class LabelCircle : public Circle, public Label
```

and accomplish the same result. However, the following variation does not accomplish the same task:

```
class LabelCircle : Circle, public Label
```

because only Label is declared public and Circle is private by default.

Beyond this, LabelCircle is provided with constructor and destructor methods and with a Create method accepting the four necessary arguments that had previously been parceled between the Label::SetLabel and Circle::Create methods.

```
  public:
    LabelCircle()  {  }
    ~LabelCircle() {  }
    void Create( int xPos, int yPos, int color,
                 char* LabelText );
};
```

The LabelSquare object type follows the same format.

The definitions and method implementations for the Location, Point, Circle, Square, and Label objects remain unchanged from previous examples, however, new implementations are provided for the LabelCircle and LabelSquare Create(...) methods.

```
void LabelCircle::Create( int xPos, int yPos, int color,
                          char* LabelText )
```

In the Create method, the SetLabel method from the Label object is called directly. Since no ambiguity occurs in the method name, a qualified name is not required.

```
{
    SetLabel( xPos, yPos, LabelText );
```

For the Circle::Create method a qualified name is necessary to prevent ambiguity and conflicts with the LabelCircle::Create method. Also, unresolved ambiguity exists several generations back with the Location::Create and Point::Create methods.

```
    Circle::Create( xPos, yPos, color, get_width()+10 );
```

While C and C++ permit overloading of functions and methods to resolve references according to the calling parameter lists, this overload resolution does not function across generations of objects. Such ambiguities must be resolved directly by using fully qualified method names.

The last task in the LabelCircle::Create method is to call the Label::Write method and since no ambiguity exists the call can be made directly, without qualification.

```
    Write();

}
```

The LabelSquare::Create method is implemented in a parallel fashion.

There is a deliberate error in the program as it is shown. When you compile OOPTest8, two compiler error messages should result, pointing out unresolved ambiguities in the lines

```
    for( i=0; i<=6; i++ ) LCircle[i].Erase();
```

and

```
    for( i=0; i<=6; i++ ) LSquare[i].Erase();
```

In OOPTest8, neither LabelCircle nor LabelSquare have declared an Erase method. Following the ancestry of both objects, Erase methods are found in both the Label, Circle, and Square objects. The compiler does not know whether the reference is to Label::Erase or Circle::Erase in the first case or to Label::Erase or Square::Erase in the second case.

Since the intention is to erase both the shape and the text, OOPTest9 corrects this problem by adding a new method to both the LabelCircle and LabelSquare objects:

```
void LabelCircle::Erase()
{
   Label::Erase();
   Circle::Erase();
}
```

Here LabelCircle::Erase calls both ancestor Erase methods, completing the dual-descendance object. LabelSquare::Erase, of course, works in the same fashion.

One more special provision has been added in OOPTest9: a pair of loops which erase the LabelCircle and LabelSquare objects before redrawing them with new captions using the same coordinate locations as the original objects:

```
for( i=0; i<=6; i++ )
{
   LCircle[i].Erase();
   LCircle[i].Create( LCircle[i].Label::get_x(),
                      LCircle[i].Label::get_y(),
                      i+1, "Changing" );
   delay( 100 );
}
```

A separate provision could have been made for changing the text of the label without having to reenter the screen coordinates. The point illustrated here is the qualified name referencing necessary to ask for the coordinates:

```
            LCircle[i].Label::get_x(),
```

Again, this is a conflict because more than one get_x and get_y method exists in the Location and Label ancestors. At the same time, having two pairs of redundant methods is unnecessary since both do exactly the same task.

In this case, it would be simpler to revise the Location method by deleting the get_x and get_y methods and changing the calls to the Create method as

```
      LCircle[i].Create( LCircle[i].get_x(),
                         LCircle[i].get_y(),
                         i+1, "Changing" );
```

This last change is left as an exercise for the reader.

Friends of Classes

In C++, the *friend* declaration makes it is possible for an object or a function to have access to an object's members without being a descendant object of that class or related to the object class.

The keyword friend gives a specified function full access rights to the object but remains a normal function without change in scope, declarations, or definition. The following example declares a function, Obj-Friend, as a friend of the object class, XObj.

```
class XObj
{
   . . .
   friend void ObjFriend( ... );
   . . .
}
```

With this declaration, ObjFriend has full access to XObj but Obj-Friend cannot be referenced from XObj, is not a member of XObj, and does not come within the scope of XObj. The implementation of Obj-Friend must be declared somewhere else, not within XObj's implementation.

Object classes may also have friend relationships to other objects. If another object class method, such as YObj::YFriend, is desired as friend to XObj, the scope resolution operator would be used in the friend declaration:

```
class XObj
{
   . . .
   friend void YObj::YFriend( ... );
   . . .
}
```

The YObj::YFriend method would be defined and implemented in YObj, not in XObj. An entire object class can also be a friend of a declared class:

```
class YObj
{
    ...

    friend class ZObj;

    ...
}
```

If ZObj is a friend of YObj and YObj::YFriend is a friend of XObj, the relationship is not transitive. While ZObj has access to YObj and YObj::YFriend has access to XObj, ZObj does not have access to XObj.

Use of the friend declaration is intended as an exception rather than a general purpose operation. If the friend declaration is required frequently, this probably means that your entire object structure should be reorganized, possibly by creating an object class descended from two or more of the existing objects as a substitute for the friend relationships.

The friend operator is not used in any example programs here.

The this Reference

The keyword this is a local variable belonging to any non-static object instance and is a self-referencing point ("self" or "pointer-to-self" in OOP jargon and called self in object-oriented Pascal).

The keyword this does not require declaration and is not generally referenced explicitly. It is used implicitly for member references and holds the address of the object instance as well. For an object, XObj with a member YMethod, the keyword this has the address &Xobj and YMethod is set to this->YMethod, equivalent to XObj.YMethod.

Remember, the keyword this is available only to object member functions, but not to friend functions.

Summary

Chapter 3 has covered many of the miscellaneous aspects of C++, demonstrating how derived class access works and how to override derived access using qualified names in redeclarations.

Qualified names also figure in another major topic, multiple inheritance, where ambiguities in ancestor method names require resolution. Friends of classes were introduced as a variant means of accessing an object's elements.

Finally, the keyword this was touched on briefly.

This concludes the introductory chapters on object-oriented programming. In Chapter 4, OOP will be used to create working objects, beginning with an object-oriented mouse and then moving on to graphics and non-graphics object applications.

```
//===============================//
//   OOPTest7 Program Listing    //
//        interactive objects    //
//===============================//

#include ...                  // include references unchanged //

class Location                              // unchanged //

class Point : public Location               // unchanged //

class Circle : public Point                 // unchanged //

class Square : public Point                 // unchanged //

class Label                                      // new //

{

    protected:

        char   TextLabel[15];

        int    x, y;

    public:

        Label()   { x = 0; y = 0; }

        ~Label() {    }

        void   SetLabel( int xPos, int yPos, char* Text );

        void   Write();

        void   Erase();
```

```
        int    get_width();

        int    get_height();

        int    get_x();

        int    get_y();

};


            // methods for Location, Point, //
            // Circle and Square unchanged  //

              // methods for Label object //

void   Label::SetLabel( int xPos, int yPos, char* Text )

{

    x = xPos;

    y = yPos;

    strcpy( TextLabel, Text );

}


void   Label::Write()

{

    settextjustify( CENTER_TEXT, CENTER_TEXT );

    outtextxy( x, y, TextLabel );

}


void   Label::Erase()

{

    setcolor( BLACK );

    Write();
```

```
}

int    Label::get_width()
{  return( textwidth( TextLabel ) );   }

int    Label::get_height()
{  return( textheight( TextLabel ) );  }

int    Label::get_x()   { return( x ); }

int    Label::get_y()   { return( y ); }

                    // end of methods //
main()
{
   static Circle aCircle[7];

   static Square aSquare[7];

   static Label  aLabel[7];

   int graphdriver = DETECT, graphmode, grapherror;

   int i, j, maxx, maxy, maxc;

   clrscr();

   initgraph( &graphdriver, &graphmode, "C:\\TC\\BGI" );

   grapherror = graphresult();

   if ( grapherror )

   {

      cout << "Graphics error: "
```

```
            << grapherrormsg( grapherror ) << "\n";

    cout << "Program aborted ...\n";

    exit( 1 );

}

maxx = getmaxx();

maxy = getmaxy();

maxc = getmaxcolor();

randomize();

                // create a background //
cleardevice();

for( i=1; i<=1000; i++ )

    putpixel( random(maxx)+1, random(maxy)+1,

            random(maxc)+1 );

                // draw random circles //
for( i=0; i<=6; i++ )

{

    aLabel[i].SetLabel( random(2*maxx/3)+maxx/6,

                        random(2*maxy/3)+maxy/6,

                        "Circle" );

    aCircle[i].Create( aLabel[i].get_x(),

                        aLabel[i].get_y(),

                        i+9,

                        aLabel[i].get_width()/2+10 );

    aLabel[i].Write();
```

```
  }

getch();

for( i=0; i<=6; i++ )

{

    aCircle[i].Erase();

    aLabel[i].Erase();

}

                // draw random squares //
for( i=0; i<=6; i++ )

{

    aLabel[i].SetLabel( random(2*maxx/3)+maxx/6,

                        random(2*maxy/3)+maxy/6,

                        "Square" );

    aSquare[i].Create( aLabel[i].get_x(),

                       aLabel[i].get_y(),

                       i+9,

                       aLabel[i].get_width()+10 );

    aLabel[i].Write();

}

getch();

for( i=0; i<=6; i++ )

{

    aSquare[i].Erase();

    aLabel[i].Erase();
```

```
    }

  getch();

}



              //==============================//
              //    OOPTest8 Program Listing    //
              //       multiple inheritance     //
              //    with unresolved references  //
              //==============================//

#include ...              // include references unchanged //

class Location                              // unchanged //

class Point : public Location               // unchanged //

class Circle : public Point                 // unchanged //

class Square : public Point                 // unchanged //

class Label                                 // unchanged //

class LabelCircle : public Circle, Label          // new //
{
   public:
      LabelCircle()  {  }
      ~LabelCircle() {  }
      void Create( int xPos, int yPos, int color,
                   char* LabelText );
};
```

```
class LabelSquare : public Square, public Label      // new //
{
   public:
      LabelSquare()  {  }
      ~LabelSquare() {  }
      void Create( int xPos, int yPos, int color,
                    char* LabelText );
};

        // methods for Location, Point, Circle, //
        // Square and Label objects unchanged    //

          // methods for LabelCircle object //
void LabelCircle::Create( int xPos, int yPos, int color,
                           char* LabelText )
{
   SetLabel( xPos, yPos, LabelText );
   Circle::Create( xPos, yPos, color, get_width()+10 );
   Write();
}

           // methods for LabelSquare object //
void LabelSquare::Create( int xPos, int yPos, int color,
                           char* LabelText )
{
   SetLabel( xPos, yPos, LabelText );
```

```
    Square::Create( xPos, yPos, color, get_width()+10 );

    Write();

}

                    // end of methods //

main()

{

    static LabelCircle LCircle[7];

    static LabelSquare LSquare[7];

    int graphdriver = DETECT, graphmode, grapherror;

    int i, j, maxx, maxy, maxc;

    clrscr();

    initgraph( &graphdriver, &graphmode, "C:\\TC\\BGI" );

    grapherror = graphresult();

    if ( grapherror )

    {

        cout << "Graphics error: "

            << grapherrormsg( grapherror ) << "\n";

        cout << "Program aborted ...\n";

        exit( 1 );

    }

    maxx = getmaxx();

    maxy = getmaxy();

    maxc = getmaxcolor();
```

```
randomize();

            // create a background //
cleardevice();

for( i=1; i<=1000; i++ )

    putpixel( random(maxx)+1, random(maxy)+1,

            random(maxc)+1 );

            // draw random circles //
for( i=0; i<=6; i++ )

    LCircle[i].Create( random(2*maxx/3)+maxx/6,

                        random(2*maxy/3)+maxy/6,

                        i+9, "Circle" );

getch();

for( i=0; i<=6; i++ ) LCircle[i].Erase();

            // draw random squares //
for( i=0; i<=6; i++ )

    LSquare[i].Create( random(2*maxx/3)+maxx/6,

                        random(2*maxy/3)+maxy/6,

                        i+9, "Square" );

getch();

for( i=0; i<=6; i++ ) LSquare[i].Erase();

getch();

}
```

```
//==============================//
//   OOPTest9 Program Listing   //
//     multiple inheritance     //
//        ** corrected **       //
//==============================//

#include ...                // include references unchanged //

class Location                          // unchanged //

class Point : public Location           // unchanged //

class Circle : public Point             // unchanged //

class Square : public Point             // unchanged //

class Label                             // unchanged //

class LabelCircle : public Circle, Label

{                                           // revised //

   public:

      LabelCircle()  {   }

      ~LabelCircle() {   }

      void Create( int xPos, int yPos, int color,
                   char* LabelText );

      void Erase();                         // new //

};

class LabelSquare : public Square, public Label

{                                           // revised //
```

```
    public:

       LabelSquare()  {   }

       ~LabelSquare() {   }

       void Create( int xPos, int yPos, int color,

                    char* LabelText );

       void Erase();                              // new //

};


            // methods for Location, Point, Circle, //
            // Square and Label objects unchanged   //

                // methods for LabelCircle object //

void LabelCircle::Create...                    // no changes //


void LabelCircle::Erase()                          // new //

{

   Label::Erase();

   Circle::Erase();

}


                // methods for LabelSquare object //

void LabelSquare::Create...                    // no changes //


void LabelSquare::Erase()                          // new //

{

   Label::Erase();

   Square::Erase();
```

```
}

                        // end of methods //

main()

{

    ...

                    // draw random circles //
    for( i=0; i<=6; i++ )

        LCircle[i].Create( random(2*maxx/3)+maxx/6,

                           random(2*maxy/3)+maxy/6,

                           i+9, "Circle" );

    getch();

    for( i=0; i<=6; i++ )

    {

        LCircle[i].Erase();

        LCircle[i].Create( LCircle[i].Label::get_x(),

                           LCircle[i].Label::get_y(),

                           i+1, "Changing" );

        delay( 100 );

    }

    getch();

    for( i=0; i<=6; i++ ) LCircle[i].Erase();

                    // draw random squares //
    for( i=0; i<=6; i++ )

        LSquare[i].Create( random(2*maxx/3)+maxx/6,
```

```
                                random(2*maxy/3)+maxy/6,

                                i+9, "Square" );

   getch();

   for( i=0; i<=6; i++ )

   {

      LSquare[i].Erase();

      LSquare[i].Create( LSquare[i].Label::get_x(),

                         LSquare[i].Label::get_y(),

                         i+1, "Changing" );

      delay( 100 );

   }

   getch();

   for( i=0; i<=6; i++ ) LSquare[i].Erase();

   getch();

}

}
```

CHAPTER 4

AN OBJECT-ORIENTED MOUSE

Since most graphics programs use the mouse as a primary interface device, this book will begin the graphics programming applications with an object-oriented mouse unit (MOUSE.I) and a utility (MOUSEPTR.CPP) to create mouse cursor images that can be incorporated in the mouse unit or directly into your applications.

The programs in this chapter assume that your computer has a bus or serial mouse and mouse driver (Microsoft, Logitech, or compatible) installed. The mouse unit created in this chapter is not a mouse driver itself, but is an interface object that uses the driver utility supplied with your mouse hardware.

When creating an object unit, it is helpful to provide descriptive documentation listing what functions are available via the unit, the parameters required to call these functions, and any data structures that are used by the object unit and are available to the calling program.

The Case of the Bashful Mouse

If you are using VGA or higher resolution graphics and the mouse pointer does not appear in the graphics application, the problem may be in your mouse driver. This can be cured by installing a newer driver package. The problem can be tested, however, using Turbo C's setgraphmode command to select a lower-resolution graphics mode.

For example, using VGA graphics with a vertical resolution of 480 pixels, the graphics mouse cursor does not appear on screen, however, when using the SetGraphMode(1) command to select medium resolution VGA graphics with a 350 vertical resolution, the mouse cursor does appear. If this is the case, contact Microsoft, Logitech, or your mouse supplier to obtain a new version mouse driver or purchase one of the new "HiRes" mice. With the Logitech mouse, mouse driver version 4.0 or later supports all VGA resolutions.

Using an Object Include File

Object include files are called in precisely the same manner as conventional include files:

```
#include `mouse.i"
```

By convention, quotes are used in the include declaration in place of the familiar angle brackets to designate a custom library file rather than a header file referencing a stock library. But there is nothing hard and fast about this convention and, if you prefer, you may use angle brackets in place of the quote marks.

There are a few other differences as well. For one, object methods are not directly accessible but must be referenced through specific object instances that normally are declared in the main program or in subprocedures. For another, object include files may often contain structure definitions, constants, or even object instances for general use by applications using the object.

In MOUSE.I, the type definitions declared by the unit are available to the applications using the unit:

```
typedef struct
    {  unsigned   flag,
                button,
                xaxis, yaxis;
    }  mouse_event;

typedef struct
    {  unsigned   int
        ScreenMask[16],
```

```
        CursorMask[16],
        xkey, ykey;
}   g_cursor;
```

Two Buttons Versus Three

The mouse object provides compatibility for both two- and three-button mice, principally by providing definitions for all three buttons:

```
#define ButtonL  = 0;
#define ButtonR  = 1;
#define ButtonM  = 2;
```

If you have worked with OS/2's Presentation Manager, the mouse buttons are defined under as 1-2-3, from left to right, with a system option to reverse the order for southpaws. Conventional mouse button ordering began when computer mice had only two buttons, left and right (and some had only one), thus, the middle button is out of order and is numbered 2. For two-button mice the middle button is not available.

Two other constants are provided for general use: software and hardware which are used to set the cursor in text mode.

```
#define Software = 0;
#define Hardware = 1;
```

Four additional constants are provided for general convenience:

```
#define  FALSE     0
#define  TRUE      1
#define  OFF       0
#define  ON        1
```

Graphics Mouse Cursors

Five graphics cursors are predefined in the mouse unit for use with graphics mouse applications. The Arrow cursor is an angled arrow similar to the default graphics cursor. The Check cursor is a check mark with the hot-spot at the base of the angle. The Cross cursor is a circle with crosshairs marking a centered hot-spot. The Glove cursor is a hand image with the hot-spot at the tip of the extended index finger and the Ibeam cursor duplicates the popular vertical bar marker used with graphics text applications. The hot-spot for the IBEAM cursor is centered roughly on the vertical bar.

All of the graphics cursors are available to applications using the mouse unit and are defined as follows:

```
static  g_cursor  ARROW =
        {  0x1FFF, 0x0FFF, 0x07FF, 0x03FF,       // screen mask
           0x01FF, 0x00FF, 0x007F, 0x003F,
           0x001F, 0x003F, 0x01FF, 0x01FF,
           0xE0FF, 0xF0FF, 0xF8FF, 0xF8FF,
           0x0000, 0x4000, 0x6000, 0x7000,       // cursor mask
           0x7800, 0x7C00, 0x7E00, 0x7F00,
           0x7F80, 0x7C00, 0x4C00, 0x0600,
           0x0600, 0x0300, 0x0300, 0x0000,
           0x0001, 0x0001  };                    // hot-spot coordinates
```

The MOUSEPTR program creates an ASCII text file following this same format and can be imported directly to any Turbo C or C++ program listing or added to the MOUSE.I unit source listings.

The Object Definitions

The object definitions begin with a general mouse object type, Mouse, which contains 14 methods belonging to the Mouse object:

```
class Mouse
{
   int     Mview;

   protected:
      Mouse();
      ~Mouse();
   public:
      static mouse_event far *Mevents;

      Mmovement *Mmotion();
      Mresult    *Mreset();
      Mstatus    Mpos();
      Mstatus    Mpressed( int button );
```

```
Mstatus   Mreleased( int button );
void Mshow( int showstat );
void Mmoveto( int xaxis, int yaxis );
void Mxlimit( int min_x, int max_x );
void Mylimit( int min_y, int max_y );
void Mmove_ratio( int xsize, int ysize );
void Mspeed( int speed );
void Mconceal( int left, int top,
               int right, int bottom );
};
```

The Mouse object type is the base object type containing methods common to all mouse objects. Notice, however, that the Mouse object does not contain any data elements, only methods which return data structures. Also, the Mouse object is not intended to be called by any applications; instead, two descendant object types, which will actually be used by applications, are declared. They include the GMouse object type which adds three new procedures (one private, two public) that are specific to graphics mouse applications:

```
class GMouse : public Mouse
{
   private:
      void set_cursor( int xaxis,
                       int yaxis,
                       unsigned mask_Seg,
                       unsigned mask_Ofs );
   public:
      void Set_Cursor( g_cursor ThisCursor );
      void Mlightpen( int set );
};
```

The TMouse object type (text mouse) is also a descendant of the GMouse type, adding two text specific procedures:

```
class TMouse : public Mouse
{
   public:
```

```
      void Set_Cursor( int cursor_type,
                       unsigned s_start,
                       unsigned s_stop  );
      void Mlightpen( int set );
};
```

The GMouse and TMouse object types each include Mlightpen methods to support the rare, but still occasional, applications that require lightpen support for either graphics or text applications.

Method Implementations

The object methods defined in the object declaration also require specific implementation. This includes the code specific to each procedure or function, and any types, constants, variables, or local procedures or functions that are private to specific methods and, therefore, not directly available to the application using the object.

```
Mouse::Mouse()    {   }

Mouse::~Mouse()    {   }
```

The Mouse object is given constructor and destructor method that are the first two methods implemented even though neither has any actual code provided. Still, this implementation must be provided, either here or in the declaration, before the object can be compiled.

The Reset Function

The Mouse implementations begin with the Mreset method which calls the mouse driver, resetting the driver to default conditions and returning a mouse status argument in the AX register (–1 if mouse present, 0 if not available). The argument is tested and, if the mouse is present, the mouse cursor is turned on.

The BX register returns the button count (2 or 3) for the mouse and both results are returned in the *Mresult* data structure.

```
Mresult *Mouse::Mreset()
{
   static Mresult  m;

   Mview = OFF;
```

```
    inreg.x.ax = 0;
    call_mouse;
    m.present = outreg.x.ax;
    m.buttons = outreg.x.bx;
    if( m.present ) Mshow( TRUE );
    return ( &m );
}
```

The Mshow Method

The Mshow method is used to turn the mouse cursor on and off by calling mouse functions 1 and 2, respectively.

Any time a screen update is being executed in an area which may include the mouse cursor, the mouse cursor should be turned off before repainting the screen and restored afterwards. Otherwise, the effects can be surprising, but not desirable. If you would like to see examples caused by omission, comment out the second half of the body of this procedure and then run the MousePtr program:

```
void Mouse::Mshow( int showstat )
{
    if( showstat )
    {
        inreg.x.ax = 1;                    // mouse function 1  //
        if( !Mview ) call_mouse;           // show mouse cursor //
        Mview = ON;
    }
    else
    {
        inreg.x.ax = 2;                    // mouse function 2  //
        if( Mview ) call_mouse;            // hide mouse cursor //
        Mview = OFF;
    } }
```

Mouse functions 1 and 2 have been combined here in a single method to provide convenience and safety lacking the in the original functions. Using the original functions, multiple calls to hide the mouse cursor require multiple calls before the cursor is restored (and vice versa). Alternatively, the Mshow method permits the hide and show cursor functions to be called only once, thus insuring that a single call can always be depended on to reverse the cursor state.

Note that hiding the mouse cursor does not affect tracking operations or button operation—the mouse position is tracked even if the mouse is invisible.

The Mpos Method

The Mpos method reports the mouse cursor position and the status of the mouse buttons. Position coordinates are always reported in pixels.

The button_status element (in Mstatus) is an integer value with the three least-significant bits indicating the current status of the left, right, and (if present) middle buttons. The corresponding bits in button_status, starting with bit 0, will be set if the button is down or clear if the button is up:

```
Mstatus Mouse::Mpos()
{                   // returns pointer to Mstatus structure with //
                    // mouse cursor position and button status   //
    static Mstatus  m;

    inreg.x.ax = 3;                        // mouse function 3 //
    call_mouse;
    m.button_status = outreg.x.bx;      // button status   //
    m.xaxis = outreg.x.cx;              // xaxis coordinate //
    m.yaxis = outreg.x.dx;              // yaxis coordinate //
    return (m);
}
```

The Mmoveto Method

The Mmoveto method is used to move the mouse cursor to a specific location on the screen. The coordinates used are always absolute screen coordinates in pixels. In text modes, pixel coordinates are still used, but the coordinates are rounded off to position the cursor to the nearest character cell (for example with an 8x8 text display, x/y pixel coordinates of 80/25 would correspond to the 11th column and 4th row of the screen).

```
void Mouse::Mmoveto( int xaxis, int yaxis )
{                               // mouse cursor to new position //
```

```
    inreg.x.ax = 4;                    // mouse function 4 //

    inreg.x.cx = xaxis;

    inreg.x.dx = yaxis;

    call_mouse;

}
```

The Mpressed Method

The Mpressed method reports the current status of all of the buttons, a count of the number of times the requested button has been pressed since the last call to Mpressed for this button and the mouse coordinates when the requested button was last pressed:

```
Mstatus Mouse::Mpressed( int button )

{

    static Mstatus  m;

    inreg.x.ax = 5;

    inreg.x.bx = button;

    call_mouse;

    m.button_status = outreg.x.ax;

    m.button_count = outreg.x.bx;

    m.xaxis = outreg.x.cx;

    m.yaxis = outreg.x.dx;

    return (m);

}
```

The Mreleased Method

The Mreleased method is the equivalent of Mpressed except for reporting the number of times the requested button was released:

```
Mstatus Mouse::Mreleased( int button )

{

    static Mstatus  m;

    inreg.x.ax = 6;

    inreg.x.bx = button;

    call_mouse;

    m.button_status = outreg.x.ax;
```

```
    m.button_count = outreg.x.bx;
    m.xaxis = outreg.x.cx;
    m.yaxis = outreg.x.dx;
    return (m);
}
```

The Mxlimit/Mylimit Methods

The Mxlimit and Mylimit methods establish screen limits, in pixels, for the mouse movement. This is particularly important when using higher resolution graphics because the default limits may not include the entire screen and, if it does not, portions of the screen cannot be reached with the mouse.

When restricting the mouse to a portion of the screen in an application using an exit button either ensure that an alternate exit procedure is supplied or that some method of reaching the exit button is always available:

```
void Mouse::Mxlimit( int min_x, int max_x )
{
    inreg.x.ax = 7;                          // mouse function 7 //
    inreg.x.cx = min_x;
    inreg.x.dx = max_x;
    call_mouse;
}

void Mouse::Mylimit( int min_y, int max_y )
{                                            // sets vertical boundaries //
    inreg.x.ax = 8;                          // mouse function 8 //
    inreg.x.cx = min_y;
    inreg.x.dx = max_y;
    call_mouse;
}
```

The Mxlimit and Mylimit methods could also be combined in a single method accepting four arguments.

The Mmotion Method

The Mmotion method returns a total horizontal and vertical step count since the last call to Mmotion. For a normal mouse, the step count varies from a low of $^1/_{100}$ inch increments (100 mickeys/inch) for older mice to $^1/_{200}$ inch (200 mickeys/inch) for more modern mice and $^1/_{320}$ inch increments (320 mickeys/inch) for a HiRes mouse.

Movement step counts are always within the range −32,768..32,767. A positive value indicates a left to right horizontal motion or, vertically, a motion towards the user (assuming the cable is pointed away from the user). Both horizontal and vertical step counts are reset to zero after this call:

```
Mmovement* Mouse::Mmotion()
{
    static Mmovement  m;

    inreg.x.ax = 11;
    call_mouse;
    m.x_count = _CX;
    m.y_count = _DX;
    return (&m);
}
```

Since the mouse graphics or text cursors are updated automatically Mmotion is not required to control the screen presentation, but may be used for special applications.

See also the Mmove_ratio and Mspeed functions.

The Mmove_ratio Method

The Mmove_ratio method controls the ratio of physical mouse movement to screen cursor movement with the x- and y-axis arguments (*xsize* and *ysize*) expressed as the number of mickeys (units of mouse motion) required to cover eight pixels on the screen. Allowable values are 1 to 32,767 mickeys, but the appropriate values are dependent on the number of mickeys per inch reported by the physical mouse; values which may be 100, 200, or 320 mickeys per inch depending on the mouse hardware.

Default values are 8 mickeys/8 pixels horizontal and 16 mickeys/8 pixels vertical. For a mouse reporting 200 mickeys/inch, this requires

3.2 inches horizontally and 2.0 inches vertically to cover a 640x200 pixel screen:

```
void Mouse::Mmove_ratio( int xsize, int ysize )
{
   inreg.x.ax = 15;
   inreg.x.cx = xsize;
   inreg.x.dx = ysize;
   call_mouse;
}
```

The Mspeed Method

The Mspeed method establishes a threshold speed (in physical mouse velocity units, mickeys/second) above which the mouse driver adds an acceleration component, allowing fast movements with the mouse to move the cursor further than slow movements. The acceleration component varies according to the mouse driver installed. For some drivers, acceleration is a constant multiplier, usually a factor of two, while other drivers, including the Logitech mouse, use variable acceleration with multiplier values increasing on an acceleration curve:

```
void Mouse::Mspeed( int speed )
{
   inreg.x.ax = 19;
   inreg.x.dx = speed;
   call_mouse;
}
```

The threshold value can be any value in the range 0..7FFFh with an average value in the range of 300 mickeys/second. Acceleration can be disabled by setting a high threshold (7FFFh) or restored by setting a low or zero threshold.

The Mconceal Method

The Mconceal method designates a rectangular area of the screen where the mouse cursor will automatically be hidden and is used principally to guard an area of the screen that will be repainted:

```
void Mouse::Mconceal( int left, int top,
                      int right, int bottom )
{
   inreg.x.ax = 16;
   inreg.x.cx = left;
   inreg.x.dx = top;
   inreg.x.si = right;
   inreg.x.di = bottom;
   call_mouse;
}
```

The mouse cursor is automatically hidden if it is in or moves into the area designated. The Mconceal function is temporary; functioning by decrementing the mouse counter in the same manner as a call to the Mshow(FALSE) function. The area set by calling Mconceal will be cleared and the mouse cursor enabled over the entire screen by calling Mshow(TRUE).

The GMouse Method Implementations

The GMouse implementation adds three graphics-specific methods to the general mouse functions inherited from the Mouse object type. Two of these new methods are public and are accessible to applications using the object, but the third is private and can only be called by another object method.

```
class GMouse : public Mouse
{
   private:                          // graphic cursor shape  //
      void set_cursor( int xaxis,
                       int yaxis,
                       unsigned mask_Seg,
                       unsigned mask_Ofs );
   public:
      void Set_Cursor( g_cursor ThisCursor );
      void Mlightpen( int set );
};
```

The set_cursor Method

The set_cursor method is private and is called indirectly through the
Set_Cursor method. The set_cursor method is the actual mechanism for
changing the graphics mouse cursor and is called with the x- and y-axis
coordinates for the cursor's hot-spot and the segment and offset address
of the cursor image.

```
void GMouse::set_cursor( int xaxis, int yaxis,
                         unsigned mask_Seg,
                         unsigned mask_Ofs )
{
   struct SREGS  seg;

   inreg.x.ax = 9;
   inreg.x.bx = xaxis;
   inreg.x.cx = yaxis;
   inreg.x.dx = mask_Ofs;
   seg.es     = mask_Seg;
   int86x( 0x33, &inreg, &outreg, &seg );
}
```

The Set_Cursor Method

The Set_Cursor method loads a new cursor screen and mask, making it
the active graphics mouse pointer:

```
void GMouse::Set_Cursor( g_cursor ThisCursor )
{
   set_cursor( ThisCursor.xkey,
               ThisCursor.ykey,
               _DS,
               (unsigned) ThisCursor.ScreenMask );
}
```

The selected graphics cursor may be one of the predefined cursors
supplied with the mouse unit (MOUSE.I) or may be a cursor defined by
the application program.

The Set_Cursor method (public) is used by applications to call the
set_cursor method (private) for the actual operation. It provides the

simplicity of changing cursors with a single argument identifying the cursor image name, instead of having to specify the offset, segment, and hot-spot coordinates for the cursor image.

The Mlightpen Methods

While lightpens are relatively scarce, a few applications do continue to use them, and the mouse driver package offers a pair of functions supporting lightpen emulation.

Though rarely needed, two methods have been created—one for the GMouse object and the other for the TMouse object type. Both implement the lightpen functions in exactly the same manner:

```
void GMouse::Mlightpen( int set )
{
   if( set ) inreg.x.ax = 13;
       else   inreg.x.ax = 14;
   call_mouse;
}
```

Light pen emulation is turned off by default. When enabled, simultaneous down states of both the right and left buttons emulate the pen-down state and release of both buttons emulates the pen-up state.

The TMouse Methods

While three functions were added to create a graphics mouse object descended from the general mouse object, only two procedures are provided to do the same for the text mouse, paralleling two of the graphic mouse procedures: Set_Cursor, a method for setting the text cursor type (see Figure 4-1), and Mlightpen.

```
class TMouse : public Mouse
{
   public:
      void Set_Cursor( int cursor_type,
                       unsigned s_start,
                       unsigned s_stop  );
      void Mlightpen( int set );
};
```

Figure 4-1: The Mouse Cursor Editor

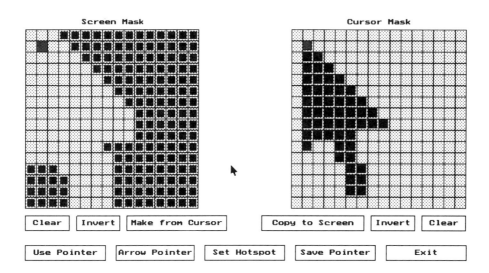

While the Set_Cursor method has the same name as the GMouse function, this version is implemented in an entirely different manner. Strictly speaking, however, this is not an example of polymorphism because both the GMouse and TMouse are descended from Mouse and not from each other (these are siblings, not descendants).

The Set_Cursor Method

The text version of the Set_Cursor method can be used to select either hardware or software cursors and set the cursor parameters:

```
void TMouse::Set_Cursor( int cursor_type,
                         unsigned s_start,
                         unsigned s_stop  )
{
   inreg.x.ax = 10;
   inreg.x.bx = cursor_type;
   inreg.x.cx = s_start;
   inreg.x.dx = s_stop;
   call_mouse;
}
```

The hardware cursor uses the video controller to create the cursor with the arguments c1 and c2, identifying the start and stop scan lines for the cursor. The number of scan lines in a character cell is determined by the hardware video controller (and monitor). As a general rule, for monochrome systems the range is 0..7 and for CGA the range is 0..14, top to bottom.

In general, a start scan line of six and a stop scan line of seven will produce an underline cursor. A start scan line of two and a stop scan line of five or six produces a block cursor and works well even on high resolution VGA systems.

The software cursor is slightly more complicated. Using the software cursor, the c1 and c2 parameters create a character or character attributes which are, respectively, ANDed and XORed with the existing screen character.

The c1 parameter (screen mask) is ANDed with the existing screen character and attributes at the mouse cursor location, determining which elements are preserved. Next, the c2 parameter (cursor mask) is XORed with the results of the previous operation, determining which characteristics are changed.

In actual practice, a screen mask value of $7F00 might be used to preserve the color attributes, while a cursor mask value of $8018 would establish a blinking up-arrow cursor or $0018 for a non-blinking up arrow. In either case the existing foreground and background color attributes are preserved. In the same fashion, a screen mask of $0000 and a cursor mask of $FFFF will produce a flashing white block cursor. See Table 4-1 for more information.

As a general rule, the eight least-significant bits of the screen mask should be either $..00 or $..FF; with the former preferred.

Table 4-1: Software Cursor Parameter Format

BIT	DESCRIPTION
0..7	Extended ASCII character code
8..10	Foreground color
11	Intensity: 1 = high, 0 = medium
12..14	Background color
15	Blinking (1) or non-blinking (0)

The Mouse Pointer Utility

A mouse cursor editor (MOUSEPTR.CPP), the second example in this chapter, is a program providing both a useful utility to create mouse cursor images and a means of demonstrating the use of the mouse unit.

While MOUSEPTR could have been created as an object-oriented program, this utility is written largely in conventional C format, aside from calls to the object-oriented mouse unit. This is done for two reasons: to avoid complicating the utility itself and, because portions of the code used in this program will serve to contrast the object-oriented graphics button structures that will be created in Chapter 5. You are, however, welcome to practice object-oriented programming by revising the MOUSEPTR program using the object-oriented button utilities that will be presented shortly.

The MOUSEPTR program is generally self-explanatory and provides two grid structures for editing the screen and cursor masks to create a mouse pointer image. Naturally, editing is accomplished using the mouse to toggle squares in the grids or to select the option buttons below the grids. Tables 4-2 and 4-3 list the options.

Table 4-2: Cursor Mask Option Buttons

CURSOR MASK OPTIONS	DESCRIPTION
Clear	Resets all bits in the cursor mask grid to FALSE (zero).
Invert	Reverses all bits in the cursor mask grid.
Copy to Screen	Copies the cursor mask grid to the screen mask grid.

Table 4-3: General Mask Options

GENERAL OPTIONS	DESCRIPTION
Invert	Reverses all bits in the screen mask grid.
Make from Cursor	Creates a screen mask grid image from the cursor mask grid. For each point in the screen mask grid, if the corresponding point in the cursor mask grid or any adjacent point in the cursor mask grid is TRUE, the screen mask grid point is FALSE.
Set Hot-spot	The next point selected in either the screen or cursor mask grids will be the hot-spot for the mouse cursor and will appear in red on both grids. Any existing hot-spot is cleared.
Use Pointer	Makes the edited cursor image the active mouse pointer on the screen.
Arrow Pointer	Restores the arrow mouse pointer.

GENERAL OPTIONS	DESCRIPTION
Save Pointer	Saves the current screen and cursor grid images to an ASCII file using hexadecimal format. The output file can be imported directly for use by any Turbo C or C++ program. The current directory is used and the filename extension .CUR is automatically supplied.
Exit	Exits from the program—no safety features are supplied to prevent accidental exits.

The control options affect both the screen and cursor masks.

The .CUR File Format

The mouse cursor image is saved in an ASCII format that is suitable for direct inclusion in any program using the MOUSE.I unit:

```
static  g_cursor  ARROW =                        // screen mask //
        {   0x1FFF,  0x0FFF,  0x07FF,  0x03FF,
            0x01FF,  0x00FF,  0x007F,  0x003F,
            0x001F,  0x003F,  0x01FF,  0x01FF,
            0xE0FF,  0xF0FF,  0xF8FF,  0xF8FF,
                                                 // cursor mask //
            0x0000,  0x4000,  0x6000,  0x7000,
            0x7800,  0x7C00,  0x7E00,  0x7F00,
            0x7F80,  0x7C00,  0x4C00,  0x0600,
            0x0600,  0x0300,  0x0300,  0x0000,
            0x0001,  0x0001   };                  // xkey, ykey //
```

All values are written in hexadecimal format, simplifying any manual editing or revising that might be desired. The *xkey* and *ykey* values are written as word values though these are actually only integer values (and never exceed $000F). Conversion is handled automatically by Turbo C.

Conventional Style Button Operations

The MOUSEPTR utility is operated by the series of button controls previously listed, but these are buttons only in a limited sense. An outline and label are written to the screen with a separate function arbitrarily matching the mouse pointer location coordinates at the time a mouse button is pressed to the corresponding screen images. The screen and cursor grids are treated in a similar fashion.

In Chapter 5, this dichotomy will be resolved in an object type named Button. Also, image, screen positions and control responses will be merged into a single control object. The Button object type could be used to replace a large part of the programming instructions in the MOUSEPTR utility program, replacing not only the screen, cursor, and general control buttons, but also replacing the screen and cursor grids with arrays of blank buttons.

For the moment, however, the topic is the conventional or non-object-oriented control structure that begins by using the gmouse object (type GMouse) to enable graphics mouse operations:

```
Result = gmouse.Mreset();
if( Result->present )
{
    do {
```

Within the loop, only the left mouse button is used and the loop begins by calling Mpressed to test for a left button pressed event:

```
Position = gmouse.Mpressed( ButtonL );
if( Position.button_count )
{
```

If the returned button_count is not zero, the next step is to decide where the mouse cursor was located when the button was pressed. This is accomplished with nested if statements.

```
if( TPos( Position.yaxis, 30, 270 ) )
{                              // screen or cursor grids //
   if( TPos( Position.xaxis,  15, 255 ) )
      ScreenSet( Position.xaxis,
               Position.yaxis );
   if( TPos( Position.xaxis, 384, 624 ) )
      CursorSet( Position.xaxis,
               Position.yaxis );
} else
if( TPos( Position.yaxis, 280, 300 ) )
                         // screen or cursor commands //
                                // screen mask items //
{
```

```
        if( TPos( Position.xaxis,  15,  75 ) )
            ClearScreen(); else
        if( TPos( Position.xaxis,  85, 145 ) )
            InvertScreen(); else
        if( TPos( Position.xaxis, 155, 295 ) )
            ScreenFromCursor(); else
                                      // cursor mask items //
        if( TPos( Position.xaxis, 364, 484 ) )
            CursorToScreen(); else
        if( TPos( Position.xaxis, 494, 554 ) )
            InvertCursor(); else
        if( TPos( Position.xaxis, 564, 624 ) )
            ClearCursor();
      } else
      if( TPos( Position.yaxis, 320, 340 ) )
      {                          // general command options //
        if( TPos( Position.xaxis,  15, 125 ) )
            UseNewCursor(); else
        if( TPos( Position.xaxis, 140, 250 ) )
            gmouse.Set_Cursor( ARROW ); else
        if( TPos( Position.xaxis, 265, 375 ) )
            SetHotSpot(); else
        if( TPos( Position.xaxis, 390, 500 ) )
            SavePointer(); else
        if( TPos( Position.xaxis, 515, 625 ) )
            Exit = TRUE;
  } } }
  while( !Exit );
}
```

While this response structure works well it has a serious deficiency. A popular adage holds that "if it works, don't fix it!" But sometimes what works in one situation does not work in all situations. The coding used in this example is a case in point. For an EGA or higher resolution graphics system, the MOUSEPTR program works just fine, but, for a CGA video, extensive conversions would have to be made before the image grids and the control buttons could fit within a 200 pixel vertical resolution.

While it would be possible to write formulas to provide adaptation to different vertical (and horizontal) resolutions for the screen images, it would also be necessary to have a series of variables associated with each of these screen elements and to assign screen coordinate values to each corresponding to the video resolution in use. In conventional programming, however, this is awkward and unwieldy. This is also an excellent example of how object-oriented programming provides tremendous advantages, as will be shown in Chapter 5.

The remainder of the MOUSEPTR.CPP program is generally self-explanatory and appears in the listings at the end of this chapter.

Summary

In this chapter, an object-mouse was created as an include file, MOUSE.I, and will be used in examples to provide general mouse control. Before proceeding further, you should have a working mouse unit, containing both the graphics and text mouse object methods, compiled and ready for use.

Either the MOUSEPTR program or the demo programs in Chapter 5 can be used to test the object-mouse:

```
//=====================================================//
// MOUSE.I: Turbo C++ source code for mouse interface //
//   object. #include dos.h before this #include to   //
//   define the register set to pass args to driver   //
//=====================================================//

#include <dos.h>

#include <stddef.h>


#define  call_mouse int86(0x33, &inreg, &outreg)

                    // interrupt call for mouse device driver //
#define  EVENTMASK  0x54

#define  lower (x, y)  (x < y) ? x : y
```

```
#define   upper (x, y)   (x > y) ? x : y

#define   ButtonL     0

#define   ButtonR     1

#define   ButtonM     2

#define   SOFTWARE    0                    // text cursor types //

#define   HARDWARE    1

#define   FALSE       0

#define   TRUE        1

#define   OFF         0

#define   ON          1


union   REGS   inreg, outreg;              // static registers //

typedef struct {   int present,           // TRUE if present  //

                       buttons;           // # of buttons      //

               }  Mresult;

typedef struct

    { int button_status,      // bits 0-2 on if button down //

         button_count,        // # times button was clicked //

         xaxis, yaxis;        // mouse cursor position       //

    }  Mstatus;

typedef struct

    {  int x_count,           // net horizontal movement //

          y_count;            // net vertical movement    //
```

```
    }   Mmovement;                          // returned by mMotion      //

typedef struct
    {   unsigned  flag,                      // mouse event record //
                  button,
                  xaxis, yaxis;
    }  mouse_event;

typedef struct               // graphics cursor descriptor //
    {   unsigned  int
            ScreenMask[16],
            CursorMask[16],
            xkey, ykey;
    }  g_cursor;

static  g_cursor  ARROW =                    // screen mask //
            {  0x1FFF, 0x0FFF, 0x07FF, 0x03FF,
               0x01FF, 0x00FF, 0x007F, 0x003F,
               0x001F, 0x003F, 0x01FF, 0x01FF,
               0xE0FF, 0xF0FF, 0xF8FF, 0xF8FF,

                                             // cursor mask //
               0x0000, 0x4000, 0x6000, 0x7000,
               0x7800, 0x7C00, 0x7E00, 0x7F00,
               0x7F80, 0x7C00, 0x4C00, 0x0600,
               0x0600, 0x0300, 0x0300, 0x0000,
               0x0001, 0x0001  };            // xkey, ykey  //
```

```
static  g_cursor CHECK =                    // screen mask //

       {  0xFFF0, 0xFFE0, 0xFFC0, 0xFF81,

          0xFF03, 0x0607, 0x000F, 0x001F,

          0x803F, 0xC07F, 0xE0FF, 0xF1FF,

          0xFFFF, 0xFFFF, 0xFFFF, 0xFFFF,


                                            // cursor mask //
          0x0000, 0x0006, 0x000C, 0x0018,

          0x0030, 0x0060, 0x70C0, 0x3980,

          0x1F00, 0x0E00, 0x0400, 0x0000,

          0x0000, 0x0000, 0x0000, 0x0000,

          0x0005, 0x000A  };                // xkey, ykey  //

static  g_cursor CROSS =                    // screen mask //

       {  0xF01F, 0xE00F, 0xC007, 0x8003,

          0x0441, 0x0C61, 0x0381, 0x0381,

          0x0381, 0x0C61, 0x0441, 0x8003,

          0xC007, 0xE00F, 0xF01F, 0xFFFF,


                                            // cursor mask //
          0x0000, 0x07C0, 0x0920, 0x1110,

          0x2108, 0x4004, 0x4004, 0x783C,

          0x4004, 0x4004, 0x2108, 0x1110,

          0x0920, 0x07C0, 0x0000, 0x0000,

          0x0007, 0x0007  };                // xkey, ykey  //

static  g_cursor GLOVE =                    // screen mask //

       {  0xF3FF, 0xE1FF, 0xE1FF, 0xE1FF,
```

```
          0xE1FF,  0xE049,  0xE000,  0x8000,

          0x0000,  0x0000,  0x07FC,  0x07F8,

          0x9FF9,  0x8FF1,  0xC003,  0xE007,

                                                  // cursor mask //
          0x0C00,  0x1200,  0x1200,  0x1200,

          0x1200,  0x13B6,  0x1249,  0x7249,

          0x9249,  0x9001,  0x9001,  0x8001,

          0x4002,  0x4002,  0x2004,  0x1FF8,

          0x0004,  0x0000  };                     // xkey, ykey  //

static  g_cursor IBEAM =                          // screen mask //
        {  0xF39F,  0xFD7F,  0xFEFF,  0xFEFF,

           0xFEFF,  0xFEFF,  0xFEFF,  0xFEFF,

           0xFEFF,  0xFEFF,  0xFEFF,  0xFEFF,

           0xFEFF,  0xFEFF,  0xFD7F,  0xF39F,

                                                  // cursor mask //
           0x0C60,  0x0280,  0x0100,  0x0100,

           0x0100,  0x0100,  0x0100,  0x0100,

           0x0100,  0x0100,  0x0100,  0x0100,

           0x0100,  0x0100,  0x0280,  0x0C60,

           0x0007,  0x0008 };                     // xkey, ykey  //

class Mouse

{

   int    Mview;                      // mouse cursor status flag //
```

```
    protected:

        Mouse();                        // constructor method    //

        ~Mouse();                       // destructor method     //

    public:

        static mouse_event far *Mevents;

                        // Global far ptr to mouse event record //

        Mmovement *Mmotion();           // net cursor motion     //

        Mresult    *Mreset();

        Mstatus    Mpos();

        Mstatus    Mpressed( int button );

        Mstatus    Mreleased( int button );

        void Mshow( int showstat );

        void Mmoveto( int xaxis, int yaxis );

        void Mxlimit( int min_x, int max_x );

        void Mylimit( int min_y, int max_y );

        void Mmove_ratio( int xsize, int ysize );

        void Mspeed( int speed );

        void Mconceal( int left, int top,

                        int right, int bottom );
};

class GMouse : public Mouse
{
    private:                            // graphic cursor shape   //
```

```
      void set_cursor( int xaxis,

                       int yaxis,

                       unsigned mask_Seg,

                       unsigned mask_Ofs );

   public:

      void Set_Cursor( g_cursor ThisCursor );

      void Mlightpen( int set );

};

class TMouse : public Mouse

{

   public:                          // text cursor shape        //

      void Set_Cursor( int cursor_type,

                       unsigned s_start,

                       unsigned s_stop  );

      void Mlightpen( int set );

};


   //=======================================================//
   //  implementations of the standard mouse functions    //
   //=======================================================//

Mouse::Mouse()

{

}


Mouse::~Mouse()
```

```
{

}


            // resets mouse default status, returns pointer to  //
            // Mresult structure indicating if mouse installed  //
            // and, if present, number of buttons - always call //
            // during initialization                            //
Mresult *Mouse::Mreset()
{

    static Mresult  m;

    Mview = OFF;

    inreg.x.ax = 0;                          // mouse function 0 //

    call_mouse;

    m.present = outreg.x.ax;

    m.buttons = outreg.x.bx;

    if( m.present ) Mshow( TRUE );

    return ( &m );

}


void Mouse::Mshow( int showstat )
{

    if( showstat )

    {

        inreg.x.ax = 1;                      // mouse function 1  //

        if( !Mview ) call_mouse;             // show mouse cursor //

        Mview = ON;
```

```
    }

    else

    {

        inreg.x.ax = 2;                    // mouse function 2  //

        if( Mview ) call_mouse;            // hide mouse cursor //

        Mview = OFF;

}   }


Mstatus Mouse::Mpos()

{                   // returns pointer to Mstatus structure with //

                    // mouse cursor position and button status   //

    static Mstatus   m;

    inreg.x.ax = 3;                        // mouse function 3 //

    call_mouse;

    m.button_status = outreg.x.bx;         // button status    //

    m.xaxis = outreg.x.cx;                 // xaxis coordinate //

    m.yaxis = outreg.x.dx;                 // yaxis coordinate //

    return (m);

}


void Mouse::Mmoveto( int xaxis, int yaxis )

{                              // mouse cursor to new position //

    inreg.x.ax = 4;                        // mouse function 4 //

    inreg.x.cx = xaxis;

    inreg.x.dx = yaxis;
```

```
        call_mouse;

}

        // return button pressed info; current status (up/dn),  //
        // times pressed since last call, cursor position at    //
        // last press - resets count and position info          //
        //              button 0 - left, 1 - right, 2 - center  //

Mstatus Mouse::Mpressed( int button )

{

        static Mstatus  m;

        inreg.x.ax = 5;                      // mouse function 5    //

        inreg.x.bx = button;                 // request for button //

        call_mouse;

        m.button_status = outreg.x.ax;

        m.button_count = outreg.x.bx;

        m.xaxis = outreg.x.cx;

        m.yaxis = outreg.x.dx;

        return (m);

}


Mstatus Mouse::Mreleased( int button )

{                               // returns release info about button //

        static Mstatus  m;

        inreg.x.ax = 6;                         // mouse function 6    //

        inreg.x.bx = button;                    // request for button //
```

```
    call_mouse;

    m.button_status = outreg.x.ax;

    m.button_count = outreg.x.bx;

    m.xaxis = outreg.x.cx;

    m.yaxis = outreg.x.dx;

    return (m);

}


        // Set min / max horizontal range for cursor. Moves  //
        // cursor inside range if outside when called. Swaps //
        // values if min_x and max_x are reversed.           //

void Mouse::Mxlimit( int min_x, int max_x )

{

    inreg.x.ax = 7;                          // mouse function 7 //

    inreg.x.cx = min_x;

    inreg.x.dx = max_x;

    call_mouse;

}


void Mouse::Mylimit( int min_y, int max_y )

{                                    // sets vertical boundaries //

    inreg.x.ax = 8;                          // mouse function 8 //

    inreg.x.cx = min_y;

    inreg.x.dx = max_y;

    call_mouse;
```

```
}

void GMouse::set_cursor( int xaxis, int yaxis,

                         unsigned mask_Seg,

                         unsigned mask_Ofs )

{                                    // Sets graphic cursor shape //

   struct SREGS  seg;

   inreg.x.ax = 9;                         // mouse function 9 //

   inreg.x.bx = xaxis;             // xaxis cursor hot-spot //

   inreg.x.cx = yaxis;             // yaxis cursor hot-spot //

   inreg.x.dx = mask_Ofs;

   seg.es     = mask_Seg;

   int86x( 0x33, &inreg, &outreg, &seg );

}


       // set text cursor type, 0 = software, 1 = hardware  //
       // software cursor, arg1 and arg2 are the screen and //
       //    cursor masks.                                  //
       // hardware cursor, arg1 and arg2 specify scan line  //
       //    start/stop - i.e. cursor shape.                //

void TMouse::Set_Cursor( int cursor_type,

                         unsigned s_start,

                         unsigned s_stop  )

{

   inreg.x.ax = 10;                        // mouse function 10 //
```

```
    inreg.x.bx = cursor_type;

    inreg.x.cx = s_start;

    inreg.x.dx = s_stop;

    call_mouse;

}


Mmovement* Mouse::Mmotion()

{                   // reports net cursor motion since last call //

    static Mmovement  m;

    inreg.x.ax = 11;                    // mouse function 11  //

    call_mouse;

    m.x_count = _CX;                    // net xaxis movement //

    m.y_count = _DX;                    // net yaxis movement //

    return (&m);

}


void GMouse::Mlightpen( int set )

{

    if( set ) inreg.x.ax = 13;         // function 13  ON //

        else   inreg.x.ax = 14;        // function 14 OFF //

    call_mouse;

}


void TMouse::Mlightpen( int set )

{
```

```
    if( set )  inreg.x.ax = 13;              // function 13  ON //

        else   inreg.x.ax = 14;              // function 14 OFF //

    call_mouse;

}


void Mouse::Mmove_ratio( int xsize, int ysize )

{                         // motion-to-pixel ratio with ratio R/8 //

    inreg.x.ax = 15;                        // Default 16 vert //

    inreg.x.cx = xsize;                     //          8 horiz //

    inreg.x.dx = ysize;

    call_mouse;

}


void Mouse::Mconceal( int left, int top,

                      int right, int bottom )

{                                    // area where mouse hidden //

    inreg.x.ax = 16;                     // use for scr update //

    inreg.x.cx = left;

    inreg.x.dx = top;

    inreg.x.si = right;

    inreg.x.di = bottom;

    call_mouse;

}


void Mouse::Mspeed( int speed )

{                                    // sets speed threshold   //
```

```
    inreg.x.ax = 19;              // in mickeys/second for  //

    inreg.x.dx = speed;            // for accelerated mouse //

    call_mouse;                    // movement response      //

}

void GMouse::Set_Cursor( g_cursor ThisCursor )

{

    set_cursor( ThisCursor.xkey,

                ThisCursor.ykey,

                _DS,

                (unsigned) ThisCursor.ScreenMask );

}

        // type definitions for use by applications //

GMouse   gmouse;

TMouse   tmouse;



        //====================================//
        //              MOUSEPTR.PAS          //
        //   Demo program for Mouse Object    //
        // and utility to create mouse cursor //
        //====================================//

#ifdef __TINY__

#error Graphics demos will not run in the tiny model

#endif


#include <conio.h>
```

```
#include <stdio.h>

#include <stdlib.h>

#include <stdarg.h>

#include <graphics.h>

#include <string.h>

#include "mouse.i"


Mstatus    Position;

g_cursor   NewCursor;

int        Buttons, XIndex, YIndex, HotSpotX = 0,

           HotSpotY = 0, HotSpotSelect, Screen[16][16],

           Cursor[16][16];


int TPos( int TP, int Low, int High )

{

   return( ( TP >= Low ) && ( TP <= High ) );

}


void BoxItem( int x, int y, int w, int h, char* text )

{

   settextjustify( CENTER_TEXT, CENTER_TEXT );

   rectangle( x, y, x+w, y+h );

   outtextxy( x+(w/2), y+(h/2), text );

}


void FillSquare( int x1, int y1, int x2, int y2,
```

```
                      int FillStyle,   int Color )
{

  int  outline[10];

  outline[0] = outline[6] = outline[8] = x1;

  outline[2] = outline[4] = x2;

  outline[1] = outline[3] = outline[9] = y1;

  outline[5] = outline[7] = y2;

  setfillstyle( FillStyle, Color );

  fillpoly( 5, outline );

}

void EraseSquare( int x1, int y1, int x2, int y2 )
{

  FillSquare( x1, y1, x2, y2, EMPTY_FILL, 0 );

}

void Beep()
{

  sound( 220 ); delay( 100 ); nosound();

                  delay(  50 );

  sound( 440 ); delay( 100 ); nosound();

}

void MakeCursor()
{
```

```
    int   i, j;

    unsigned int TBit;

    NewCursor.xkey = HotSpotX;

    NewCursor.ykey = HotSpotY;

    for( i=0; i<=15; i++ )

    {

        NewCursor.ScreenMask[i] = 0x0000;

        NewCursor.CursorMask[i] = 0x0000;

        for( j=0; j<=15; j++ )

        {

            NewCursor.CursorMask[i] <<= 1;

            if( Cursor[j][i] ) NewCursor.CursorMask[i]++;

            NewCursor.ScreenMask[i] <<= 1;

            if( Screen[j][i] ) NewCursor.ScreenMask[i]++;

} } }

void UseNewCursor()

{

    MakeCursor();

    gmouse.Mshow( FALSE );

    gmouse.Set_Cursor( NewCursor );

    gmouse.Mshow( TRUE );

}

void PaintScreen( int X, int Y )
```

```
{
   int Color = WHITE;

   if ( ( X == HotSpotX ) && ( Y == HotSpotY ) )
      Color = LIGHTRED;

   gmouse.Mshow( FALSE );

   if( Screen[X][Y] )
      FillSquare( X*15+18, Y*15+33, X*15+27, Y*15+42,
                 SOLID_FILL, Color );
   else
   {
      EraseSquare( X*15+15, Y*15+30, X*15+30, Y*15+45 );
      FillSquare(  X*15+15, Y*15+30, X*15+30, Y*15+45,
                 CLOSE_DOT_FILL, Color );
   }

   gmouse.Mshow( TRUE );

   setcolor( WHITE );
}

void PaintCursor( int X, int Y )
{
   int Color = WHITE;

   if( ( X == HotSpotX ) && ( Y == HotSpotY ) )
      Color = LIGHTRED;

   gmouse.Mshow( FALSE );
```

```
    if( Cursor[X][Y] )

        FillSquare( (X+1) * 15 + 369, (Y+2) * 15,

                    (X+2) * 15 + 366, (Y+3) * 15 - 3,

                    SOLID_FILL, Color );

    else

        FillSquare( (X+1) * 15 + 369, (Y+2) * 15,

                    (X+2) * 15 + 369, (Y+3) * 15,

                    CLOSE_DOT_FILL, Color );

    gmouse.Mshow( TRUE );

    setcolor( WHITE );

}


void HotSpotComplete()

{

    PaintCursor( HotSpotX, HotSpotY );

    PaintScreen( HotSpotX, HotSpotY );

    gmouse.Mshow( FALSE );

    HotSpotSelect = FALSE;

    setcolor( WHITE );

    settextjustify( CENTER_TEXT, CENTER_TEXT );

    BoxItem( 265, 320, 110, 20, "Set Hotspot" );

    gmouse.Mshow( TRUE );

}


void SetHotSpot()
```

```
{
    int X, Y;

    X = HotSpotX;

    Y = HotSpotY;

    HotSpotX = -1;

    HotSpotY = -1;

    PaintCursor( X, Y );

    PaintScreen( X, Y );

    gmouse.Mshow( FALSE );

    HotSpotSelect = TRUE;

    setcolor( RED );

    settextjustify( CENTER_TEXT, CENTER_TEXT );
    BoxItem( 265, 320, 110, 20, "Set Hotspot" );

    setcolor( WHITE );

    gmouse.Mshow( TRUE );
}

void ScreenLayout()
{
    int i, j;

    settextjustify( CENTER_TEXT, CENTER_TEXT );
    outtextxy( 135, 20, "Screen Mask" );

    outtextxy( 504, 20, "Cursor Mask" );

    HotSpotComplete();
```

```
                    // screen mask items //
   BoxItem(  15, 280,  60, 20, "Clear" );

   BoxItem(  85, 280,  60, 20, "Invert" );

   BoxItem( 155, 280, 140, 20, "Make from Cursor" );

                    // cursor mask items //
   BoxItem( 564, 280,  60, 20, "Clear" );

   BoxItem( 494, 280,  60, 20, "Invert" );

   BoxItem( 344, 280, 140, 20, "Copy to Screen" );

                    // control options //
   BoxItem(  15, 320, 110, 20, "Use Pointer" );

   BoxItem( 140, 320, 110, 20, "Arrow Pointer" );

   BoxItem( 265, 320, 110, 20, "Set Hotspot" );

   BoxItem( 390, 320, 110, 20, "Save Pointer" );

   BoxItem( 515, 320, 110, 20, "Exit" );

   for( i=0; i<=15; i++ )

      for( j=0; j<=15; j++ )

      {

         Screen[i][j] = FALSE;

         PaintScreen( i, j );

         Cursor[i][j] = FALSE;

         PaintCursor( i, j );

}       }

void ClearScreen()

{
```

```
    int   i, j;

    for( i=0; i<=15; i++ )

       for( j=0; j<=15; j++ )

          if( Screen[i][j] )

          {

              Screen[i][j] = FALSE;

              PaintScreen( i, j );

}          }

void ClearCursor()

{

    int   i, j;

    for( i=0; i<=15; i++ )

       for( j=0; j<=15; j++ )

          if( Cursor[i][j] )

          {

              Cursor[i][j] = FALSE;

              PaintCursor( i, j );

}          }

void InvertScreen()

{

    int   i, j;

    for( i=0; i<=15; i++ )
```

```
        for( j=0; j<=15; j++ )

        {

            if( Screen[i][j] ) Screen[i][j] = FALSE;

                        else Screen[i][j] = TRUE;

            PaintScreen( i, j );

}       }

void InvertCursor()

{

    int i, j;

    for( i=0; i<=15; i++ )

        for( j=0; j<=15; j++ )

        {

            if( Cursor[i][j] ) Cursor[i][j] = FALSE;

                        else Cursor[i][j] = TRUE;

            PaintCursor( i, j );

}       }

void ScreenSet( int xaxis, int yaxis )

{

    int x, y;

    x = ( xaxis / 15 ) - 1;

    y = ( yaxis / 15 ) - 2;

    if( HotSpotSelect )
```

```
    {

       HotSpotX = x;

       HotSpotY = y;

       HotSpotComplete();

    }

    else

    {

       if( Screen[x][y] ) Screen[x][y] = FALSE;

                    else Screen[x][y] = TRUE;

       PaintScreen( x, y );

}   }

void CursorSet( int xaxis, int yaxis )

{

    int x, y;

    x = ( xaxis - 384 ) / 15;

    y = ( yaxis / 15 ) - 2;

    if( HotSpotSelect )

    {

       HotSpotX = x;

       HotSpotY = y;

       HotSpotComplete();

    }

    else
```

```
    {
        if( Cursor[x][y] ) Cursor[x][y] = FALSE;
                    else Cursor[x][y] = TRUE;
        PaintCursor( x, y );
}   }

void CursorToScreen()
{
    int i, j;

    for( i=0; i<=15; i++ )
        for( j=0; j<=15; j++ )
        {
            Screen[i][j] = Cursor[i][j];
            PaintScreen( i, j );
}       }

void ScreenFromCursor()
{
    int i, j, x, y, Test;

    for( i=0; i<=15; i++ )
        for( j=0; j<=15; j++ )
        {
            Test = TRUE;
            for( x=-1; x<=1; x++ )
```

```
            for( y =-1; y<=1; y++ )

                if( ( TPos( i+x, 0, 15 ) ) &&

                    ( TPos( j+y, 0, 15 ) ) &&

                    ( Cursor[i+x][j+y] ) ) Test = FALSE;

        Screen[i][j] = Test;

        PaintScreen( i, j );

}    }


int SavePointer()

{

    int  i, Done = FALSE;

    char Ch, CursorName[8]="", FileName[12]="";

    FILE *CF;

    strcpy( CursorName, "........" );

    setviewport( 269, 0, 369, 42, TRUE );

    settextjustify( CENTER_TEXT, CENTER_TEXT );

    gmouse.Set_Cursor( IBEAM );

    gmouse.Mmoveto( 277, 30 );

    i = 0;

    do

    {

        gmouse.Mshow( FALSE );

        clearviewport();

        setcolor( LIGHTRED );
```

```
        rectangle( 0, 0, 100, 40 );

        outtextxy( 50, 10, "Save As" );

        outtextxy( 50, 20, "File Name?" );

        outtextxy( 50, 30, CursorName);

        gmouse.Mmoveto( 277+i*8,30 );

        gmouse.Mshow( TRUE );

        Ch = getch();

        if( Ch == 0x0D ) Done = TRUE;

        else if( ( Ch == 0x08 ) && ( i > 1 ) ) i-=2;

        else if( i > 7 ) { Beep(); i - -; }

        else CursorName[i] = Ch;

        i++;

    }

    while( !Done );

    gmouse.Set_Cursor( ARROW );

    gmouse.Mshow( FALSE );

    clearviewport();

    setviewport( 0, 0, getmaxx(), getmaxy(), TRUE );

    gmouse.Mshow( TRUE );

    for( i=7; i>=0; i - - )

    {

        if( CursorName[i] == '.' ) CursorName[i] = '\0';

        if( CursorName[i] == ' ' ) CursorName[i] = '\0';

    }
```

```
if( strlen( CursorName ) == 0 ) { Beep(); return(0); }

MakeCursor();

strcpy( FileName, CursorName );

strcat( FileName, ".CUR" );

outtextxy( 320, 10, FileName );

CF = fopen( FileName, "w" );

fprintf( CF, "static  g_cursor %s = \n", CursorName );

fprintf( CF,
    "         {   0x%04X, 0x%04X, 0x%04X, 0x%04X,\n",
    NewCursor.ScreenMask[0], NewCursor.ScreenMask[1],
    NewCursor.ScreenMask[2], NewCursor.ScreenMask[3] );

for( i=1; i<=3; i++ )
    fprintf( CF,
        "             0x%04X, 0x%04X, 0x%04X, 0x%04X,\n",
        NewCursor.ScreenMask[i*4],
        NewCursor.ScreenMask[i*4+1],
        NewCursor.ScreenMask[i*4+2],
        NewCursor.ScreenMask[i*4+3] );

for( i=0; i<=3; i++ )
    fprintf( CF,
        "             0x%04X, 0x%04X, 0x%04X, 0x%04X,\n",
        NewCursor.CursorMask[i*4],
        NewCursor.CursorMask[i*4+1],
        NewCursor.CursorMask[i*4+2],
```

```
                NewCursor.CursorMask[i*4+3] );

    fprintf( CF, "              0x%04X, 0x%04X };\n",
                NewCursor.xkey,  NewCursor.ykey );

    fprintf( CF, "\n" );

    fclose( CF );

    return( 1 );
}

main()
{
    int GDriver = DETECT, GMode, GError,
        Exit = FALSE, i, j;
    Mresult* Result;

    initgraph( &GDriver, &GMode, "C:\\TC\\BGI" );

    GError = graphresult();

    if( GError != grOk )
    {
        printf( "Graphics error: %s\n",
                grapherrormsg(GError) );

        printf( "Program aborted...\n" );

        exit(1);
    }

    cleardevice();

    ScreenLayout();
```

```
Result = gmouse.Mreset();

setwritemode( COPY_PUT );

if( Result->present )

{

   do

   {

      Position = gmouse.Mpressed( ButtonL );

      if( Position.button_count )

      {

         if( TPos( Position.yaxis, 30, 270 ) )

         {                          // screen or cursor grids //

            if( TPos( Position.xaxis,  15, 255 ) )

               ScreenSet( Position.xaxis,

                     Position.yaxis );

            if( TPos( Position.xaxis, 384, 624 ) )

               CursorSet( Position.xaxis,

                     Position.yaxis );

         } else

         if( TPos( Position.yaxis, 280, 300 ) )

                           // screen or cursor commands //
                              // screen mask items //
         {

            if( TPos( Position.xaxis,  15,  75 ) )

               ClearScreen(); else

            if( TPos( Position.xaxis,  85, 145 ) )
```

```
                     InvertScreen(); else

          if( TPos( Position.xaxis, 155, 295 ) )

               ScreenFromCursor(); else

                                    // cursor mask items //
          if( TPos( Position.xaxis, 364, 484 ) )

               CursorToScreen(); else

          if( TPos( Position.xaxis, 494, 554 ) )

               InvertCursor(); else

          if( TPos( Position.xaxis, 564, 624 ) )

               ClearCursor();

     } else

     if( TPos( Position.yaxis, 320, 340 ) )

     {                        // general command options //
          if( TPos( Position.xaxis,  15, 125 ) )

               UseNewCursor(); else

          if( TPos( Position.xaxis, 140, 250 ) )

               gmouse.Set_Cursor( ARROW ); else

          if( TPos( Position.xaxis, 265, 375 ) )

               SetHotSpot(); else

          if( TPos( Position.xaxis, 390, 500 ) )

               SavePointer(); else

          if( TPos( Position.xaxis, 515, 625 ) )

               Exit = TRUE;

}   }   }
```

```
        while( !Exit );

    }

    tmouse.Mreset();

    tmouse.Set_Cursor( HARDWARE, 11, 12 );

    Beep();

}
```

CHAPTER 5

OBJECT BUTTON CONTROLS

By itself, the object mouse created in Chapter 4 is interesting but useless until applied to a practical task. The next step is to create two types of control objects, BUTTONS and TBOXES, that respond to mouse hit events; and to create a simple demo program, BTNTEST, to show how these control objects work. Before going into details on the creation of these two object types, I'll begin with an overview of the operations of each.

Graphics and Text Button Operations

While the graphics and text button operations are provided as independent units, there are similarities between the two object types. Examples of the text button objects appear in Figure 5-1 and the graphics button objects appear in Figure 5-2.

For both object types, several elements are assigned when each object instance is created. For the text buttons, the parameters include the outline type, size, position, color, and text label. For text buttons, the box outline is created using the extended ASCII character set and may be a single, double, or blank outline. For graphic buttons, the button style may be Square, Rounded, or ThreeD.

For text buttons, only the horizontal size (in columns) is selected, with the vertical size fixed at three rows. For graphics buttons, both vertical and horizontal sizes are set (in pixels) and, if the vertical size is greater than the horizontal, the text orientation is set as vertical.

Both the text and graphics buttons accept string arguments for the text label, but the handling is slightly different in each case. For the text button, the label is truncated if it will not fit within the button outline. For the graphics button, labels may also be truncated if necessary, but typefaces may also be sized for the best fit for the label within the button.

Position arguments are accepted by both button types. For the text buttons the coordinates are row/column positions and, for the graphic buttons they are pixel positions; both setting the upper-left corner positions.

Text Button States and Colors

Foreground and background colors are also assigned when each instance of the object is created. In this implementation, however, the assigned background color is used immediately but the foreground color is used only when the text button's state is set as Select. Initially, each text button is set as Off and must be explicitly changed to Select, either by the program or by mouse-selection, before the assigned color will be used for highlighting. In the default Off state, the button is drawn using the LightGray color.

A third text button state, Invalid (shown in Figure 5-1), is also provided. This causes the button to be drawn using the DarkGray color. This particular provision is often useful when an option should be shown but is selectable in the present circumstances.

Graphic Button States and Colors

For the graphics button objects, only two states are provided, true or false, and no Invalid state is implemented. As before, a default state of false is assigned when the button is created and must be explicitly changed.

The graphic buttons differ from the text buttons in another respect; the graphic button images are always drawn using the assigned color and, for highlighting to show selection, the background and foreground colors are swapped (button 3 in Figure 5-2) and the buttons are redrawn.

Figure 5-1: Text Button Images

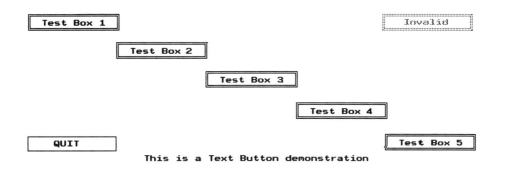

Figure 5-2: Graphic Button Images

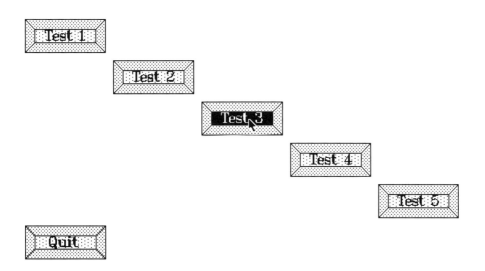

Button Mouse Selection

Both the text (TBoxes) and graphic (Buttons) button objects have provisions to recognize mouse hits, but in the current programs, neither object type tests the mouse position or interrogates mouse button events directly. Instead, the application program must watch for mouse button events, passing the event coordinates to each instance of the object for testing.

When the object detects a mouse hit, by comparing the event coordinates with its own position and size, a Boolean hit result is returned to the application program. Either the text or graphics object button automatically changes its own state and redisplays itself accordingly.

In the present demo, the tests and responses are limited. The only mouse button tested is a left-button down event. When the left button is pressed, the first response is to test all of the text or graphic buttons. If any are set as Select then the button's Invert procedure is called to turn it off. After all screen buttons have been reset, a second loop polls each of the screen buttons for a mouse hit. If the mouse button event did coincide with a screen button, the screen button turns itself on and the application program responds with an audible prompt.

If a text button with the Invalid state set is mouse-selected, the only result is an audio prompt generated by the button object—not by the application.

The TBoxes Unit

The TBoxes unit is the first control object created. This provides a text-oriented object type displaying a box outline and text label (see Figure 5-1). TBoxes begins by declaring the two data types:

```
typedef enum { UNSEL, SELECT, INVALID } BoxState;
typedef enum { NONE, SINGLE, DOUBLE } BoxType;
```

In this case, the object type Box is not created as a descendant of any other object type:

```
class Box
{
   protected:
      int   x, y, Color, BackColor, SizeX, Exist;
      BoxState State;
      BoxType  ThisBox;
      char     BtnTxt[40];
```

The Box object has several variables as shown, most of which are self-explanatory. The Boolean variable, *Exist*, however, deserves a few comments and a few cautions.

The Exist Variable

In the demo program, BTNTEST, two arrays of objects are declared as:

```
Button   GButton[10];
Box      TBox[10];
```

Because these are object-type variables, they are often expected to carry out semi-independent operations, but if the variable has not been initialized, the operations executed can be surprising at best and, at worst, may cause a system hang-up.

In the demo programs used in this book, there is little chance for a declared, but uninitialized object to be called. In other circumstances, however, you may prefer to err on the side of safety and, after declaring an array of object, declare the Exist variables for all elements in the array as false by calling the Initialize method:

```
for( i=1; i<=10; i++ )
{
    GButton[i].Initialize;
    TBox[i].Initialize;
}
```

Many of the critical methods in the object do not execute unless the Exist variable has been set to true, which is done when the Create method is called for each object instance.

If you examine the source code for each of these objects, you will note that more than the Exist flag is affected by the Initialize method. Also, the Box::Initialize method is more elaborate than the Button::Initialize method. In either case, the Exist flag setting is the primary objective of the Initialize method, while the remaining method code is either optionally redundant or might be handled equally well by the object's Create method.

Using the graphic button object as an example, suppose that a nonexistent button is called by any of several instructions, resulting in the Draw method being called. If the button size has not been assigned by a call to the Create method, it could result in an extremely long wait while graphics operations are attempted over an indeterminate area or, in other cases, a system hang-up may be the result (see Table 5-1).

Table 5-1: Random Results Returned by 10 Uncreated Buttons

WIDTH		HEIGHT		EXIST	
Width =	1024	Height =	0	Exist =	TRUE
Width =	191	Height =	7680	Exist =	TRUE
Width =	-24240	Height =	0	Exist =	FALSE
Width =	232	Height =	-30464	Exist =	TRUE
Width =	30464	Height =	24044	Exist =	TRUE
Width =	-442	Height =	-4983	Exist =	TRUE
Width =	0	Height =	17923	Exist =	TRUE
Width =	154	Height =	0	Exist =	TRUE
Width =	-30463	Height =	3590	Exist =	FALSE
Width =	1654	Height =	-6130	Exist =	TRUE

In the worst case the size of the button object is 30,464 by 24,044—a total of 732,476,416 pixels, over 3,000 times the size of the average screen. Drawing or erasing an image of this size can take a bit longer than expected, or worse, operations may extend to critical memory locations, disrupting the system. Another method of preventing such accidents is by using constructor and destructor calls and dynamic allocation. This will be demonstrated later.

Box Object Methods

Nineteen methods are declared for the object-type Box; most are self-explanatory. A few of these, however, deserve at least a brief mention.

The Create method for the text button accepts arguments setting the initial position, size, foreground and background colors, and text label for a text button object. The Create procedure sets *Exist* as TRUE for the current instance, ensures that a text string has been provided and finally, calls the Draw method to create a text button on the screen.

No position tests are provided, but if desired, would be better implemented in the Draw method than here in the Create method.

The Initialize method requires no arguments, but resets all variables to zero or to false, clearing the object instance for further use. No screen operations are executed.

The DrawBox method is the heart of the Box object, writing the text button screen image:

```
void Box::DrawBox()
{
    char    BoxStr[6];
```

```
int        i, XPos, YPos, C;

XPos = wherex();
YPos = wherey();
C = getbkcolor();
```

Since the text buttons are intended for use with applications that will have other text material on screen, before a button is created, the current screen background color and cursor position are saved and will be restored before the DrawBox method is completed.

The current text color is determined by the button's state and the button's assigned background color:

```
switch( State )
{
    case INVALID:
    case    UNSEL: textattr( LIGHTGRAY + BackColor );
                   break;
    case    SELECT: textattr( Color + BackColor );
                   break;
}
```

Here, the textattr function is called to set the foreground and background color attributes but the BackColor value has already been left-shifted four places and, therefore, can be added to the foreground color directly. Next, the local variable, BoxStr, is given the characters appropriate to the assigned box style:

```
switch( ThisBox )
{
    case    NONE: strcpy( BoxStr, "        "); break;
    case SINGLE: strcpy( BoxStr,
                        "\xDA\xBF\xC0\xD9\xC4\xB3" );
                 break;
    case DOUBLE: strcpy( BoxStr,
                        "\xC9\xBB\xC8\xBC\xCD\xBA" );
}
```

At this point, all that's left is to write the screen image:

```
                      // top of box //
   gotoxy( x, y );
   cprintf( "%c", BoxStr[0] );
   for( i=2; i<=SizeX-1; i++ )
       cprintf( "%c", BoxStr[4] );
   cprintf( "%c", BoxStr[1] );
                      // center of box //
   gotoxy( x, y+1 );
   cprintf( "%c", BoxStr[5] );
   for( i=2; i<=SizeX-1; i++ ) cprintf( " " );
   cprintf( "%c", BoxStr[5] );
```

The interior of the box is written as spaces to clear anything that might already appear on the screen, then the new label is written, centered.

```
   gotoxy( x + ( SizeX - strlen( BtnTxt ) ) / 2, y+1 );
   cprintf( "%s", BtnTxt );
                      // bottom of box //
   gotoxy( x, y+2 );
   cprintf( "%c", BoxStr[2] );
   for( i=2; i<SizeX; i++ ) cprintf( "%c", BoxStr[4] );
   cprintf( "%c", BoxStr[3] );
```

Finally, the saved cursor position and background color attributes are restored, leaving the system ready for other operations.

```
   textbackground( C );
   gotoxy( XPos, YPos );
}
```

cprintf Versus printf

The printf instruction is the default method used by most programmers to write text information to the screen. There is one limitation which you should be aware of here. The printf instruction does not set the screen attributes but uses the existing screen attributes which, in this demonstration would be a Black background and a Lightgray foreground.

The text button objects, however, are designed to have specific background and foreground colors and to change these color attributes to show button states. Therefore, the cprintf instruction is used to insure that the current color settings are actually written to the screen.

The BoxHit Method

One more method deserves explanation; the BoxHit method, which is called by the application with two parameters giving the coordinates of a mouse button event and returning a Boolean result:

```
int  Box::BoxHit( int MouseX, int MouseY )
{
   MouseX = MouseX / 8 + 1;
   MouseY = MouseY / 8 + 1;
```

Because the coordinates reported by the mouse event are in pixel units, the *MouseX* and *MouseY* parameters are converted to character positions (row/column units) before testing:

```
   if( ( MouseX >= x ) && ( MouseX < x+SizeX ) &&
       ( MouseY >= y ) && ( MouseY <= y+2 ) )
   {
      Invert();
      return( TRUE );
   } else return( FALSE );
}
```

If the reported coordinates fall within the button object's parameters, BoxHit calls the Invert method to show that the button has been hit; finally returning true to the calling application. If not, then false is returned.

The remaining 15 methods used by the Box object can be found in the program listings at the end of this chapter. Several methods are provided but not utilized by the demo program. Remember, any methods that are not used by an application are not included by Turbo C++ in the compiled program. Nothing is saved by being skimpy about declaring methods.

The Button Object

The Button object is the graphics parallel of the TBoxes object, providing graphic button images that can be tested for mouse event hits, responding with a visual cue as well as returning a Boolean result.

Note, however, that the methods provided for the text and graphic button features are only approximately parallel. The graphic buttons differ from the text buttons in two principal respects; buttons may be any size (within the limits of the screen or window), and the button caption may be oriented vertically instead of horizontally.

A variety of graphic button examples appear in Figure 5-3, in varying sizes, styles, and orientations with button 5 (ThreeD style) showing the selected state.

Figure 5-3: Assorted Graphics Buttons

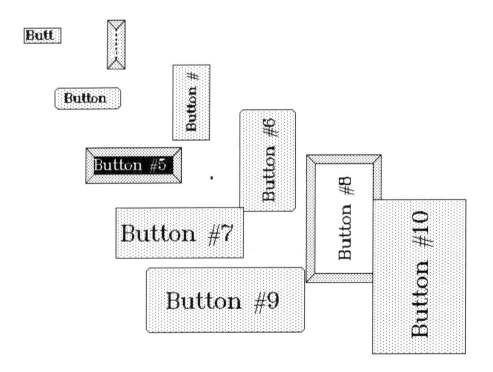

Notice also that buttons 1 and 2 are actually too small to properly display labels, but attempt to do so anyway. The demo generating the illustration in Figure 5-3 used Borland's TriplexFont which, sometimes, is too large for many applications. The SmallFont (LITT.CHR) provides an alternate stroked character font approximately half the size of the triplex font and, in general, more useful for small button labels. For more details on Borland's fonts and sizing examples, refer to *Graphics Programming In Turbo C 2.0*, Addison-Wesley Publishing Company, 1988.

Depending on your application, you may prefer to modify the Button object to use this smaller font, or to adapt the label algorithm to switch fonts for smaller labels.

As can be seen in Figure 5-3, button labels are oriented vertically any time the button image is taller (in pixel units) than it is wide. This is an optional feature and the graphics button unit could be redesigned for closer similarities to the text buttons. If the vertical orientation is eliminated, the revision should probably include restrictions on button height.

Like the text version, the graphic buttons are established by calling the Create method, but the parameter list is different in that Button::Create is called as:

```
void Button::Create( int PtX, int PtY, int Width,
                     int Height, int C, char* Text )
```

Unlike the text version, no explicit background color is assigned, but a width parameter is required.

Like the text button version, the Create method is primarily concerned with assigning values derived from the calling parameters before calling the Draw method to execute the actual screen operations. One difference, however, is the Boolean Rotate variable that is set by testing the width against the height:

```
{
    setviewport( 0, 0, getmaxx(), getmaxy(), TRUE );
    settextjustify( CENTER_TEXT, CENTER_TEXT );
    x = PtX;
    y = PtY;
    SizeX = Width;
    SizeY = Height;
    if( SizeX < 20 ) SizeX = 20;
    if( SizeY < 20 ) SizeY = 20;
```

```
     if( Height > Width ) Rotate = TRUE;
                      else Rotate = FALSE;
     Color  = C;
     State  = FALSE;
     Exist  = TRUE;
     strcpy( BtnTxt, Text );
     Draw();
}
```

The Draw method for the graphics buttons is somewhat more complicated than the text counterpart and begins with two constants, radius
and offset, used for the rounded corners and to control the fill area:

```
void Button::Draw()
{
    int      radius = 6, offset = 3, AlignX, AlignY,
             TempSize, TextLen, i, TextDir;
    Outline RectArr;
```

The RectArr variable is an array of integers used to define and fill a
rectangular outline:

The Draw method begins by setting a viewport (a graphics window)
to the button size and further restricting graphics drawing operations to
the viewport limits:

```
    setviewport( x, y, x+SizeX, y+SizeY, TRUE );
    setcolor( Color );
```

A switch/case statement using the Style variable selects the appropriate drawing routines beginning with the simplest case of the Square
style:

```
    switch( ThisButton )
    {
       case SQUARE:
          {
             rectangle( 0,  0,  SizeX, SizeY );
             break;
          }
```

The ThreeD style begins by drawing the outer rectangle and filling the entire rectangle using the CLOSE_DOT_FILL pattern:

```
case THREE_D:
    {
        rectangle( 0, 0, SizeX, SizeY );
        RectArr[0] = RectArr[2] = RectArr[8] =
        RectArr[1] = RectArr[7] = RectArr[9] = 1;
        RectArr[4] = RectArr[6] = SizeX-1;
        RectArr[3] = RectArr[5] = SizeY-1;
        setfillstyle( CLOSE_DOT_FILL, Color );
```

The next step is drawing the inner rectangle (on top of the dot-filled rectangle) and the four diagonal lines defining the sloped corner edges of the button:

```
        setlinestyle( USERBIT_LINE, 0, NORM_WIDTH );
        fillpoly( 5, RectArr );
        setlinestyle( SOLID_LINE, 0, NORM_WIDTH );
        rectangle( 2*radius, 2*radius,
                    SizeX-2*radius, SizeY-2*radius );
        line( 0, 0, 2*radius, 2*radius );
        line( 0, SizeY, 2*radius, SizeY-2*radius );
        line( SizeX, 0, SizeX-2*radius, 2*radius );
        line( SizeX, SizeY, SizeX-2*radius,
                            SizeY-2*radius );
        break;

    }
```

If you are running the demo program while reading this text, you may wish to change line 25 in BTNTEST.CPP from SetButtonType(THREE_D) to SetButtonType(ROUNDED) to view this button style.

The default style, Rounded, is the most complex of the three button styles and begins by drawing three quarter-circle arcs at the corner positions for the button image:

```
case ROUNDED:
    {
```

```
arc( SizeX-radius, radius, 0, 90, radius );
arc( radius, radius, 90, 180, radius );
arc( radius, SizeY-radius, 180, 270, radius );
arc( SizeX-radius, SizeY-radius, 270, 360,
        radius );
```

After the corners are drawn, the straight sides are drawn connecting the ends of the arcs:

```
line( radius, 0, SizeX-radius, 0 );
line( radius, SizeY, SizeX-radius, SizeY );
line( 0, radius, 0, SizeY-radius );
line( SizeX, radius, SizeX, SizeY-radius );
}    }
```

To complete the button fill, the Square and Rounded button styles use the same rectangular coordinates while the ThreeD style requires adjustment to limit fill to the raised center of the button.

```
switch( ThisButton )
{
    case SQUARE:
    case ROUNDED:
        {
            RectArr[0] = RectArr[2] = RectArr[8] =
            RectArr[1] = RectArr[7] = RectArr[9] =
                offset;
            RectArr[4] = RectArr[6] = SizeX-offset;
            RectArr[3] = RectArr[5] = SizeY-offset;
            break;
        }
    case THREE_D:
        {
            RectArr[0] = RectArr[2] = RectArr[8] =
            RectArr[1] = RectArr[7] = RectArr[9] =
                2*radius+1;
            RectArr[4] = RectArr[6] = SizeX-2*radius;
```

```
        RectArr[3] = RectArr[5] = SizeY-2*radius;
        break;
}      }
```

After the RectArr structure is set, a fill style is selected to show the button state, using a solid fill for a selected button or a close dot pattern for a button that is off:

```
if( State ) setfillstyle( SOLID_FILL, Color );
        else setfillstyle( CLOSE_DOT_FILL, Color );
setlinestyle( USERBIT_LINE, 0, NORM_WIDTH );
fillpoly( 5, RectArr );
```

Finally, the RectArr structure is passed to the FillPoly procedure to fill the interior of the button with the selected pattern. Next, the typeface, font size, and text direction are set and the label position calculated within the button outline.

```
setlinestyle( SOLID_LINE, 0, NORM_WIDTH );
 settextstyle( TypeFace, Rotate, FontSize );
AlignX = (SizeX/2)-3;
AlignY = (SizeY/2)-3;
```

If the button's state is set, then the drawing color is set to the background color, since the button has been filled solid, before writing the button label and then resetting the original color value and restoring the viewport settings to encompass the entire screen.

```
if( State ) setcolor( getbkcolor() );
outtextxy( AlignX, AlignY, BtnTxt );
if( State ) setcolor( Color );
setviewport( 0, 0, getmaxx(), getmaxy(), TRUE );
}
```

The remaining methods provided for the Buttons object are largely self-explanatory, providing inquiries for various button parameters or options to change parameters for an existing button without having to explicitly erase one button and create another.

The Button Test Program

The button test program, BTNTEST.CPP, is a simple demo utility that creates graphic and text button displays (see Figures 5-1 and 5-2) using the mouse object created in Chapter 4 as the control I/O. If your system lacks a mouse, a keyboard mouse emulator can be created as a substitute. In addition to several Turbo C header files, three include files are required: MOUSE.I, BUTTONS.I, and TBOXES.I.

The button test demo begins with the graphics buttons display. If when you execute the program, the graphics mouse cursor does not appear, you may have a problem mentioned in Chapter 4—a high resolution monitor and a low resolution mouse driver. If so, a one-line revision (shown below) should reset the graphics driver to a resolution that is compatible with the mouse driver:

```
GDriver = DETECT;
initgraph( &GDriver, &GMode, "\\TC\\BGI" );
setgraphmode( 1 );              // for low-res mouse drivers //
GError = graphresult();
```

For a long-term solution, the mouse driver may be upgraded—with or without purchasing a Hi-Res Mouse. Contact Microsoft, Logitech, or your mouse manufacturer for more details. If this does not work, you might simply comment out the graphics portion of the demonstration and proceed directly with the text button demo.

The BTNTEST program itself should require no special explanations.

Summary

With the mouse object unit created in the previous chapter, the basics of control button operations were demonstrated using the text and graphics button objects.

One potential problem mentioned was the issue of calling an uninitiated object. In many cases, depending on the object type defined, this may be no problem at all. In other cases, this can be only an annoyance or possibly a disaster. In either case, it is bad programming practice. As an alternative, the practice of providing a boolean flag for each object type was suggested, with the flags for all elements of an array of object initialized as false until each instance of the object has been assigned values for any critical variables.

More practically, critical default values can simply be assigned in the object constructor method.

```
//============//
//  TBOXES.I  //
//============//

typedef enum { UNSEL, SELECT, INVALID } BoxState;

typedef enum { NONE, SINGLE, DOUBLE } BoxType;

class Box

{

    protected:

        int  x, y, Color, BackColor, SizeX, Exist;

        BoxState State;

        BoxType  ThisBox;

        char     BtnTxt[40];

    public:

        void Move( int PtX, int PtY );

        void DrawBox();

        void Create( int PtX, int PtY, int Width,

                     int C1, int C2, char* Text );

        void Initialize();

        void Erase();

        void Invert();

        void SetColor( int C );

        void SetBackColor( int C );
```

```
            void SetState( BoxState BState );

            void SetLabel( char* Text );

            void SetBoxType( BoxType  WhatType );

            int  GetColor();

            int  GetBackColor();

            int  GetX();

            int  GetY();

            int  GetWidth() ;

            BoxState GetState();

            BoxType  GetType();

            int  BoxHit( int MouseX, int MouseY );
};


            //=====================================//
            // implementation for object type Box //
            //=====================================//

void Box::Initialize()

{

    State = UNSEL;

    Exist = FALSE;

    x = 0;

    y = 0;

    SizeX = 0;

    Color = 0;

    BackColor = 0;
```

```
        strcpy( BtnTxt, "" );
}

void Box::DrawBox()
{
    char     BoxStr[6];
    int      i, XPos, YPos, C;

    XPos = wherex();
    YPos = wherey();
    C = getbkcolor();
    switch( State )
    {
        case INVALID:
        case   UNSEL: textattr( LIGHTGRAY + BackColor );
                      break;
        case  SELECT: textattr( Color + BackColor );
                      break;
    }
    switch( ThisBox )
    {
        case   NONE: strcpy( BoxStr, "       "); break;
        case SINGLE: strcpy( BoxStr,
                            "\xDA\xBF\xC0\xD9\xC4\xB3" );
                     break;
```

```
    case DOUBLE: strcpy( BoxStr,

                        "\xC9\xBB\xC8\xBC\xCD\xBA" );

  }
// top of box //

  gotoxy( x, y );

  cprintf( "%c", BoxStr[0] );

  for( i=2; i<=SizeX-1; i++ )

    cprintf( "%c", BoxStr[4] );

  cprintf( "%c", BoxStr[1] );
// center of box //

  gotoxy( x, y+1 );

  cprintf( "%c", BoxStr[5] );

  for( i=2; i<=SizeX-1; i++ ) cprintf( " " );

  cprintf( "%c", BoxStr[5] );

  gotoxy( x + ( SizeX - strlen( BtnTxt ) ) / 2, y+1 );

  cprintf( "%s", BtnTxt );
// bottom of box //

  gotoxy( x, y+2 );

  cprintf( "%c", BoxStr[2] );

  for( i=2; i<SizeX; i++ ) cprintf( "%c", BoxStr[4] );

  cprintf( "%c", BoxStr[3] );

  textbackground( C );

  gotoxy( XPos, YPos );

}
```

```
void Box::Create( int PtX, int PtY, int Width, int C1, int
C2, char* Text )
{
    x = PtX;

    y = PtY;

    SizeX = Width;

    Color = C1;

    BackColor = C2 << 4;

    State = UNSEL;

    Exist = TRUE;

    strcpy( BtnTxt, Text );

    DrawBox();

}

void Box::Erase()
{
    int  i, j, XPos, YPos, C;

    XPos = wherex();

    YPos = wherey();

    if( Exist )

    {
        C = getcolor();

        textcolor( 0 );

        for( j=0; j<=2; j++ )
```

```
            {
                gotoxy( x, y+j );
                for( i=1; i<=SizeX; i++ ) printf( " " );
            }
            textcolor( C );
        }
    gotoxy( XPos, YPos );
}

void Box::Move( int PtX, int PtY )
{
    Erase();
    x = PtX;
    y = PtY;
    DrawBox();
}

void Box::SetLabel( char* Text )
{
    strcpy( BtnTxt, Text );
    DrawBox();
}

void Box::SetColor( int C )
{
    Color = C;
```

```
   DrawBox();

}

void Box::SetBackColor( int C )

{

   BackColor = C;

   DrawBox();

}

void Box::SetState( BoxState BState )

{

   if( State != BState )

   {

      State = BState;

      DrawBox();

}   }

void Box::SetBoxType( BoxType WhatType )

{

   ThisBox = WhatType;

}

void Box::Invert()

{

   switch( State )

   {
```

```
        case    UNSEL: SetState( SELECT );   break;

        case   SELECT: SetState( UNSEL );    break;

        case INVALID: {   sound( 440 );

                          delay( 200 );

                          nosound();        }
}   }


int   Box::GetColor()        { return( Color ); }

int   Box::GetBackColor()    { return( BackColor ); }

int   Box::GetX()            { return( x ); }

int   Box::GetY()            { return( y ); }

int   Box::GetWidth()        { return( SizeX ); }

BoxState Box::GetState()   { return( State ); }

BoxType  Box::GetType()    { return( ThisBox ); }

int   Box::BoxHit( int MouseX, int MouseY )
{
   MouseX = MouseX / 8 + 1;

   MouseY = MouseY / 8 + 1;

   if( ( MouseX >= x ) && ( MouseX < x+SizeX ) &&
       ( MouseY >= y ) && ( MouseY <= y+2 ) )

   {

      Invert();
```

```
            return( TRUE );

      }  else return( FALSE );

}


        //=======================================//
        // BUTTONS.I - Button object include file //
        //=======================================//

typedef enum { ROUNDED, SQUARE, THREE_D } ButtonType;

typedef   int   Outline[9];

class Point

{

   protected:

      int   x, y, Color;

   public:

      void Move( int PtX, int PtY );

      void Create( int PtX, int PtY, int C );

      void Set_Color( int C );

      int   GetColor();

      int   GetX();

      int   GetY();

};

class Button : public Point

{

   protected:
```

```
        int   Exist, State, Rotate, ThisButton,

              FontSize, TypeFace, SizeX, SizeY;

        char BtnTxt[40];

    public:

        void Draw();

        void Create( int PtX, int PtY, int Width,

                        int Height, int C, char* Text );

        void Initialize();

        void Erase();

        void Invert();

        void Move( int PtX, int PtY );

        void Set_Color( int C );

        void SetState( int BState );

        void SetLabel( char* Text );

        void SetButtonType( ButtonType WhatType );

        void SetTypeSize( int TxtSize );

        void SetTypeFace( int TxtFont );

        int GetWidth();

        int GetHeight();

        int GetState();

        int GetTextSize();

        ButtonType GetType();

        int ButtonHit( int MouseX, int MouseY );

};
```

```
//=====================================//
// implementation for object type Point //
//=====================================//

void Point::Create( int PtX, int PtY, int C )
{
   x = PtX;

   y = PtY;

   Color = C;

   putpixel( x, y, Color );
}

void Point::Move( int PtX, int PtY )
{
   Create( PtX, PtY, Color );
}

void Point::Set_Color( int C )
{
   Color = C;

   putpixel( x, y, Color );
}

int Point::GetColor()
{
   return( Color );
}
```

```
int Point::GetX()

{

   return( x );

}

int Point::GetY()

{

   return( y );

}


        //=====================================//
        // implementation for object type Button //
        //=====================================//

void Button::Initialize()

{

   Exist = FALSE;

   Rotate = FALSE;

   SetTypeSize( 2 );

   SetTypeFace( TRIPLEX_FONT );

}

void Button::Draw()

{

   int     radius = 6, offset = 3, AlignX, AlignY,
           TempSize, TextLen, i, TextDir;

   Outline RectArr;
```

```
setviewport( x, y, x+SizeX, y+SizeY, TRUE );

setcolor( Color );

switch( ThisButton )

{
    case SQUARE:

        {
            rectangle( 0,  0,  SizeX, SizeY );

            break;

        }

    case THREE_D:                         // THREE_D Outline //

        {
            rectangle( 0, 0, SizeX, SizeY );

            RectArr[0] = RectArr[2] = RectArr[8] = 1;

            RectArr[1] = RectArr[7] = RectArr[9] = 1;

            RectArr[4] = RectArr[6] = SizeX-1;

            RectArr[3] = RectArr[5] = SizeY-1;

            setfillstyle( CLOSE_DOT_FILL, Color );

            setlinestyle( USERBIT_LINE, 0, NORM_WIDTH );

            fillpoly( 5, RectArr );

            setlinestyle( SOLID_LINE, 0, NORM_WIDTH );

            rectangle( 2*radius, 2*radius,
                        SizeX-2*radius, SizeY-2*radius );

            line( 0, 0, 2*radius, 2*radius );

            line( 0, SizeY, 2*radius, SizeY-2*radius );
```

```
            line( SizeX, 0, SizeX-2*radius, 2*radius );

            line( SizeX, SizeY, SizeX-2*radius,

                                SizeY-2*radius );

        break;

      }

   case ROUNDED:

      {                                   // draw corners //

        arc( SizeX-radius, radius, 0, 90, radius );

        arc( radius, radius, 90, 180, radius );

        arc( radius, SizeY-radius, 180, 270, radius );

        arc( SizeX-radius, SizeY-radius, 270, 360,

            radius );

                                          // draw sides //

        line( radius, 0, SizeX-radius, 0 );

        line( radius, SizeY, SizeX-radius, SizeY );

        line( 0, radius, 0, SizeY-radius );

        line( SizeX, radius, SizeX, SizeY-radius );

}    }

switch( ThisButton )                     // fill button //

{

   case SQUARE:

   case ROUNDED:

      {

          RectArr[0] = RectArr[2] = RectArr[8] =
```

```
                RectArr[1] = RectArr[7] = RectArr[9] =
                    offset;

                RectArr[4] = RectArr[6] = SizeX-offset;

                RectArr[3] = RectArr[5] = SizeY-offset;

                break;

            }

        case THREE_D:

            {

                RectArr[0] = RectArr[2] = RectArr[8] =

                RectArr[1] = RectArr[7] = RectArr[9] =
                    2*radius+1;

                RectArr[4] = RectArr[6] = SizeX-2*radius;

                RectArr[3] = RectArr[5] = SizeY-2*radius;

                break;

        }       }

// show State //

    if( State ) setfillstyle( SOLID_FILL, Color );

            else setfillstyle( CLOSE_DOT_FILL, Color );

    setlinestyle( USERBIT_LINE, 0, NORM_WIDTH );

    fillpoly( 5, RectArr );

    setlinestyle( SOLID_LINE, 0, NORM_WIDTH );

// adjust fonts and string to fit //

    settextstyle( TypeFace, Rotate, FontSize );

    AlignX = (SizeX/2)-3;
```

```
      AlignY = (SizeY/2)-3;

      if( State ) setcolor( getbkcolor() );
// add label //
      outtextxy( AlignX, AlignY, BtnTxt );

      if( State ) setcolor( Color );

      setviewport( 0, 0, getmaxx(), getmaxy(), TRUE );

}


void Button::Create( int PtX, int PtY, int Width,
                     int Height, int C, char* Text )
{
      setviewport( 0, 0, getmaxx(), getmaxy(), TRUE );

      settextjustify( CENTER_TEXT, CENTER_TEXT );

      x = PtX;

      y = PtY;

      SizeX = Width;

      SizeY = Height;

      if( SizeX < 20 ) SizeX = 20;

      if( SizeY < 20 ) SizeY = 20;

      if( Height > Width ) Rotate = TRUE;

                      else Rotate = FALSE;

      Color  = C;

      State  = FALSE;

      Exist  = TRUE;
```

```
      strcpy( BtnTxt, Text );

      Draw();

}

void Button::Erase()

{

   if( Exist )

   {

      setviewport( x, y, x+SizeX, y+SizeY, TRUE );

      clearviewport();

      Exist = FALSE;

      setviewport( 1, 1, getmaxx(), getmaxy(), TRUE );

}   }

void Button::Move( int PtX, int PtY )

{

   Erase();

   x = PtX;

   y = PtY;

   Draw();

}

void Button::SetLabel( char* Text )

{

   strcpy( BtnTxt, Text );

   Draw();
```

```
}

void Button::Set_Color( int C )
{
   Color = C;
   Draw();
}

void Button::SetState( int BState )
{
   if( State != BState ) Invert();
}

void Button::SetTypeSize( int TxtSize )
{
   FontSize = TxtSize;
}

void Button::SetTypeFace( int TxtFont )
{
   TypeFace = TxtFont;
}

void Button::SetButtonType( ButtonType WhatType )
{
   ThisButton = WhatType;
}
```

```
void Button::Invert()

{

    if( State ) State = FALSE;

            else State = TRUE;

    Draw();

}

int Button::GetWidth()     { return( SizeX ); }

int Button::GetHeight()    { return( SizeY ); }

int Button::GetState()     { return( State ); }

int Button::GetTextSize() { return( FontSize ); }

ButtonType Button::GetType()      { return( ThisButton ); }

int Button::ButtonHit( int MouseX, int MouseY )

{

    if( ( MouseX >= x ) && ( MouseX <= x+SizeX ) &&

        ( MouseY >= y ) && ( MouseY <= y+SizeY ) )

    {

        Invert();

        return( TRUE );

    }

    else return( FALSE );

}
```

```
//===================================//
// program Button_Test - BTNTEST.CPP //
//===================================//

#include <conio.h>

#include <stdio.h>

#include <stdlib.h>

#include <stdarg.h>

#include <string.h>

#include <graphics.h>

#include "mouse.i"

#include "button.i"

#include "tboxes.i"

Mstatus Position;

Button  GButton[10];

Box     TBox[10];

int     Status, SButtons, BtnCount;

void Create_Buttons()
{
    int  i;

    char TempStr[10], Temp2[2];

    for( i=1; i<=5; i++ )
    {
        GButton[i].Initialize();
```

```
        strcpy( TempStr, "Test " );

        itoa( i, Temp2, 10 );

        strcat( TempStr, Temp2 );

        GButton[i].SetButtonType( THREE_D );

        GButton[i].Create( (i-1)*110+10, (i-1)*50+10,
                           100, 40, i+8, TempStr );

    }

    GButton[6].SetButtonType( THREE_D );

    GButton[6].Initialize();

    GButton[6].Create( 10, 260, 100, 40, WHITE, "Quit" );

}


void Create_TBox()

{

    int  i;

    char TempStr[10], Temp2[2];

    for( i=1; i<=5; i++ )

    {

        strcpy( TempStr, "Test " );

        itoa( i, Temp2, 10 );

        strcat( TempStr, Temp2 );

        TBox[i].Initialize();

        TBox[i].SetBoxType( DOUBLE );

        TBox[i].Create( (i-1)*15+1, (i-1)*5+1,
```

```
                              15, i+8, i, TempStr );

    }

    TBox[6].SetBoxType( SINGLE );

    TBox[6].Initialize();

    TBox[6].Create( 1, 21, 15, WHITE, 0, "Quit" );

    TBox[7].SetBoxType( DOUBLE );

    TBox[7].Initialize();

    TBox[7].Create( 61, 1, 15, WHITE, 0, "Invalid" );

    TBox[7].SetState( INVALID );

}

main()

{

    int i, GDriver = DETECT, GMode, GError, Exit;

    Mresult* Result;

    initgraph( &GDriver, &GMode, "C:\\TC\\BGI" );

    GError = graphresult();

    if( GError )

    {

        printf( "Graphics error: %s\n",

                grapherrormsg( GError ) );

        printf( "Program aborted...\n" );

        exit(1);

    }
```

```
setviewport(0,0,getmaxx(),getmaxy(),TRUE);

cleardevice();

Create_Buttons();

Result = gmouse.Mreset();

if( Result->present )

{

   Exit = FALSE;

   do

   {

      Position = gmouse.Mpressed( ButtonL );

      if( Position.button_count )

      {

         gmouse.Mshow( FALSE );

         for( i=1; i<=6; i++ )

         {

            if( GButton[i].GetState() )

               GButton[i].Invert();

            if( GButton[i].ButtonHit( Position.xaxis,

                                      Position.yaxis ) )

            {

               gmouse.Mshow( TRUE );

               sound( i*220 ); delay(100); nosound();

                               delay(100);

               sound( i*110 ); delay(100); nosound();
```

```
                          if( i == 6 ) Exit = TRUE;

                 }  }

                 gmouse.Mshow( TRUE );

        }  }

        while( !Exit );

        gmouse.Mshow( FALSE );

        for( i=1; i<=6; i++ ) GButton[i].Erase();

        gmouse.Mshow( TRUE );

        delay( 1500 );

    }

    closegraph();

// close graphics and restore //

// text mouse operation        //

    Result = tmouse.Mreset();

    if( Result->present )

    {

        Exit = FALSE;

        clrscr();

// set up for text button operation //

        gotoxy( 20, 24);

        cprintf("This is a Text Button test routine");

        tmouse.Mshow( FALSE );

        Create_TBox();

        tmouse.Mshow( TRUE );
```

```
    do

    {

        Position = tmouse.Mpressed( ButtonL );

        if( Position.button_count )

        {

            tmouse.Mshow( FALSE );

            for( i=1; i<=7; i++ )

                if( TBox[i].GetState() == SELECT )

                    TBox[i].Invert();

            for( i=1; i<=7; i++ )

                if( TBox[i].BoxHit( Position.xaxis,

                                        Position.yaxis ) )

                {

                    tmouse.Mshow( TRUE );

                    sound( i*220 ); delay(100); nosound();

                                        delay(100);

                    sound( i*110 ); delay(100); nosound();

                    if( i == 6 ) Exit = TRUE;

                }

            tmouse.Mshow( TRUE );

    }    }

    while( !Exit );

}

tmouse.Mshow( FALSE );
```

```
for( i=1; i<=7; i++ ) TBox[i].Erase();

tmouse.Mshow( TRUE );

delay( 1500 );
}
```

CHAPTER 6

EXTENDING OBJECTS IN C++

The basic principles of object-oriented programming shown thus far are applicable to all object types. You have seen how an object can be created and then extended to form a new object type. Some degree of data abstraction has been used in previous examples.

In this chapter, the theory of data abstraction will be discussed in more detail, along with the theory and practice of extending objects and the potential problems and opportunities inherent in doing so.

Object Data Abstraction

While the theory and principles of data abstraction were explained earlier (See the "Encapsulation" section in Chapter 1), this topic will recur periodically. You have seen how an object can be referenced indirectly through methods rather than calling its values directly, and how an object can be prevented from relying on global variables. I will again emphasize the importance of providing complete object methods.

In the example objects presented in Chapters 4 and 5, a complete series of methods was provided for all conceivable accesses required, even though the demo programs themselves did not require all of them. The units created contain several unreferenced object methods. Since the Turbo C++ linker does not include any methods that are not actually used by the program, there is no penalty—in terms of the compiled program size or performance of the program—for being thorough.

The big advantage in designing the object with complete access methods is that the object itself can later be redesigned internally, as long as the original access methods are retained. This can be done without requiring any applications using the object to be rewritten; they only need to be recompiled in order to include the revised object.

Later, if it becomes necessary to add a new access method or to expand the performance of the object, it can be done with complete freedom as long as the object's original methods continue to be supported.

The degree of freedom afforded by providing complete access methods is virtually unlimited. Since none of the object's internal variables are accessed directly by name, all of them can be renamed or restructured as necessary; their internal handling rewritten entirely or any manner of alteration performed as long as it does not affect the manner in which the object responds to the calling application. Remember, this freedom of revision is not totally unlimited. There is one caution to keep in mind: *any descendants of an altered object* will be affected by the revisions.

The degree to which revisions will require updating descendant objects depends on the parent and child objects and the nature of the revisions. In general, renaming internal variables will require revision of child objects, but rewriting the procedures used internally should not require revisions of child procedures as long as the same inputs are used and the same objective result is achieved.

If it does become necessary to drop previously existing object methods, forward compatibility can still be maintained by replacing these with dummy methods; that is, methods which emulate the calling performance of discarded methods but actually accomplish little or nothing aside from providing compatibility for applications expecting these method calls to exist.

For the same reason, the example objects previously created used internal method calls wherever possible (for example, the implementation of an object method may call another method belonging to the same object rather than using duplicate code). As a secondary benefit, this also produces economy both in the source code and compiled program and is good practice in any type of programming, not merely object-oriented programming.

Other aspects of methods provisions will be discussed later in this chapter.

Extending Objects

Objects are extended by defining a new object type as a descendant of an existing object—a technique shown in Chapter 1 and again in Chapter 5. Extending objects can take many different forms.

In standard C, the printf function accepts a variable number of parameters and varying parameters types, such as:

```
printf( "A string message\n" );
printf( "The cursor is at: %2d : %2d\n", X, Y );
```

In graphics applications, however, the corresponding functions outtext and outextxy do not accept variable parameter lists. However, the text printf function can be extended to provide the graphics gprintf function which duplicates the convenience of the original function in a new environment. The gprintf function appears in *Graphics Programming In Turbo C* 2.0, available from Addison-Wesley.

In like fashion, object-oriented programming provides a similar flexibility through inheritance; each descendant object type inherits the methods and data fields of its ancestor type, but can add whatever new methods and data fields are necessary for a specific application. It does so without having to totally recreate the parent object.

Also, the parent object's methods may be overwritten and replaced with new methods applicable to the specific requirements of the new object.

Static Method Inheritance and Overrides

Axiomatically, each descendant object inherits all of the methods belonging to the parent object, but this does not mean that the descendant object is bound to perform exactly like the parent. Instead, any inherited method which is inappropriate to the new object's purpose can either be ignored or overwritten—the latter being the more appropriate choice.

As an example, in Chapter 5 the Button object was created as a descendant of the Point object type and inherited the Move, Create, SetColor, GetColor, GetX, and GetY methods defined for Point. But, for the Button object, the Move, Create, and SetColor methods were overwritten by defining new methods, using the same names but not always

with the same calling parameters. For the Point object, the three methods in question were defined as:

```
void Move( int PtX, int PtY );
void Create( int PtX, int PtY, int C );
void SetColor( int C );
```

And for the Button object, the same three method names were defined
as:

```
void Move( int PtX, int PtY );
void Create( int PtX, int PtY, int Width,
             int Height, int C, char* Text );
void SetColor( int C );
```

The changes in the Create method are obvious: three new parameters,
two integers, and one string, which did not appear in the Point method
have been added, thus requiring a new implementation for the method.

What about the Move and SetColor methods? These do not appear to
have changed. And, examining their implementations, only one immediate difference is apparent:

```
void Point::Move( int PtX, int PtY )
{
    x = PtX;
    y = PtY;
    Draw();
}

void Button::Move( int PtX, int PtY )
{
    Erase();
    x = PtX;
    y = PtY;
    Draw();
}

void Point::SetColor( int C )
{
```

```
      Color = C;
      Draw();
   }

   void Button::SetColor( int C )
   {
      Color = C;
      Draw();
   }
```

But, if there are no differences, why are these methods redeclared and reimplemented?

Actually, the similarities are misleading. As created, the Point object type, which has not been used for real applications except to serve as a convenient parent for other object types, is relatively unsophisticated. As it stands, the Point::Move method simply creates a new point on the screen but does nothing to erase the earlier screen image. This programming flaw is provided to point out one type of possible error.

The Button object type, however, has been provided with the mechanisms necessary (in the Move method), to erase an existing button before recreating a new image at a new position.

But, suppose the Point object was given the same sophistication as the Button object—the ability to erase an existing point in response to a Move. If this were done, the two pairs of procedures could look like this:

```
   void Point::Move( int PtX, int PtY )
   {
      Erase();
      x = PtX;
      y = PtY;
      Draw();
   }

   void Button::Move( int PtX, int PtY )
   {
      Erase();
      x = PtX;
      y = PtY;
```

```
    Draw();
}
```

Now that the paired methods are identical is there any further reason for redefining the Move and SetColor methods for the Button object?

Static Method Inheritance

Obviously, the previous question is intended as a trap. If you answered "No", consider yourself snared. It is vitally important for the Move and SetColor methods to be redefined even if the reasons are not immediately obvious.

The object methods appearing here are called *static methods* as opposed to *virtual methods* and the conflicts discussed in this section are specific to static methods. Virtual methods, which provide a second solution to these problems, will be discussed later.

Using static methods, the flaw in not redefining the Move method for the Button object is simply that the Point::Move method calls the Point::Erase and Point::Draw methods, not the Button::Erase and Button::Draw methods (see also the "Compiler Operations" section). Since the Point::Erase and Point::Draw methods have very little to do except to erase and draw a single screen pixel, they have virtually no relevance to the Button object. The same is true of the two SetColor methods that call two separate, and far from identical, Draw methods.

On the other hand, the GetColor, GetX, and GetY methods defined for the Point object do not need to be redefined for the Button object and can be used as is with perfect accuracy. Thus, which methods must be redefined for child objects depends entirely on the parent and child objects and the tasks that must be implemented by the methods.

The Scope Resolution Operator

In general, any inherited method can be explicitly referenced using the form, Ancestor::Method. For example, assume that the Point object has been rewritten and includes a method titled SetLoc which is defined as:

```
void SetLoc( int PtX, int PtY )
{
    x = PtX;
    y = PtY;
}
```

With the SetLoc method provided, the Point::Move method can be simplified:

```
void Point::Move( int PtX, int PtY )
{
    Erase();
    SetLoc( PtX, PtY );
    Draw();
}
```

Since the SetLoc method belongs to the Point object, scope resolution is not required here. In like fashion, the Button::Move method can be rewritten to also call the parent method SetLoc:

```
void Button::Move( PtX, PtY : integer );
}
    Erase();
    Point::SetLoc( PtX, PtY );
    Draw();
{
```

In this particular case, the scope resolution operator is again redundant because the Button object has not redefined the inherited SetLoc method. Thus, the call would automatically go to the Point object's method. Suppose, however, that the Button object has its own version of SetLoc:

```
void Button::SetLoc( int PtX, int PtY )
{
    ... Button specific handling provisions ...
    Point::SetLoc( PtX, PtY );
    ... Button specific handling provisions ...
}
```

In this case, the Point::SetLoc scope resolution is absolutely necessary both to prevent a recursive loop, and in the Button::Move method (unless, of course, Button::Move was intended to call Button::SetLoc). In conclusion, scope resolution may be used for three purposes:

- To resolve conflicts between methods with the same name but belonging to different object classes.
- To allow child methods to explicitly call ancestor methods which have been overwritten in the child object.
- To allow a child method to call an explicit ancestor method where several generations of objects have redefined the method two or more times.

Global Variables

Global variables should not be referenced or required by objects. Having stated this, I will proceed to qualify the statement in several fashions.

First, all variables declared within an object definition are global to the object and its methods. Within the object, variables may be treated in the same fashion as variables declared for a procedure that are global to the procedure's subprocedures. (The variables declared within the object's methods are valid only within the method.)

The second qualification is broader because there can be cases where a true global variable is simply the best solution to a program's needs. For example, an editor utility might be written as an object using dynamic memory allocation to store text data, so that the data is available to the calling application with the object returning pointers to the data's location in memory.

For simplicity, a variety of memory pointers might be global to both the object and to the application. If so, the declaration of the pointer variables should be made within the object unit, not by the calling application I am assuming that an object of this type would be compiled as a referenced unit and not included within the main program's source code or used as an include file, as has been done with the MOUSE.INC file and the gmouse and tmouse object instances.

Third, predefined constants and flag values (or even flag variables) are more convenient if declared globally. However, these should always be declared within the object unit, not by the calling application.

The original statement stands as rephrased: no object should reference nor require externally declared global variables. Attempting to do so will: limit the portability from application to application of the object; will prevent the object and its descendants from being compiled as program units.

Inheriting Data Fields

Data fields, as well as methods, are inherited by child objects, but unlike inherited methods, cannot be overwritten or redefined. If necessary, inherited data fields can be ignored or used for purposes not originally intended. You cannot define a new data field with the same identifier as an inherited data field or change the structure of an inherited data field.

There are other limitations. If an object's data field has been declared private (the default), then these data fields are not accessible to descendant object types, except through the object methods defined by the ancestor type.

When an ancestor object type has declared private data fields, however, the names of the data fields can be redeclared by descendant object types and may be declared as any data type. But a word of caution—while this redeclaration is permissible and will not produce compiler errors, it may easily produce errors in the operation of the object. Therefore, this freedom should be exercised with extreme care.

Compiler Operations for Static Methods

Several of the preceding inheritance problems are a product of the C++ compiler/linker operations specific to static methods. Virtual methods are handled in a different fashion, but before the solution is explained, it helps to understand the problem.

The source of the problem is the means by which the compiler resolves method calls (or function calls in conventional C). When the compiler encounters the Point::Move method implementation, the Erase, SetLoc and Draw methods already have addresses within the code segment. Later, when another method or the main program makes a call to the Move method:

```
Move( PtX, PtY );
```

becomes the equivalent of:

```
Erase();                    { Point::Erase address  }
SetLoc( PtX, PtY );         { Point::SetLoc address }
Draw();                     { Point::Draw address   }
```

The reason that forward declarations are used is to provide addresses to functions for the compiler's use before the actual code is encountered.

This also reduces the need for the multiple passes required by some compiler languages.

Now, assume that the Erase and Draw methods are also reimplemented for the Button object, but the Move method has not been reimplemented. In this case, when a Button object calls the Move method, the result is still a series of calls to the Point methods, not the Button methods.

When the compiler encounters the reference Button::Move, it looks first in the Button method definitions. If no Move has been defined for the Button method, the compiler moves up to the immediate ancestor of the current object type, continuing to regress until the method referenced is found. Of course, if no such method is encountered or if the named method is private to an ancestor type, the compiler terminates, issuing an error message that the method named is not defined.

Even though the Button object has its own Erase and SetLoc methods, the Move method called is Point::Move. With static methods, the reference addresses of the Erase and Draw methods refer only to the Point implementations, not the Button implementations.

When the Button::Move method is implemented (see Figure 6-1) ,the compiled result correctly becomes:

```
Erase();                    { Button::Erase address }
SetLoc( PtX, PtY );         { Point::SetLoc address }
Draw();                     { Button::Draw address  }
```

The SetLoc method, which simply assigns the calling parameters to the x- and y-axis location variables, is not redefined for the Button object.

Remember, when the inherited methods are static methods, the method called is the method precisely as it was defined and compiled for the ancestor type. If the ancestor type calls other methods, the addresses of the subsequent methods called will be those of the ancestor type, even when the descendant object has defined methods overriding the ancestor methods.

As Brian Flamig says in *HyperGuide to Turbo Pascal 5.5*, "...to bind a method to a message (that is, a function call), the compiler must look at the type of the object involved and select the appropriate method for the message." (*HyperGuide to Turbo Pascal 5.5* is a public-domain utility available on CompuServe in the BPROGA forum.)

Figure 6-1: Statically-Linked Object Method Calls

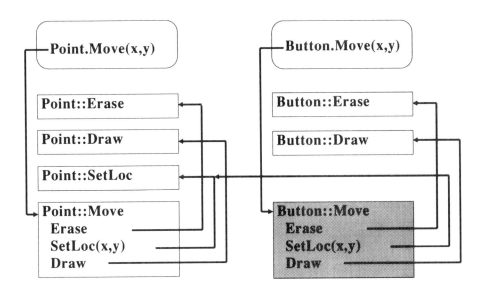

Static Versus Virtual Methods

While static methods work and should be considered basic tools, they do not provide the optimum flexibility that we desire for object-oriented programming. There are more versatile tools available and virtual methods offer an alternative in which the structure and programming demands are not so rigid.

The main difference between a static and a virtual method lies in the point at which the methods are linked or bound. Static methods, as shown, are subject to a process called *early binding* with their links determined at the time a program (or unit) is compiled. This is shown in Figure 6-1.

Alternatively, *late binding*, used with virtual methods, does not create any fixed links between methods and calling procedures. Instead, at compile time, a binding mechanism is installed which will link the method and the calling process at the time the call is actually executed.

How virtual methods are created and how the mechanisms for virtual methods work will be shown in Chapter 7.

Summary

This chapter reviewed the basic elements of object-oriented programming using static object methods and suggested a number of revisions for the Point and Button object types originally created in Chapter 5.

In Chapter 7, we will discuss virtual methods and the Point and Button objects will modified once again, this time with previously static methods becoming virtual methods.

The revisions suggested in Chapter 6 appear in the following listings.

```
//=============================================//
//  BUTTON2.I == Button object include file //
//=============================================//

typedef enum { ROUNDED, SQUARE, THREE_D }  ButtonType;

typedef int  Outline[9];


class Point

{

    protected:

        int    x, y, Color;

    public:

        void Move( int PtX, int PtY );

        void Draw();

        void Create( int PtX, int PtY, int C );

        void SetColor( int C );

        void SetLoc( int PtX, int PtY );

        void Erase();

        int  GetColor();

        int  GetX();
```

```
        int    GetY();

};

class Button : public Point

{

    protected:

        int             Exist, State, Rotate, FontSize,

                        TypeFace, SizeX, SizeY;

        ButtonType  ThisButton;

        char            BtnTxt[40];

    public:

        void Create( int PtX, int PtY, int Width,

                        int Height, int C, char* Text );

        void Initialize();

        void Draw();

        void Erase();

        void Invert();

        void Move( int PtX, int PtY );

        void SetColor( int C );

        void SetState( int BState );

        void SetLabel( char* Text );

        void SetButtonType( ButtonType WhatType );

        void SetTypeSize( int TxtSize );

        void SetTypeFace( int TxtFont );
```

```
        int   GetWidth();

        int   GetHeight();

        int   GetState();

        int   GetTextSize();

        int   ButtonHit( int MouseX, int MouseY );

        ButtonType  GetType();

};


        //=====================================//
        // implementation for object type Point //
        //=====================================//

void Point::SetLoc( int PtX, int PtY )

{

   x = PtX;

   y = PtY;

}


void Point::Draw()

{

   putpixel( x, y, Color );

}


void Point::Create( int PtX, int PtY, int C )

{

   SetLoc( PtX, PtY );

   Color = C;
```

```
        Draw();

}

void Point::Erase()

{

    int Temp;

    Temp = Color;

    Color = getbkcolor();

    Draw();

    Color = Temp;

}

void Point::Move( int PtX, int PtY )

{

    Erase();

    SetLoc( PtX, PtY );

    Draw();

}

void Point::SetColor( int C )

{

    Color = C;

    Draw();

}

int  Point::GetColor...                      // no changes //
```

```
int   Point::GetX...                        // no changes //

int   Point::GetY...                        // no changes //


        //======================================//
        // implementation for object type Button //
        //======================================//

void Button::Initialize...                   // no changes //

void Button::Draw...                         // no changes //


void Button::Create( int PtX, int PtY, int Width,

                     int Height, int C, char* Text )

{

    setviewport( 0, 0, getmaxx(), getmaxy(), TRUE );

    settextjustify( CENTER_TEXT, CENTER_TEXT );

    SetLoc( PtX, PtY );

    SizeX = Width;

    SizeY = Height;

    if( SizeX < 20 ) SizeX = 20;

    if( SizeY < 20 ) SizeY = 20;

    if( Height > Width ) Rotate = TRUE;

                    else Rotate = FALSE;

    Color  = C;

    State  = FALSE;

    Exist  = TRUE;

    strcpy( BtnTxt, Text );

    Draw();
```

```
}

void Button::Erase...                              // no changes //

void Button::Move( int PtX, int PtY )              // revised //
{
    Erase();

    SetLoc( PtX, PtY );

    Draw();
}

void Button::SetLabel...                           // no changes //

void Button::SetColor...                           // no changes //

void Button::SetState...                           // no changes //

void Button::SetTypeSize...                        // no changes //

void Button::SetTypeFace...                        // no changes //

void Button::SetButtonType...                      // no changes //

void Button::Invert...                             // no changes //

int Button::GetWidth...                            // no changes //

int Button::GetHeight...                           // no changes //

int Button::GetState...                            // no changes //

int Button::GetTextSize...                         // no changes //

ButtonType Button::GetType...                      // no changes //

int Button::ButtonHit...                           // no changes //

        // ========= end of methods =========== //
```

The BTNTEST2 demo program requires only one change to access the revised include file, thus:

```
//=====================================//
// program Button_Test_2 - BTNTEST2.CPP //
//=====================================//
```

```
#include <conio.h>

    . . .

#include <graphics.h>

#include "mouse.i"

#include "button2.i"                        // <-changed //

#include "tboxes.i"

                              // no further changes required //
```

CHAPTER 7

VIRTUAL OBJECT METHODS

While static methods are addressed and resolved at compile time and use fixed references, virtual methods are dynamically referenced. Using virtual methods at compile time, the method implementations are compiled. However, references calling the virtual methods or references within one virtual method calling another virtual method are not resolved. In other words, the references are not replaced by link addresses at this time.

For example, assume that the Point and Button objects previously demonstrated are recreated with Erase and Draw changed from static to virtual methods. In this case, instead of addresses replacing the method references in Move, virtual references are made which will be resolved at run time instead of at compile time.

But, if method addresses are not resolved at compile time, how can they be resolved at run time?

The Virtual Method Table

Instead of replacing method calls with method addresses, the compiler creates a new element for each virtual object type—the Virtual Method Table or VMT which become part of the data segment of each object type definition.

Each VMT contains a variety of information including the object type's size and, for each of the virtual methods belonging to the object type, a pointer to the virtual method's implementation code. These pointers to the implementation codes for the methods are used at run time to resolve the method calls, linking each to the appropriate implementation.

Figure 7-1 shows a partial diagram for the Point and Button object methods and the Virtual Method Tables created for each. Compare this figure with the static implementation links shown previously in Figure 6-1.

Figure 7-1: Methods Using VMT References

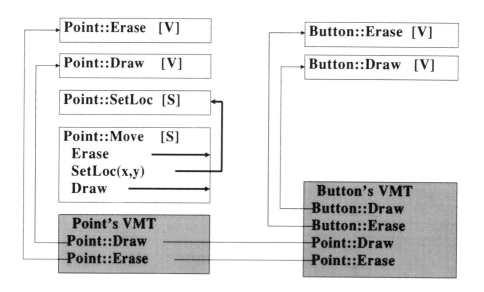

In the static version even though both versions were defined identically, the Move method was still redefined for the Button object so that Button's version would call Button::Erase and Button::Draw instead of Point::Erase and Point::Draw.

For the virtual methods version, notice that while Point::Move is still static, no Button::Move method is defined and the Point::Move method has unresolved references to the virtual Erase and Draw methods. The SetLoc method, which also remains static and is not redeclared by the Button object, is still referenced directly by its implementation address.

To satisfy the unresolved references, Point's VMT contains implementation addresses for Point's Draw and Erase methods. Button's VMT inherits Point's method addresses, but adds its own Draw and Erase addresses. In this fashion, at run time, a Button instance calling Point's Move method still uses the Button::Erase and Button::Draw methods while a Point instance calling Move uses Point::Erase and Point::Draw methods (see Figures 7-2 and 7-3).

Figure 7-2: A Point Instance Calling the Move Method

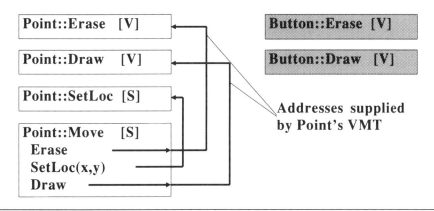

Figure 7-3: A Button Instance Calling the Move Method

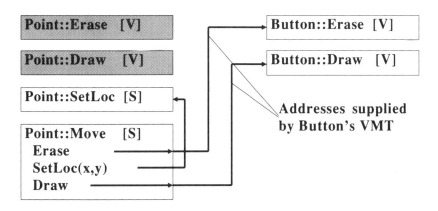

This is precisely what virtual methods are for! Using virtual methods, when a new descendant of either Point or Button is created, the Move method does not need to be redefined, not even when the new object has its own versions of Erase or Draw, because these will be used automatically.

Virtual Descendants

Suppose another descendant object, titled ScrollBar, defines a new version of SetLoc? So far, the SetLoc method has been statically linked. What happens now?

Two possibilities occur here, depending on whether the new Scroll-Bar::SetLoc method is created as a static or virtual method, but in either case the solution is the same.

First, the Move method will need to be redefined (as ScrollBar::Move for the descendant object type) before the ScrollBar::SetLoc method will be used because the Point::Move method is still statically linked to Point::SetLoc.

Second, it is preferable, when ScrollBar redefines SetLoc, to make SetLoc a virtual method so that future revisions and/or descendants will not need to further redefine the Move method which is already a virtual method. Keep this in mind, it will be important later.

Assuming that only these two redefinitions are required (SetLoc redefined as a virtual method; Move redefined, but still static; and the Erase and Draw methods remaining unchanged), an instance of Scroll-Bar calling the Move method appears in Figure 7-4.

This time, the Point::Move method is not referenced at all. Instead, the ScrollBar::Move method is linked by virtual reference to the Button::Erase, ScrollBar::SetLoc, and Button::Draw methods. Any descendant objects of ScrollBar will not need to redefine the Move method, even if they redefine the Erase, SetLoc, or Draw methods. What about the Move method itself? Should it have been a virtual method from the start? Or should ScrollBar::Move be declared as a virtual method?

So far, nothing has been done that actually requires either of the Move methods to be virtual and, even if both were virtual methods, their execution would not be affected. Instead, it is the *virtual* nature of the methods called by the two Move methods which accomplishes the principal task.

On the other hand, if the Point::SetLoc method had originally been defined as a virtual method, only the original Point::Move method would be needed and no redefinition of the ScrollBar::Move method would be required. So why not declare all methods virtual and simply be done with it?

Figure 7-4: A ScrollBar Instance Calling the Move Method

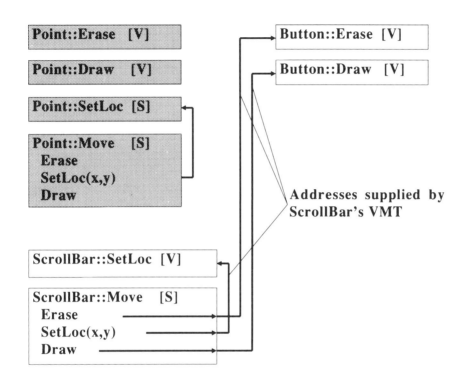

It could be done, but with two small flaws. First, each virtual method requires an entry in the object's Virtual Methods Table, which requires a small, but real amount of space. Second, execution of the program would be slightly slower with each instance of an object requiring a small slice of time for the its constructor to consult the VMT and link the virtual method calls to the appropriate addresses.

Static Methods Versus Virtual Methods

Static methods are used to optimize speed and memory efficiency, while virtual methods provide extensibility. As a general rule, if any method is likely to be redefined by a descendant object and the redefined method needs to be accessible to the ancestor, then the method should be created as virtual rather than static.

If an object has any virtual methods, a VMT is created for that object type in the data segment and every instance of the object will possess a link to it. Every call to a virtual method references the VMT, while static methods are called directly by the address.

While the VMT is efficient, the static method calls remain slightly faster than virtual calls and, if no VMT is required or created, then a small savings in code size is realized.

In the end, one of the points of object-oriented programming is *extensibility*, allowing the extension of existing code without recompiling the source code. This is achieved, in part, by using virtual methods. Don't forget the possibility that users of your object types will probably think of ways of employing the object type which were not anticipated when the object type was created. This, in the final analysis, is what extensibility is all about!

Static Methods Redefined as Virtual

Despite the preceding cautions, static methods are not necessarily dead-ends and, instead of all methods being initially and unnecessarily declared as virtual, any descendant object type can redeclare a static method as a virtual method.

If you refer back to Figures 7-1, 7-2, and 7-3, notice that both Point::Erase and Button::Erase, and Point::Draw and Button::Draw are indicated as virtual methods (indicated in the diagrams by [V]). Once any method is defined as a virtual method, all descendant redefinitions of the method must also be virtual.

Once Virtual, Always Virtual

In C++, once a method has been defined as virtual, the descendant method is also virtual. It does not need to be specified as virtual though the virtual declaration can be repeated without conflict.

In Turbo Pascal 5.5, this same rule held for virtual methods and descendants with the single difference that the virtual identifier was required for all descendant method definitions.

The drawback, of course, in redeclaring a static method as a virtual method, is that complete information about the original declaration is required in order to redefine the complete method. An initial virtual declaration permits extensibility without revealing the original method's source. Static to virtual redefinition is a one-way street and a method which was previously virtual, cannot be redefined as static!

Creating Virtual Methods

Having talked about the theory of virtual methods, it's time to move on to the practical aspects, beginning with how a virtual method is declared.

Virtual methods are declared simply by appending the reserved word virtual to the method declaration. Beginning with the Point object declaration in BUTTON3.I, the changes appear as follows:

```
class Point
{
  protected:
    int   x, y, Color;
  public:
    Point();                                  // new //
    void Move( int PtX, int PtY );
    virtual void Draw();                       // revised //
    void Create( int PtX, int PtY, int C );
    void SetColor( int C );
    virtual void SetLoc( int PtX, int PtY );   // revised //
    virtual void Erase();                      // revised //
    int   GetColor();
    int   GetX();
    int   GetY();
};
```

In addition to the keyword virtual preceding the SetLoc, Draw, and Erase method declarations, you should also notice that a new method, Point::Point, has been declared as a constructor method. A *constructor* is a special type of procedure provided to handle some of the initial setup work required for virtual methods and will be discussed in a moment. For the present, simply remember that in C++ an object's constructor method is called automatically; either implicitly when instances of the object class are declared or, for dynamically allocated object instances, by the invocation of the new operator.

Further, as an advantage of C++ over Turbo Pascal, it becomes effectively impossible for virtual methods to be called before the object constructor has been referenced.

For the Button object, the Draw and Erase methods are redefined, but are again defined as virtual, not static, methods. Remember, once a method has been defined as virtual, all descendant methods must also be defined as virtual. The explicit definition as virtual is optional because, once made, the virtual assignment is carried forward to all descendant methods. The remaining virtual method defined in the Point object, SetLoc, is not redefined in the Button object.

The Initialize method defined in previous versions has now become the constructor method, Button::Button, though the tasks previously executed by the Button::Initialize method have not been changed:

```
class Button : public Point
{
    protected:
        int         Exist, State, Rotate, FontSize,
                    TypeFace, SizeX, SizeY;
        ButtonType  ThisButton;
        char        BtnTxt[40];
    public:
        Button();                              // new //
        virtual void Draw();                   // revised //
        virtual void Erase();                  // revised //
        virtual void Move( int PtX, int PtY ); // revised //
                { no further declaration changes }

    }
```

Aside from these four changes in the declarations, the remainder of the methods are declared exactly as they appeared in previous versions of the Button object. But there are additional revisions. First, the Point::Point constructor method is new and has to be implemented:

```
Point::Point()
    {
    }
```

Please note that the preceding code is not an error. The fact that the Point::Point method implementation does not contain any instruction is perfectly correct because, in this case, nothing is required except the constructor call itself.

Constructor Methods

The constructor method is vital to objects using virtual methods because it is the constructor call that establishes the link between an object instance and the object type's Virtual Method Table. Without this link, any call to a virtual method simply leads to some never-never-land where it cannot be resolved.

Each object type using virtual methods has a single VMT, but the individual instances of an object type do not contain copies of the VMT itself. The only way that an object instance can access the VMT is through the link created by the constructor call.

Obviously, the constructor method cannot be a virtual method; each object type constructor has the same method name as the object class and the constructor implementation could not be called by the object until after the constructor had supplied the link to the VMT. The link identifies the address of the constructor implementation which is only done in response to the constructor call. While recursion is permitted, this type of circular bootstrap recursion is not. The constructor methods, therefore, are always static.

As mentioned previously, constructor methods once declared, are called automatically; either implicitly by the declaration of an object instance or, for dynamic object instances, by the invocation of the new function to create the object instance.

Summary

This chapter has provided an introduction to virtual methods, discussing the theory behind virtual methods, the reasons for using virtual methods instead of static methods, and some of the trade-offs involved. The constructor method type has also been introduced and explained. Finally, the Button object appears in a third revision using virtual methods.

Next, the ScrollBar object, cited as an example in the current chapter, will finally be created as a descendant (however unlikely) of the Button type. This will be accomplished using BUTTON4.I (a slight modification of the BUTTON3.I), rather than adding to the source code, to show how object extensibility actually works.

```
//==========================================//
//   BUTTON3.I — Button object include file  //
//==========================================//

typedef enum { ROUNDED, SQUARE, THREE_D }  ButtonType;

typedef int  Outline[9];

class Point
{
  protected:
    int    x, y, Color;
  public:
    Point();                                         // new //
    void Move( int PtX, int PtY );
    virtual void Draw();                             // revised //
    void Create( int PtX, int PtY, int C );
    void SetColor( int C );
    virtual void SetLoc( int PtX, int PtY );     // revised //
    virtual void Erase();                        // revised //
    int  GetColor();
    int  GetX();
    int  GetY();
};

class Button : public Point
{
    protected:
```

```cpp
    int         Exist, State, Rotate, FontSize,

                TypeFace, SizeX, SizeY;

    ButtonType  ThisButton;

    char        BtnTxt[40];

public:

    Button();                                       // new //

    virtual void Draw();                            // revised //

    void Create( int PtX, int PtY, int Width,

                 int Height, int C, char* Text );

    virtual void Erase();                           // revised //

    void Invert();

    virtual void Move( int PtX, int PtY );      // revised //

    void SetColor( int C );

    void SetState( int BState );

    void SetLabel( char* Text );

    void SetButtonType( ButtonType WhatType );

    void SetTypeSize( int TxtSize );

    void SetTypeFace( int TxtFont );

    int  GetWidth();

    int  GetHeight();

    int  GetState();

    int  GetTextSize();

    int  ButtonHit( int MouseX, int MouseY );

    ButtonType  GetType();
```

```
};


        //=======================================//
        // implementation for object type Point  //
        //=======================================//

Point::Point()                                    // new //

{

        //  even though nothing is done here,   //
        //   this implementation must still be  //
        //  provided for the constructor method //

}

void Point::SetLoc...                             // no changes //

void Point::Draw...                              // no changes //

void Point::Create...                            // no changes //

void Point::Erase...                             // no changes //

void Point::Move...                              // no changes //

void Point::SetColor...                          // no changes //

int  Point::GetColor...                          // no changes //

int  Point::GetX...                              // no changes //

int  Point::GetY...                              // no changes //


        //=======================================//
        // implementation for object type Button //
        //=======================================//
```

```
Button::Button()                                 // new //
{
    Exist = FALSE;

    Rotate = FALSE;

    SetTypeSize( 2 );

    SetTypeFace( TRIPLEX_FONT );
}

void Button::Draw...                             // no changes //

void Button::Create...                           // no changes //

void Button::Erase...                            // no changes //

void Button::Move...                             // no changes //

void Button::SetLabel...                         // no changes //

void Button::SetColor...                         // no changes //

void Button::SetState...                         // no changes //

void Button::SetTypeSize...                      // no changes //

void Button::SetTypeFace...                      // no changes //

void Button::SetButtonType...                    // no changes //

void Button::Invert...                           // no changes //

int Button::GetWidth...                          // no changes //
```

```
int Button::GetHeight...                    // no changes //

int Button::GetState...                     // no changes //

int Button::GetTextSize...                  // no changes //

ButtonType Button::GetType...               // no changes //

int Button::ButtonHit...                    // no changes //


        // =========== end of methods ============= //



        //======================================//
        // program Button_Test_3 — BTNTEST3.CPP //
        //======================================//
#include <conio.h>

...

#include <graphics.h>

#include "mouse.i"

#include "button3.i"                     // <- changed //

#include "tboxes.i"

                            // no further changes required //
```

CHAPTER 8

SCROLLBARS AND OBJECT EXTENSIBILITY
_____

To demonstrate object extensibility, two ScrollBar objects, one graphic and one text, will be developed as descendants of the Button and Box object types.

In previous chapters examples were created by building on existing source code or by modifying an existing object type. Object extensibility, however, does not depend on having the ancestor source code available. It uses a precompiled ancestor, as long as the .h header file was available.

For now I'll simply use the button4.i include file, referencing this source file from the main demo program. To compile the two scrollbar files (as .OBJ files), scrlbar.i would need references to the button4.i and graphics.h files while tscrlbar.i would require an include reference for tboxes.i.

Before going into the details of how these object descendants are created, a review of the what and why of extensibility is in order.

Object Extensibility

Object extensibility is one of the principal advantages of object-oriented programming. Using extensibility, toolbox units can be created and distributed to users in linkable .obj and .h form as modifiable sources for use in creating their own applications.

For distribution purposes, the source code of an object-oriented unit can remain the property of the developer while the distributed object code does not require release of any documentation other than a description of public and protected elements of the objects. Additional documentation, however, is suggested for clarity and the user's convenience.

Because the source code itself is not distributed, programmers are able to maintain a proprietary interest in their software development and, at the same time, can develop new versions of distributed packages without sacrificing compatibility with previous versions.

Extensibility is simply a method of distributing programming toolboxes because toolbox units can conveniently be used, modified, and extended by their original developers without recompiling the original source codes.

Extensibility is derived from two elements: *object* inheritance and *late binding*. Object inheritance allows a descendant object to possess everything the ancestor object owned. Late binding permits new and old object methods to meld together so that extensions of existing objects and methods are created without imposing performance penalties beyond a brief reference to the Virtual Method Table.

Programming for Extensibility

The Button and Point objects were created and subsequently modified to demonstrate different aspects of object-oriented programming. At the same time, any considerations not immediately relevant were ignored and some programming elements were written in the simplest possible fashion to avoid digressive explanations.

Programming for extensibility requires two parts advance planning and one part hindsight and revision. While it is impossible and impractical for a programmer to anticipate every descendant object type that will later be created from a unit, there are a few guidelines which can be applied.

Please realize that these are not hard and fast rules—defining absolute rules would be even harder than anticipating all possible descendant object types. These are suggestions that will reduce the amount of hindsight and revision required.

Tool Declarations

Any tools that will be required to implement an object should, if at all practical, be declared within the object file and not depend on the application program for declaration or inclusion.

For example, even though both the Button and Box objects use direct calls to the Mouse object, the Mouse object file does not appear in the include declarations in either object file. Instead, the demo programs called on the Mouse object file while the gmouse and tmouse objects were declared as static instances in the Mouse object file.

Before either the Button or Box object source files could be compiled as independent .obj files, include declarations would be needed for mouse.i and graphics.h.

However, by declaring static instances of both gmouse and tmouse in the Mouse file, working object instances are available not only for the other object types but for the calling application as well.

The ScrollBar Object

The ScrollBar object type should be a familiar feature since it appears in a variety of text- and graphics-based applications ranging from drawing and design utilities to the Turbo C++ Integrated Development Environment. The operation of scrollbars is, by design, self-explanatory.

In this case, the ScrollBar objects were chosen for two purposes: to demonstrate extensibility; and to create a second useful graphics control feature.

Despite the fact that Buttons and ScrollBars have relatively little in common, the ScrollBar object is defined as a descendant of the Button object type, inheriting the Button data and method elements, but also defining new methods and elements peculiar to the ScrollBar object type. Two instances of the ScrollBar object type appear in Figure 8-1.

Creating the ScrollBar Object

The ScrollBar object file begins by enumerating the data type, HitType:

```
typedef enum { NO_HIT, RIGHT, UP, HBAR,
               VBAR, LEFT, DOWN } HitType;
```

Figure 8-1: ScrollBar Control Objects

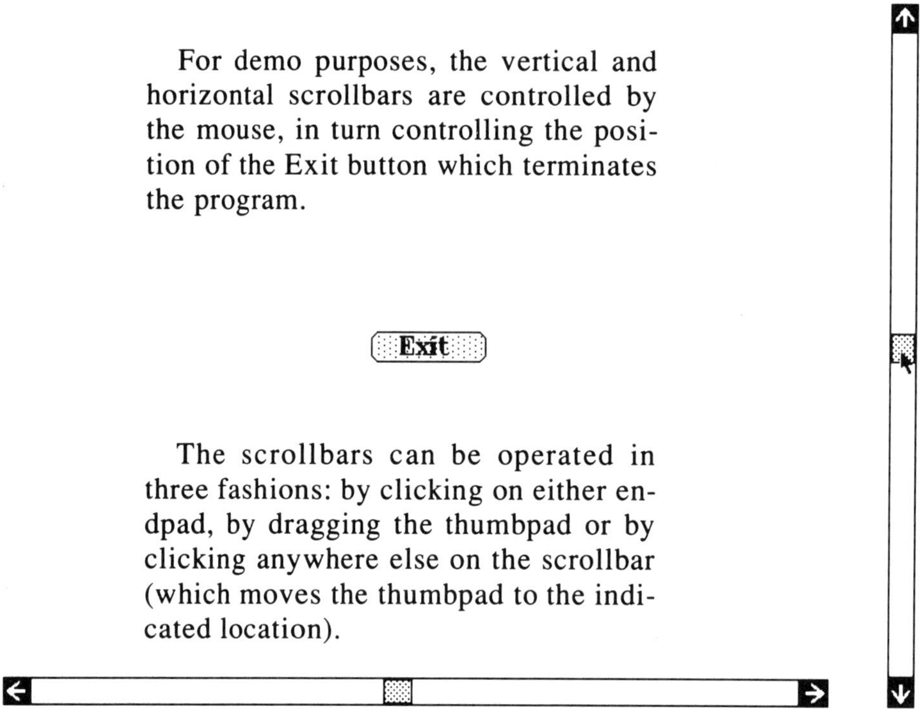

For demo purposes, the vertical and horizontal scrollbars are controlled by the mouse, in turn controlling the position of the Exit button which terminates the program.

The scrollbars can be operated in three fashions: by clicking on either endpad, by dragging the thumbpad or by clicking anywhere else on the scrollbar (which moves the thumbpad to the indicated location).

HitType provides a series of messages as integer values that can be passed to various object methods or returned to a calling application to identify scrollbar hit events. Since HitType consists of integer values, simple integer arguments can be used just as well as an enumerated type—and are the same to the computer. The enumerated mnemonics are provided for the programmer's convenience.

The ScrollBar object is declared as a descendant of the Button object and, since descendance has not been explicitly declared as public, it is private by default and this is perfectly acceptable because none of Button's methods will be needed by applications calling a ScrollBar instance.

```
class ScrollBar : Button
{
```

In like fashion, ScrollBar's data elements are also explicitly declared private.

```
    private:
        int   LineColor, SPos, Step, ScrollMove;
        viewporttype VRef;
```

But ScrollBar's methods are declared public because, otherwise, they wouldn't be accessible to the application.

```
    public:
        ScrollBar();
        ScrollBar( int PtX, int PtY, int Size,
                   int C1, int C2, int Orientation );
```

ScrollBar's constructor method is declared in two different forms (overloaded) for reasons that will be discussed in Chapter 9.

The destructor method, of course, must always be declared public (see Chapter 2) but the Init, ScrollHit, GetPosition and GetDirection methods are also public to permit access by applications.

```
        ~ScrollBar();
        void Init( int PtX, int PtY, int Size,
                   int C1, int C2, int Orientation );
        HitType  ScrollHit();
        int  GetPosition();
        int  GetDirection();
```

You may have noticed already that the second constructor method and the Init method have the same calling parameters. While this might appear redundant, remember that for static object instances the constructor method call is implicit and does not necessarily include a parameter list.

In the ScrlTest.CPP demo, it would be quite impractical to provide a parameter list at the point where the object instances are declared.

But, for dynamic object instances an explicit constructor call is more convenient but should also have the appropriate initialization parameters. This will be shown in Chapter 9.

The remaining methods are not intended to be called by applications—only by other object methods and, therefore, are declared as private.

```
    private:
        virtual void SetLoc( int PtX, int PtY );
        void RestoreViewPort();
        virtual void Draw();
        virtual void Erase();
        void SetOutline();
        void SetArrows();
        void SetThumbPad();
        void EraseThumbPad();
};
```

Alternating private, public, private declarations is perfectly legitimate even though it has not been shown previously. It would be equally appropriate to declare access individually for each method and data element.

The Draw and Erase methods are declared virtual because future descendants of ScrollBar may need to redefine these, but may also require access to the original method definitions. These are also declared private because it is unlikely for an application to need direct access to these methods. Descendant objects, of course, can always redefine access if necessary.

The ScrollHit Method

The ScrollHit method is the workhorse provision of the ScrollBar object but, as you can see from the method declaration, does not require any calling parameters. Instead, the ScrollHit method acts independently, returning an argument reporting the scrollhit event type.

When queried, if a hit has occurred, the scrollbar's thumbpad image is updated (and the original graphics window restored) before returning a message to the calling application indicating: no hit occurred (NO_HIT); that the mouse hit the endpads (RIGHT, UP, LEFT, or DOWN), or; that the hit occurred somewhere within the body of the scrollbar (HBAR or VBAR).

The HitType returned by the ScrollHit method can be used by the calling application to decide what action should be taken in response to the event.

This is not all that ScrollHit accomplishes (which is a good example of why object units should have more than minimal documentation describing the public methods calling parameters and return values).

Unlike the Button object which requires the calling application to pass mouse coordinate parameters to determine a button hit event, the ScrollHit method queries the Mouse object directly, retrieving a record of mouse button events and event coordinates. It compares this information to its own screen position and thumbpad and endpad coordinates to determine if it has been hit or not.

This is also why the gmouse object instance is declared within the Mouse object file instead of relying on the calling application to define a mouse handle or to provide mouse button event information. After seeing how the mouse is called by the ScrollBar.ScrollHit method, you may well prefer to revise the ButtonHit method for similar handling—but this is left as an exercise for the reader.

After retrieving the mouse coordinates, the ScrollHit method determines the mouse pointer position relative to the scrollbar coordinates and decides on the HitType, as well as adjusting the thumbpad position within the scrollbar. In addition to retrieving mouse coordinates, the ScrollHit method turns off (hides) the mouse pointer before updating the scrollbar image and then restores the mouse pointer image when done. All of this is smoother and faster than relying on the calling application to prevent graphics conflicts with the mouse pointer.

The ScrollBar Constructor

The ScrollBar constructor method—ScrollBar::ScrollBar—is defined in two versions—a practice referred to earlier as overloading. The first version is called without any parameters and initializes all of the object's variables as zero. Before the scrollbar image is actually drawn, the Init method must be called with the appropriate information.

In the second version, however, the constructor method is called with the initialization parameters directly, setting the color, position, size, and orientation of the object instance by passing these arguments directly to the Init method.

The ScrollBar Init Method

Since ScrollBar is designed and intended for use with application windows, the Init method begins by retrieving the current viewport settings. These viewport settings are used to restore the original window settings after the Draw, Erase, or ThumbPad routines have changed viewport settings.

```
void ScrollBar::Init( int PtX, int PtY, int Size,
                      int C1, int C2, int Orientation )
{
   getviewsettings( &VRef );
   if( Size < 100 ) Size = 100;
   ScrollMove = Orientation;
   SPos = 21;
   Step = Size / 100;
```

The Init method also sets a minimum width (or height if vertical) of 100 pixels and establishes the Step increment by dividing the overall size by 100. Both values, of course are optional. See the section titled *Omissions* later in this chapter.

Of course, the SizeX and SizeY parameters which were inherited from the Button object type have to be set according to the ScrollMove orientation:

```
switch( ScrollMove )
{
   case VERT_DIR:
   {
      SizeX = 20;
      SizeY = Size;
      while( PtX + SizeX > VRef.right ) PtX- -;
      break;
   }
   case HORIZ_DIR:
   {
      SizeX = Size;
      SizeY = 20;
      while( PtY + SizeY > VRef.bottom ) PtY- -;
   }  }
```

An arbitrary thickness of 20 pixels is also set and the initial position of the thumbpad is established at the left or top of the scrollbar. Last, the PtX and PtY parameters are passed on to the SetLoc method, the two color parameters are assigned and the Draw method is called to create the scrollbar image:

```
    SetLoc( PtX, PtY );
    LineColor = C1;
    Color = C2;
    Draw();
}
```

The RestoreViewPort Method

The RestoreViewPort method is a convenience provided to restore the original graphic window settings. It uses the VRef (ViewPortType) variable which was set when the object instance was initialized:

```
void ScrollBar::RestoreViewPort()
{
    setviewport( VRef.left,  VRef.top,
                 VRef.right, VRef.bottom,
                 VRef.clip  );
}
```

The SetLoc Method

The SetLoc method originally defined in the Point object is redefined here, making the coordinates relative and, at the same time, adjusting the SizeX and SizeY parameters to ensure that the object does not exceed the window limits:

```
void ScrollBar::SetLoc( int PtX, int PtY )
{
    x = VRef.left + PtX;
    y = VRef.top + PtY;
    while( ( x + SizeX ) > VRef.right )  SizeX- -;
    while( ( y + SizeY ) > VRef.bottom ) SizeY- -;
}
```

The Draw Method

The Draw method was defined in the Button4 unit as a virtual method, but is redefined here because the ScrollBar object has different graphic drawing requirements:

```
void ScrollBar::Draw()
{
   int  OldColor = getcolor();

   SetOutline();
   SetArrows();
   SetThumbPad();
   setcolor( OldColor );
}
```

In this version, the Draw method calls several subsidiary methods for the various tasks before restoring the original drawing color.

The SetOutline method begins by setting a new drawing color and a new viewport to accommodate the scrollbar image before drawing the scrollbar outline as a solid bar:

```
void ScrollBar::SetOutline()
{
   Outline RectArr;

   setcolor( LineColor );
   setviewport( x, y, x+SizeX, y+SizeY, TRUE );
   RectArr[0] = RectArr[2] = RectArr[8] =
   RectArr[1] = RectArr[7] = RectArr[9] = 1;
   RectArr[4] = RectArr[6] = SizeX-1;
   RectArr[3] = RectArr[5] = SizeY-1;
   setfillstyle( SOLID_FILL, Color );
   setlinestyle( SOLID_LINE, 0, NORM_WIDTH );
   fillpoly( 5, RectArr );
```

The next step is to erase the center of the bar in order to leave two solid ends (the endpads) and an outline along the length of the bar:

```
   setfillstyle( SOLID_FILL, getbkcolor() );
   switch( ScrollMove )
   {
      case VERT_DIR:
      {
         RectArr[1] = RectArr[7] = RectArr[9] = 21;
```

```
         RectArr[3] = RectArr[5] = SizeY-21;
         break;
      }
      case HORIZ_DIR:
      {
         RectArr[0] = RectArr[2] = RectArr[8] = 21;
         RectArr[4] = RectArr[6] = SizeX-21;
   }  }
   fillpoly( 5, RectArr );
}
```

This step could also be accomplished using the Bar procedure from the *graphics* unit, but since the tools are already defined from the Button methods, the established format is repeated here.

The SetArrows method is called to draw two arrow images at each of the remaining solid ends of the bar using the thick line style:

```
void ScrollBar::SetArrows()
{
   setcolor( getbkcolor() );
   setlinestyle( SOLID_LINE, 0, THICK_WIDTH );
   switch( ScrollMove )
   {
      case VERT_DIR:
      {
         line( 10, 4,    4, 12 );
         line( 10, 4,   16, 12 );
         line( 10, 4,   10, 16 );
         line( 10, SizeY-4,    4, SizeY-12 );
         line( 10, SizeY-4,   16, SizeY-12 );
         line( 10, SizeY-4,   10, SizeY-16 );
         break;
      }
      case HORIZ_DIR:
      {
         line( 4, 10, 12,    4 );
         line( 4, 10, 12, 16 );
```

```
        line( 4, 10, 16, 10 );
        line( SizeX-4, 10, SizeX-12,  4 );
        line( SizeX-4, 10, SizeX-12, 16 );
        line( SizeX-4, 10, SizeX-16, 10 );
   }  }
   setlinestyle( SOLID_LINE, 0, NORM_WIDTH );
}
```

The SetThumbPad Method

The SetThumbPad method draws a dot-patterned square within the scrollbar outline, beginning by saving the current color and then setting the viewport to the scrollbar outline:

```
void ScrollBar::SetThumbPad()
{
   Outline RectArr;
   int      OldColor = getcolor();

   setviewport( x, y, x+SizeX, y+SizeY, TRUE );
   setcolor( LineColor );
   setfillstyle( CLOSE_DOT_FILL, Color );
   switch( ScrollMove )
   {
      case VERT_DIR:
      {
         RectArr[0] = RectArr[2] = RectArr[8] = 2;
         RectArr[1] = RectArr[7] = RectArr[9] = SPos;
         RectArr[4] = RectArr[6] = 18;
         RectArr[3] = RectArr[5] = SPos+19;
         break;
      }
      case HORIZ_DIR:
      {
         RectArr[0] = RectArr[2] = RectArr[8] = SPos;
         RectArr[1] = RectArr[7] = RectArr[9] = 2;
         RectArr[4] = RectArr[6] = SPos+19;
```

```
        RectArr[3] = RectArr[5] = 19;
    }  }
    fillpoly( 5, RectArr );
```

The thumbpad image is created using the predefined CLOSE_DOT_FILL pattern and the current instance's Color, while the LineColor is used for the solid outline around the thumbpad. Finally, the original color setting and viewport are restored:

```
    setcolor( OldColor );
    RestoreViewPort();
}
```

The EraseThumbPad Method

The EraseThumbPad method could be accomplished in essentially the same fashion as the SetThumbPad method except for using the background color and the SOLID_FILL pattern, again ending by restoring the original color and viewport settings.

Instead, however, the even simpler expedient of setting the viewport to cover only the thumbpad image and then erasing the viewport contents provides a fast convenient method of erasure.

```
void ScrollBar::EraseThumbPad()
{
    switch( ScrollMove )
    {
        case VERT_DIR:
            setviewport( x+2, y+SPos,
                         x+18, y+SPos+19, TRUE );  break;
        case HORIZ_DIR:
            setviewport( x+SPos, y+2,
                         x+SPos+19, y+18, TRUE );
    }
    clearviewport();
    RestoreViewPort();
}
```

If, however, you chose to use a patterned background for the scrollbar body, a different technique would be needed to restore this area.

The ScrollHit Method

The ScrollHit method is the heart of the scrollbar operations and it begins by setting a default value (NO_HIT) for the local variable Result:

```
HitType ScrollBar::ScrollHit()
{
   HitType   Result = NO_HIT;
   Mstatus   Position;
   int       MouseX, MouseY, NPos = 0;

   Position = gmouse.Mpressed( ButtonL );
```

Instead of calling the ScrollHit method with parameters for the mouse pointer location, ScrollHit calls the gMouse::GetPosition method directly to retrieve its own mouse button status and coordinate information. For simplicity, the button status information is not presently tested by the ScrollHit method, but could be used for confirmation of button down or button release status if desired.

```
   MouseX = Position.xaxis;
   MouseY = Position.yaxis;
   switch( ScrollMove )
   {
```

Depending on whether the ScrollMove variable indicates the current instance is horizontal or vertical, the mouse coordinates are tested against the scrollbar position variables (with corrections from window coordinates to absolute screen coordinates) to decide if a scrollbar hit has occurred and if so, what type of hit has occurred:

```
      case VERT_DIR:
      {
         if( (MouseX>=x) && (MouseX<=x+20)
          && (MouseY>=y) )
            if( MouseY<=y+20 )         Result = UP;    else
            if( MouseY<=y+SizeY-31 ) Result = VBAR;  else
            if( MouseY<=y+SizeY )      Result = DOWN;
         break;
      }
```

```
    case HORIZ_DIR:
    {
        if( (MouseY>=y) && (MouseY<=y+20)
          && (MouseX>=x) )
            if( MouseX<=x+20 )        Result = LEFT;   else
            if( MouseX<=x+SizeX-31 )  Result = HBAR;   else
            if( MouseX<=x+SizeX )     Result = RIGHT;
}   }
```

The current ScrollBar method tests for a hit anywhere along the scrollbar image. If the hit is not on either of the endpads or the thumbpad, the scroll position will jump abruptly to the selected location. In some applications, you may prefer to guard against such rapid movements by restricting hits to the endpads and the thumbpad (which has not yet been tested directly).

At this point, ScrollHit has identified where the mouse hit occurred, but hasn't yet taken any action as a result. If Result is not NO_HIT, then a response is appropriate; otherwise, NO_HIT is returned directly.

```
if( Result == NO_HIT ) return( Result );
switch( Result )
{
    case  LEFT:
    case    UP: NPos = SPos-Step;      break;
    case RIGHT:
    case  DOWN: NPos = SPos+Step;      break;
    case  HBAR: NPos = MouseX-(x+10);  break;
    case  VBAR: NPos = MouseY-(y+10);
}
if( NPos < 21 ) NPos = 21;
switch( Result )
{
    case  LEFT:
    case RIGHT: if( NPos > SizeX-41 )
                    NPos = SizeX-41;  break;
    case    UP:
    case  DOWN: if( NPos > SizeY-41 )
```

```
                    NPos = SizeY-41;
     }
```

If a response is required, NPos is given the new thumbpad coordinate and tested to insure that the proper limits are not exceeded.

```
gmouse.Mshow( FALSE );
EraseThumbPad();
```

Next, the mouse pointer is turned off and the current thumbpad is erased before SPos is updated with the value in NPos and a new thumbpad drawn:

```
SPos = NPos;
SetThumbPad();
```

Last, the SetThumbPad method is called to restore the thumbpad image, the mouse pointer is turned on again and *Result* is reported back to the calling application:

```
gmouse.Mshow( TRUE );
return( Result );
```
}

The ScrlTest Demo

The ScrlTest demo program creates the screen shown in Figure 8-1, allowing you to experiment directly with the scrollbar operations. The position of the included "Exit" button is controlled directly by the two scrollbars and will maneuver around the screen in response to the scroll operations selected.

Aside from these few comments, the ScrlTest program is essentially self-explanatory. Have fun.

Omissions

To keep the present demonstration relatively simple, there are several methods not provided by the ScrollBar object definition which could be useful in actual applications.

First, while the ScrollHit method calls the Mouse object directly to retrieve the mouse button status and position information, the mouse button status is not tested or used. However, the ScrollHit method could be rewritten so that, once a scrollbar hit was established, it would loop continuously, performing its own tests and moving the thumbpad until the mouse button was released or the mouse cursor moved away from the scrollbar. I'll come back to whether this is a good or bad implementation.

Second, what about a provision, using the capabilities shown previously to change the mouse pointer from an arrow image to a glove pointer, either when the mouse pointer is over the scrollbar image or when the mouse button is pressed?

Third, how about a method provision to allow an application to directly control the thumbpad (slider pad) position along the scrollbar? This wouldn't be desired for every application, but could be quite useful in many circumstances.

Fourth, should provisions be made to change the scrollbar colors without having to recreate the scrollbar from scratch?

Fifth, what about provisions to change the thickness of the scrollbar and the size of the endpads and thumbpads.

Sixth, what other provisions could be made to improve the efficiency and/or the performance of the scrollbar?

Here are a half-dozen questions to mull over and, after you have experimented with the ScrlTest program, you may have a half-dozen of your own.

The first question concerned making the ScrollHit method essentially self-contained so that once called, it would conduct its own operations until the mouse button was released or the mouse pointer moved away from the scrollbar. What's wrong with this? Nothing, if you only want the scrollbars to control the scrollbar images. But what about the external application that is calling the scrollbar to control its own operations? In the demo program, the scrollbars are used to move the Exit button image around the screen, but if the scrollbar instance does not exit until it can return a NO_HIT result, how would the button image ever be updated?

If updating was done every time a ScrollHit method returned, regardless of the reported result, how would this look? Would it look jerky with large, sudden movements only? What about flicker when the mouse button was pressed somewhere other than over a scrollbar?

In some circumstances, a delayed response might be desired, but this would be relatively rare and could be implemented within the calling application without restricting the object methods to such a limited and unwieldy operation.

Before making a method too efficient, consider how it affects the application using the object.

A Text-Mode ScrollBar

Previously, both the Mouse and Button objects were created as parallel graphics and text versions while the ScrollBar object has been created only in its graphics version—an omission made primarily because scroll bars have previously not been associated with text presentations and because text mode does not offer the fine degrees of control that are inherently associated with scroll bar controls.

But this does not mean that a text ScrollBar cannot be created, operating in a manner analogous to the graphic control though lacking the fine degrees of position adjustment of the graphics object.

Consistent with the principles of extensibility, implementation of a text ScrollBar can be quite easily accomplished while the principal problem in doing so is deciding how the ScrollBar image will be handled.

Several options suggest themselves but the first consideration might be how many screen columns (for a vertical scrollbar) or rows (for a horizontal scrollbar) will be devoted to the control object.

If the line and box characters from the extended character set are to be totally analogous to the graphics version, the text scrollbar would need a minimum of three columns or three rows—two each for the outline and the third (center) for the moving thumbpad. And, if a fourth row or column is added as a margin, this expenditure of screen resources may excessively limit your application.

As an alternative, a single row or column could be devoted to the text scrollbar, using the left and right or up and down arrow characters (0x1A, 0x1B, 0x18, and 0x19) in inverse video as the ends of the scrollbars. At the same time, the body of the scrollbar could be composed of the half-tone block character, 0xB1, and the thumbpad could use either the heavy half-tone block, 0xB2, or the solid block character, 0xDB.

In this form, narrow but effective text scrollbars become quite practical, using only a minimum of the available display space.

But the scrollbar thumbpad will only be able to move in discrete character steps, providing 23 vertical steps (two are used for the ends) and 70+ horizontal steps (a horizontal endpad three characters wide looks much better than a single character endpad and is easier to hit).

On the other hand, if a wider range of adjustment is absolutely required in a text mode application, both coarse and fine scrollbar controls could be used. Each step of the coarse control would be the equivalent of the entire range of the fine control.

I have offered a few suggestions for constructing text scrollbar objects. In the listings at the end of this chapter and on the disk accompanying this volume, a text-based scrollbar object is provided together with demo program—ScrlTst2—which is analogous to ScrlTest.CPP.

Further implementation of this object extension is left as an exercise for the reader but, please note, the present example is quite minimal and does not presently support windows.

Summary

In this chapter, a new object type, the ScrollBar object, has been created using the extensibility feature of object-oriented programming. At the same time, several elements have been shown in the ScrollBar methods which could well be incorporated in the earlier Button and/or Point methods—including making them directly responsible for querying mouse position and button information and making each window-sensitive in terms of position.

For example, the Button object previously defined does not test the coordinates provided on either a Create or Move operation to see if these are valid for the screen size or for the window size. The ScrollBar object does possess at least a rudimentary self-test capability to decide if it can be correctly displayed. Objects can be much more powerful than conventional procedures and functions, but to balance this power, they must also exercise some care to ensure proper operation.

Also, the Button objects demonstrated were created for static object instances only and could well use an overloaded constructor method to provide better handling for dynamic instances.

In Chapter 9, dynamic objects will be demonstrated as a variation of the present scrollbar objects.

```
            //=======================================//
            // program ScrollBar_Test == SCRLTEST.CPP //
            //    graphics scrollbar demonstration    //
            //=======================================//

#include <conio.h>

#include <stdio.h>

#include <stdlib.h>

#include <stdarg.h>

#include <string.h>

#include <graphics.h>

#include "mouse.i"

#include "button4.i"

#include "scrlbar.i"

main()
{
    Mstatus     Position;
    int         Exit = FALSE, MoveButton,
                GDriver = DETECT, GMode, GError;
    ScrollBar   HScroll, VScroll;
    Button      ExitButton;

    initgraph( &GDriver, &GMode, "C:\\TC\\BGI" );
    GError = graphresult();
    if( GError )
    {
```

```
    printf( "Graphics error: %s\n",

            grapherrormsg( GError ) );

    printf( "Program aborted...\n" );

    exit(1);

}

if( !gmouse.Mreset() ) exit(1);

cleardevice();

HScroll.Init( 0, getmaxy()-40, getmaxx()-60,

            GREEN, LIGHTGREEN, HORIZ_DIR );

VScroll.Init( getmaxx()-40, 0, getmaxy()-40,

            GREEN, LIGHTGREEN, VERT_DIR );

ExitButton.SetButtonType( ROUNDED );

ExitButton.Create( HScroll.GetPosition()-20,

                VScroll.GetPosition(),

                80, 20, LIGHTRED, "Exit" );

do

{

    Position = gmouse.Mpressed( ButtonL );

    if( Position.button_count )

    {

        Exit = ExitButton.ButtonHit( Position.xaxis,

                                    Position.yaxis );

        if( !Exit )  do

        {
```

```
            MoveButton = FALSE;

            switch( HScroll.ScrollHit() )
            {
                case LEFT:

                case HBAR:

                case RIGHT: MoveButton = TRUE;
            }

            switch( VScroll.ScrollHit() )
            {
                case UP:

                case VBAR:

                case DOWN: MoveButton = TRUE;
            }

            if( MoveButton )
                ExitButton.Move( HScroll.GetPosition()-20,

                                 VScroll.GetPosition() );

            Position = gmouse.Mreleased( ButtonL );
        }
        while( !Position.button_count );
    }  }
    while( !Exit );

    closegraph();          // restore text mode and ...       //
    tmouse.Mreset();       // reset mouse for text operation //
}
```

```
//==============================//
// ScrollBar unit == SCRLBAR.I //
//   graphics scrollbar object  //
//==============================//

typedef enum { NO_HIT, RIGHT, UP, HBAR,

               VBAR, LEFT, DOWN } HitType;

typedef int   Outline[10];


class ScrollBar : Button

{

   private:

      int  LineColor, SPos, Step, ScrollMove;

      viewporttype VRef;

   public:

      ScrollBar();                         // constructor method //

      ScrollBar( int PtX, int PtY, int Size,

                 int C1, int C2, int Orientation );

                                           // 2nd constructor    //
      ~ScrollBar();                        // destructor method  //

      void Init( int PtX, int PtY, int Size,

                 int C1, int C2, int Orientation );

      virtual void SetLoc( int PtX, int PtY );

      HitType  ScrollHit();

      int  GetPosition();

      int  GetDirection();

   private:
```

```
        void RestoreViewPort();

        virtual void Draw();

        virtual void Erase();

        void SetOutline();

        void SetArrows();

        void SetThumbPad();

        void EraseThumbPad();

};


        //========================================//
        // implementation for object type ScrollBar //
        //========================================//

ScrollBar::ScrollBar()

{

   x = y = SizeX = SizeY = Color =

   LineColor = SPos = Step = ScrollMove = 0;

}


ScrollBar::ScrollBar( int PtX, int PtY, int Size,

                      int C1, int C2, int Orientation )

{

   Init( PtX, PtY, Size, C1, C2, Orientation );

}


ScrollBar::~ScrollBar()   {   Erase();   }
```

```
void ScrollBar::Init( int PtX, int PtY, int Size,
                      int C1, int C2, int Orientation )
{
   getviewsettings( &VRef );
   if( Size < 100 ) Size = 100;
   ScrollMove = Orientation;
   SPos = 21;
   Step = Size / 100;
   switch( ScrollMove )
   {
      case VERT_DIR:
      {
         SizeX = 20;
         SizeY = Size;
         while( PtX + SizeX > VRef.right ) PtX- -;
         break;
      }
      case HORIZ_DIR:
      {
         SizeX = Size;
         SizeY = 20;
         while( PtY + SizeY > VRef.bottom ) PtY- -;
   } }
   SetLoc( PtX, PtY );
```

```
   LineColor = C1;

   Color = C2;

   Draw();

}


void ScrollBar::SetLoc( int PtX, int PtY )

{

   x = VRef.left + PtX;

   y = VRef.top + PtY;

   while( ( x + SizeX ) > VRef.right )  SizeX- -;

   while( ( y + SizeY ) > VRef.bottom ) SizeY- -;

}


void ScrollBar::EraseThumbPad()

{

   switch( ScrollMove )

   {

      case VERT_DIR:
         setviewport( x+2, y+SPos,
                      x+18, y+SPos+19, TRUE );  break;
      case HORIZ_DIR:
         setviewport( x+SPos, y+2,
                      x+SPos+19, y+18, TRUE );

   }

   clearviewport();
```

```
      RestoreViewPort();

}

void ScrollBar::SetThumbPad()

{

    Outline RectArr;

    int     OldColor = getcolor();

    setviewport( x, y, x+SizeX, y+SizeY, TRUE );

    setcolor( LineColor );

    setfillstyle( CLOSE_DOT_FILL, Color );

    switch( ScrollMove )

    {

        case VERT_DIR:

        {

            RectArr[0] = RectArr[2] = RectArr[8] = 2;

            RectArr[1] = RectArr[7] = RectArr[9] = SPos;

            RectArr[4] = RectArr[6] = 18;

            RectArr[3] = RectArr[5] = SPos+19;

            break;

        }

        case HORIZ_DIR:

        {

            RectArr[0] = RectArr[2] = RectArr[8] = SPos;

            RectArr[1] = RectArr[7] = RectArr[9] = 2;
```

```
            RectArr[4] = RectArr[6] = SPos+19;

            RectArr[3] = RectArr[5] = 19;

    }  }

    fillpoly( 5, RectArr );

    setcolor( OldColor );

    RestoreViewPort();

}


void ScrollBar::SetOutline()

{

    Outline RectArr;

    setcolor( LineColor );

    setviewport( x, y, x+SizeX, y+SizeY, TRUE );

    RectArr[0] = RectArr[2] = RectArr[8] = 1;

    RectArr[1] = RectArr[7] = RectArr[9] = 1;

    RectArr[4] = RectArr[6] = SizeX-1;

    RectArr[3] = RectArr[5] = SizeY-1;

    setfillstyle( SOLID_FILL, Color );

    setlinestyle( SOLID_LINE, 0, NORM_WIDTH );

    fillpoly( 5, RectArr );

                    // clear center of bar //
    setfillstyle( SOLID_FILL, getbkcolor() );

    switch( ScrollMove )

    {
```

```
        case VERT_DIR:

        {

            RectArr[1] = RectArr[7] = RectArr[9] = 21;

            RectArr[3] = RectArr[5] = SizeY-21;

            break;

        }

        case HORIZ_DIR:

        {

            RectArr[0] = RectArr[2] = RectArr[8] = 21;

            RectArr[4] = RectArr[6] = SizeX-21;

    }   }

    fillpoly( 5, RectArr );

}

void ScrollBar::SetArrows()

{

    setcolor( getbkcolor() );

    setlinestyle( SOLID_LINE, 0, THICK_WIDTH );

    switch( ScrollMove )

    {

        case VERT_DIR:

        {

            line( 10, 4,  4, 12 );

            line( 10, 4, 16, 12 );
```

```
          line( 10, 4, 10, 16 );

          line( 10, SizeY-4,  4, SizeY-12 );

          line( 10, SizeY-4, 16, SizeY-12 );

          line( 10, SizeY-4, 10, SizeY-16 );

          break;

       }

       case HORIZ_DIR:

       {

          line( 4, 10, 12,  4 );

          line( 4, 10, 12, 16 );

          line( 4, 10, 16, 10 );

          line( SizeX-4, 10, SizeX-12,  4 );

          line( SizeX-4, 10, SizeX-12, 16 );

          line( SizeX-4, 10, SizeX-16, 10 );

    }  }

    setlinestyle( SOLID_LINE, 0, NORM_WIDTH );

}


void ScrollBar::Draw()

{

    int  OldColor = getcolor();

    SetOutline();                        // scrollbar outline  //

    SetArrows();                         // scrollbar arrows   //

    SetThumbPad();                       // draw thumbpad      //
```

```
   setcolor( OldColor );                    // restore orig color //

}

void ScrollBar::Erase()

{

   setviewport( x, y, x+SizeX, y+SizeY, TRUE );

   clearviewport();

   RestoreViewPort();

}

void ScrollBar::RestoreViewPort()

{

   setviewport( VRef.left,   VRef.top,

                VRef.right, VRef.bottom,

                VRef.clip   );

}

HitType ScrollBar::ScrollHit()

{

   HitType   Result = NO_HIT;

   Mstatus   Position;

   int       MouseX, MouseY, NPos = 0;

   Position = gmouse.Mpressed( ButtonL );

   MouseX = Position.xaxis;

   MouseY = Position.yaxis;
```

```
switch( ScrollMove )

{

   case VERT_DIR:

   {

      if( (MouseX>=x) && (MouseX<=x+20)

       && (MouseY>=y) )

         if( MouseY<=y+20 )        Result = UP;    else

         if( MouseY<=y+SizeY-31 ) Result = VBAR;  else

         if( MouseY<=y+SizeY )     Result = DOWN;

      break;

   }

   case HORIZ_DIR:

   {

      if( (MouseY>=y) && (MouseY<=y+20)

       && (MouseX>=x) )

         if( MouseX<=x+20 )        Result = LEFT;  else

         if( MouseX<=x+SizeX-31 ) Result = HBAR;  else

         if( MouseX<=x+SizeX )     Result = RIGHT;

}  }

if( Result == NO_HIT ) return( Result );

switch( Result )

{

   case  LEFT:

   case    UP: NPos = SPos-Step;        break;
```

```
      case RIGHT:

      case   DOWN: NPos = SPos+Step;        break;

      case   HBAR: NPos = MouseX-(x+10);   break;

      case   VBAR: NPos = MouseY-(y+10);

   }

   if( NPos < 21 ) NPos = 21;

   switch( Result )

   {

      case   LEFT:

      case RIGHT: if( NPos > SizeX-41 )

                      NPos = SizeX-41;  break;

      case     UP:

      case   DOWN: if( NPos > SizeY-41 )

                      NPos = SizeY-41;

   }

   gmouse.Mshow( FALSE );

   EraseThumbPad();

   SPos = NPos;

   SetThumbPad();

   gmouse.Mshow( TRUE );

   return( Result );

}


int ScrollBar::GetPosition()  { return( SPos );  }
```

```
int ScrollBar::GetDirection() { return( ScrollMove ); }

        //=========== end of methods ==============//


        //=======================================//
        // program ScrollBar_Test == SCRLTST2.CPP //
        //          text scrollbar demo           //
        //=======================================//
```

```cpp
#include <conio.h>

#include <stdio.h>

#include <stdlib.h>

#include <stdarg.h>

#include <string.h>


#include "mouse.i"

#include "tboxes.i"

#include "tscrlbar.i"

main()
{
    Mstatus    Position;

    int        Exit = FALSE, ThumbMove;

    TScrollBar HScroll, VScroll;

    Box        ExitButton;

    if( !tmouse.Mreset() ) exit(1);

    clrscr();
```

```
HScroll.Init( 1, 25, 70,

            LIGHTGRAY, LIGHTGREEN, HORIZONTAL );

VScroll.Init( 79, 1, 23,

            LIGHTGRAY, LIGHTRED, VERTICAL );

ExitButton.Create( HScroll.GetPosition(),

                VScroll.GetPosition(),

                10, LIGHTRED, BLACK, "Exit" );

do

{

    Position = tmouse.Mpressed( ButtonL );

    if( Position.button_count )

    {

        Exit = ExitButton.BoxHit( Position.xaxis,

                                Position.yaxis );

        if( !Exit )  do

        {

            ThumbMove = FALSE;

            switch( HScroll.ScrollHit() )

            {

                case LEFT:

                case HBAR:

                case RIGHT: ThumbMove = TRUE;

            }

            switch( VScroll.ScrollHit() )
```

```
            {
                case UP:

                case VBAR:

                case DOWN:    ThumbMove = TRUE;

            }
            if( ThumbMove )
                ExitButton.Move( HScroll.GetPosition(),

                                    VScroll.GetPosition() );

            Position = tmouse.Mreleased( ButtonL );

        }
        while( !Position.button_count );

    }  }

    while( !Exit );

    tmouse.Mreset();          // reset mouse for text operation //

}



        //===================================//
        // Text ScrollBar object == TSCRLBAR.I //
        //===================================//

typedef enum { NONE, RIGHT, UP, HBAR,

            VBAR, LEFT, DOWN } HitType;

typedef enum { HORIZONTAL, VERTICAL } Direction;

class TScrollBar : Box

{
```

```
    protected:

        int  Size, ScrollMove, SPos;

        unsigned char BarAttr, EndAttr;

    public:

        TScrollBar();                        // constructor method //

        TScrollBar( int PtX, int PtY, int Width,

                    int C1,  int C2,  int Orientation );

                                             // 2nd constructor     //
        ~TScrollBar();                       // destructor method   //

        void Init( int PtX, int PtY, int Width,

                    int C1,  int C2,  int Orientation );

        int  GetPosition();

        int  GetDirection();

        HitType  ScrollHit();

    private:

        void Draw();

        void Erase();

        void ThumbPad( int Show );

};
```

```
//===========================================//
// implementation for object type TScrollBar //
//===========================================//

TScrollBar::TScrollBar()

{

   x = y = Size = ScrollMove =

   BarAttr = EndAttr = SPos = 0;

}


TScrollBar::TScrollBar( int PtX, int PtY, int Width,

                        int C1, int C2, int Orientation )

{

   Init( PtX, PtY, Width, C1, C2, Orientation );

}


TScrollBar::~TScrollBar() {  Erase();  }


void TScrollBar::Init( int PtX, int PtY, int Width,

                       int C1, int C2, int Orientation )

{

   x = PtX;

   y = PtY;

   Size = Width;

   EndAttr = ( ( C2 + ( C1 << 4 ) ) & 0x7F );

   BarAttr = ( ( C1 + ( C2 << 4 ) ) & 0x7F );
```

```
    ScrollMove = Orientation;

    if( Size < 10 ) Size = 10;

    SPos = 1;

    switch( ScrollMove )

    {

       case VERTICAL:

          while( y + Size > 24 ) Size- -;   break;

       case HORIZONTAL:

          while( x + Size > 79 ) Size- -;

    }

    Draw();

}


void TScrollBar::Draw()

{

    int  i;

    struct text_info T;

    unsigned char OldAttr;


    gettextinfo( &T );

    OldAttr = T.normattr;

    textattr( BarAttr );

    for( i=0; i<=Size; i++ )

       {
```

```
     switch( ScrollMove )

     {

        case VERTICAL:    gotoxy( x, y + i );  break;

        case HORIZONTAL: gotoxy( x + i, y );

     }

     cprintf( "%c", 0xB0 );

  }

textattr( EndAttr );

gotoxy( x, y );

switch( ScrollMove )

{

   case VERTICAL:

   {

      cprintf( "%c", 0x1E );

      gotoxy( x, y+Size );

      cprintf( "%c", 0x1F );

   } break;

   case HORIZONTAL:

   {

      cprintf( "%c", 0x11 );

      gotoxy( x+Size, y );

      cprintf( "%c", 0x10 );

} }

gotoxy( 1, 1 );
```

```
   textattr( OldAttr );               // restore default color //

   ThumbPad( TRUE );

}


void TScrollBar::Erase()

{

   int   i;

   for( i=0; i<=Size; i++ )

   {

      switch( ScrollMove )

      {

         case VERTICAL:    gotoxy( x, y+i );  break;

         case HORIZONTAL:  gotoxy( x+i, y );

      }

      printf( " " );

   }

   gotoxy( 1, 1 );

}


void TScrollBar::ThumbPad( int Show )

{

   int   i;

   struct text_info T;
```

```
   unsigned char OldAttr;

   gettextinfo( &T );

   OldAttr = T.normattr;

   switch( ScrollMove )

   {

      case VERTICAL:   gotoxy( x, y + SPos );  break;

      case HORIZONTAL: gotoxy( x + SPos, y );

   }

   if( Show )

   {

      textattr( EndAttr );

      cprintf( "%c", 0xF0 );

   }

   else

   {

      textattr( BarAttr );

      cprintf( "%c", 0xB0 );

   }

   gotoxy( 1, 1 );

   textattr( OldAttr );                   // restore default color //

}


HitType TScrollBar::ScrollHit()
```

```
{
   HitType   Result;

   Mstatus   Position;

   int       xPos, yPos;

   Result = NONE;

   Position = tmouse.Mpressed( ButtonL );

   xPos = Position.xaxis / 8 + 1;        // convert pixels to //

   yPos = Position.yaxis / 8 + 1;        // to row / column   //

   switch( ScrollMove )
   {
      case VERTICAL:
      {
         if( ( xPos == x ) && ( yPos >= y ) )
            if( yPos == y )          Result = UP;    else

            if( yPos <= y+Size-1 ) Result = VBAR;  else

            if( yPos == y+Size )     Result = DOWN;  break;

      }
      case HORIZONTAL:
      {
         if( ( yPos == y ) && ( xPos >= x ) )
            if( xPos == x )          Result = LEFT;  else

            if( xPos <= x+Size-1 ) Result = HBAR;  else
```

```
            if( xPos == x+Size )    Result = RIGHT;
    }   }

    if( Result == NONE ) return( Result );

    tmouse.Mshow( FALSE );

    ThumbPad( FALSE );

    switch( Result )

    {

        case   LEFT:

        case    UP: SPos- -;            break;

        case RIGHT:

        case   DOWN: SPos++;          break;

        case   HBAR: SPos = xPos - x;  break;

        case   VBAR: SPos = yPos - y;

    }

    if( SPos < 1 ) SPos = 1;

    if( SPos > Size-1 ) SPos = Size-1;

    ThumbPad( TRUE );

    tmouse.Mshow( TRUE );

    return( Result );

}


int TScrollBar::GetPosition()    {   return( SPos );   }
```

```
int TScrollBar::GetDirection()  {  return( ScrollMove );  }


        //=========== end of methods =============//
```

CHAPTER 9

DYNAMIC OBJECT INSTANCES

So far, all of the objects used in demo programs have been static instances; that is, instances of object types declared and statically allocated in the program's data segment and stack. References to *static* instances (or *static* objects) have no connection with the type of methods, static or virtual, that belong to the objects in question.

Static allocation is restrictive and cumbersome. With conventional record data structures, static allocation requires you to determine the maximum number of records required at the time the program is written and then to declare an array of records of the anticipated size. The traditional 64K data size limit has also been an unacceptable restriction for many applications.

More often, static record allocation is replaced by dynamic record allocation—where memory pointers are used as reference links and where memory is dynamically allocated for data records as needed and deallocated when no longer wanted, thus freeing unnecessary memory for other uses.

Advantages of Dynamic Objects

Object instances, which are closely related to data records, can also be dynamically created, allocating memory as required, destroying the object, and deallocating the memory when it is no longer needed. In this fashion, an application can create, within system memory limitations, as many objects as necessary and then release these from memory when they are no longer needed.

Obviously, for the Button or ScrollBar objects used in previous demonstrations, requirements for unanticipated numbers of objects are unlikely. Instead, in Chapter 10, a data record object type will be used to demonstrate dynamic object allocation in circumstances where the prediction of the number of objects is not possible.

First, it helps to understand how objects are created using pointer references and dynamic memory allocation.

Pointers to Objects

Before dynamically creating an object instance, a handle or *pointer* to the object is necessary; otherwise, the object instance could not be referenced or called by the application. An object instance can be allocated as a pointer reference using the new procedure:

```
typedef ScrollBar* SPtr;

  SPtr  HScroll = new ScrollBar( );
```

In this example, the object pointer is declared and the object instance is allocated in the same statement. This is the usual handling for dynamic objects. Initializing the object instance will also be included in this same command.

Allocation and Initialization

With Turbo C++, the malloc function has been supplemented with the new procedure permitting dynamic allocation and initialization of an object to be executed in a single operation, as shown.

Just as with a data record, the new procedure dynamically allocates sufficient memory space on the heap to contain an instance of the ScrollBar object, according to the size of the ScrollBar base type, and returns the address of the memory space allocated to the HScroll pointer variable.

Since the ScrollBar object contains virtual methods, the Init method could be called to initialize the scrollbar instance, but an overloaded constructor method has been provided so that declaration and initialization can be accomplished in a single step:

```
SPtr HScroll = new ScrollBar( 0, getmaxy()-40,
                              getmaxx()-80, GREEN,
                              LIGHTGREEN, HORIZ_DIR );
```

Notice also that this declaration was not made until after graphics mode had been initiated so that the getmaxy() and getmaxx() procedures can be used and so that the scrollbar image can be drawn.

Arrays of object can also be allocated using the optional syntax:

```
SPtr  ScrArray[5] = new ScrollBar();
```

In this case, however, the Init method is still needed to individually initialize each array element.

After this, all further method calls are made in the normal fashion except for using the pointer name and the arrow (->) reference symbol in place of an instance name (as would have been used with a statically allocated object). Instead of

```
switch( HScroll.ScrollHit() ) ...
```

the method is called as:

```
switch( HScroll->ScrollHit() ) ...
```

Method calls internal to the object definition do not require the pointer reference and no changes to object definition files are required.

Disposing of Dynamic Objects

Traditionally, data records are deallocated using the delete procedure when they are no longer required:

```
delete DataPointer;
```

For a dynamic object, there may be more required for disposal than simply releasing the heap space. This is because an object may contain its own pointers to other dynamic structures or to objects that also need to be released or that require special clean-up methods such as closing open files or restoring file records before exiting.

Instead of calling the delete function directly, complex objects should include a clean-up method, or multiple clean-up methods, to handle the special shutdown tasks.

The Destructor Keyword

Turbo C++ provides a special method type, identified by the keyword destructor, which is used to clean up and deallocate dynamic objects. The destructor method provides the means by which a program can combine a shutdown and clean-up method call with a Dispose instruction.

However, before going into the details of what the destructor call accomplishes and how, we will look at how the destructor call is used.

Programming Destructor Methods

Continuing with the ScrollBar object as an example, the destructor method is implemented:

```
ScrollBar::~ScrollBar()
{
    Erase();
}
```

In this case, the destructor method calls the Erase method to erase the scrollbar image. The Erase method already resets the viewport (graphics window) screen by calling RestoreViewPort to restore the graphics window parameters originally found when the scrollbar was created.

Alternatively, the destructor method, like the default constructor method, could be an empty procedure:

```
ScrollBar::~ScrollBar()
{
}
```

In other applications, more complex destructor methods (or more than one destructor method) may be desired to execute different clean-up tasks. Obviously, only one destructor method can be called for any object instance.

Unlike other method types, destructors cannot be inherited, but may be either static or virtual methods. Because each object type will generally require custom clean-up handling, it is recommended that destructors always be virtual methods to ensure that the correct shutdown handling is called for each object type.

The Destructor Method

The destructor method is used in two different fashions, depending on whether the object instance is a static instance or was dynamically created.

In the case of static object instances, destructor methods are called implicitly when the scope of the object expires; for example, when the procedure or program which declared the object instance terminates. If the object instance is *global* to the entire program, the constructor is called before main and the destructor is called after main terminates. If the object is declared *within a subprocedure*, the constructor is called when the procedure begins and the destructor is called when the procedure terminates and the object goes out of scope.

In static instances, calling the destructor method is automatic and does not require explicit provisions within the program—aside from providing a destructor implementation if one is necessary. Remember, if no specific destructor implementation is provided, the compiler will create a default destructor method which is always public but which will not contain any special provisions aside from deallocating the object itself.

With dynamic objects, however, explicit destructor calls can be used to deallocate object instances and release the memory used, as well as performing other tasks that may be necessary before the object terminates.

The delete Operator

The delete operator is the counterpart of the new operator and is used to terminate any dynamic object instance that was created by calling new. The syntax for using the delete operator is:

```
delete object_pointer
```

Since C++ has no way of knowing when a dynamically created object is no longer desired , dynamic objects cannot be implicitly destroyed as static objects are when their scope terminates. It is the programmer's responsibility to explicitly deallocate dynamic object instances.

Calling the Destructor Method

The delete operator is only one means of deallocating objects because the destructor method can also be explicitly called. However, calling an object's destructor method requires a slightly different syntax than other method calls.

An object's destructor method, as previously discussed, has the same name as the object class but is preceded by a tilde (~) character identifying the method as *not*-constructor. Calling the destructor method as

```
HScroll->~ScrollBar();
```

will result in a compiler error and, to call the destructor method explicitly, the full class::method name is required:

```
HScroll->ScrollBar::~ScrollBar();
```

Destructor Tasks

In addition to deallocating the memory used by an object instance, the destructor method may also accomplish other tasks before terminating the object. As shown in examples, these could include erasing a screen image, flushing buffers, updating and closing files, saving necessary member data in some other form, and deallocating other associated dynamic objects or dynamic records.

Later, a dynamic link list object will be required to deallocate a series of associated data objects before terminating. Since the link object itself uses relatively little memory compared to the data objects which it manages, simply deallocating the link list would release very little of the memory used but would, at the same time, leave the data elements unreachable—thus the necessity for a clean and careful shutdown.

The delete Operator Versus Explicit Destructor Calls

Since the delete operator is the equivalent of the explicit destructor call and is simpler to write, why have two versions?

When the delete operator is used, no arguments can be passed to the destructor method and, in most cases, no arguments are necessary. In the case of the linked list, no arguments are necessary for the destructor to clean up correctly.

In some cases, however, it may be desirable to pass one or more arguments to the destructor method to make specific provisions for how the object is shut down. This might include instructions to update and save file lists or to simply discard the list and close the file. Or there might be other specific tasks which, depending on the application and circumstances, are required in some cases but are not in others.

By providing explicit destructor calls as well as the delete operator, the flexibility of the objects are enhanced. Either type of call may be used according to the conditions and requirements of the object.

And Versus Deallocation

Conventionally, the malloc function has been used to dynamically allocate memory and the free or realloc functions have been used to free or reassign memory. With object-oriented programming, these traditional functions have been supplanted by the new and delete operators.

The reasons for this are relatively simple. With objects, the sizes of object types vary tremendously and with polymorphic objects, the object identifier does not necessarily indicate the size of the allocated instance.

For this reason, calling the destructor rather than free offers the solution by accessing the object instance's Virtual Method Table. Each object type's VMT includes the size, in bytes, of the object type definition. The VMT for any object is available through the this reference—an invisible reference that is passed to a method on any method call, providing a handle or address to the object type's Virtual Method Table.

When the destructor method is called, it returns the size indicated by the object type's VMT (which is the size of the actual object instance). Even if the object instance is a polymorphic object where the object name no longer identifies the actual object instance, the instance's correct VMT is accessed and the appropriate instance size is still returned:

```
HScroll = new ScrollBar( 0, GetMaxY, GetMaxX-60,
                    Green, LightGreen, Horizontal );

    . . .

delete HScroll;
```

The destructor method, after calling HScroll's VMT, returns the size of the object instance to the delete procedure, ensuring that the appropriate memory deallocation is executed.

The task of returning the instance size is not accomplished by the body of the destructor method, but by an epilogue code generated by the compiler in response to the reserved word destructor.

Summary

In this chapter, two operators have been introduced: the new and delete procedures. Also, the theory of creating and handling dynamically allocated object instances has been discussed.

A final graphics example, revising the ScrlTest.CPP program to use dynamic object instances is shown below (ScrlTst3.CPP), together with a dynamic revision of the text scrollbar demo (ScrlTst4.CPP). You should notice the similarities between the earlier static object demonstrations and the present dynamic object demos.

In subsequent chapters, these techniques will be demonstrated further, together with handling practices for pointers and pointer-linked lists to create a multi-purpose address/telephone directory and to create special methods allowing a linked list to conduct its own sorting operations, as well as other custom activities.

```
//=======================================//
// program ScrollBar_Test == SCRLTST3.CPP //
//       dynamic scrollbar instances       //
//=======================================//

#include <conio.h>

#include <stdio.h>

#include <stdlib.h>

#include <stdarg.h>

#include <string.h>

#include <graphics.h>

#include "mouse.i"

#include "button4.i"

#include "scrlbar.i"

typedef ScrollBar* SPtr;
```

```
main()

{

    Mstatus Position;

    int     Exit = FALSE, MoveButton,

            GDriver = DETECT, GMode, GError;

    Button  ExitButton;

    initgraph( &GDriver, &GMode, "C:\\TC\\BGI" );

    GError = graphresult();

    if( GError )

    {

        printf( "Graphics error: %s\n",

                grapherrormsg( GError ) );

        printf( "Program aborted...\n" );

        exit(1);

    }

    if( !gmouse.Mreset() ) exit(1);

    cleardevice();

    SPtr HScroll = new ScrollBar( 0, getmaxy()-40,

                                    getmaxx()-80, GREEN,

                                    LIGHTGREEN, HORIZ_DIR );

    SPtr VScroll = new ScrollBar( getmaxx()-40, 0,

                                    getmaxy()-40, GREEN,

                                    LIGHTGREEN, VERT_DIR );
```

```
ExitButton.SetButtonType( ROUNDED );

ExitButton.Create( HScroll->GetPosition()-20,

                   VScroll->GetPosition(),

                   80, 20, LIGHTRED, "Exit" );

do

{

   Position = gmouse.Mpressed( ButtonL );

   if( Position.button_count )

   {

      Exit = ExitButton.ButtonHit( Position.xaxis,

                                   Position.yaxis );

      if( !Exit )  do

      {

         MoveButton = FALSE;

         switch( HScroll->ScrollHit() )

         {

            case LEFT:

            case HBAR:

            case RIGHT: MoveButton = TRUE;

         }

         switch( VScroll->ScrollHit() )

         {

            case UP:

            case VBAR:
```

```
          case DOWN: MoveButton = TRUE;

      }

      if( MoveButton )

         ExitButton.Move(

                    HScroll->GetPosition()-20,

                    VScroll->GetPosition() );

      Position = gmouse.Mreleased( ButtonL );

    }

    while( !Position.button_count );

}  }

while( !Exit );

VScroll->ScrollBar::~ScrollBar();

delay( 500 );

HScroll->ScrollBar::~ScrollBar();

delay( 500 );

closegraph();

tmouse.Mreset();
}


        //=====================================//
        // program ScrollBar_Test — SCRLTST4.CPP //
        //    dynamic text scrollbar instances   //
        //=====================================//

#include <conio.h>

#include <stdio.h>
```

```
#include <stdlib.h>

#include <stdarg.h>

#include <string.h>

#include "mouse.i"

#include "tboxes.i"

#include "tscrlbar.i"

typedef TScrollBar* TPtr;

main()
{
    Mstatus       Position;
    int            Exit = FALSE, ThumbMove;
    Box           ExitButton;

    if( !tmouse.Mreset() ) exit(1);
    clrscr();
    TPtr   HScroll = new TScrollBar( 1, 25, 70,

                                     DARKGRAY, GREEN,

                                     HORIZONTAL );
    TPtr   VScroll = new TScrollBar( 80, 1, 23,

                                     DARKGRAY, LIGHTRED,

                                     VERTICAL );
    ExitButton.Create( HScroll->GetPosition(),

                       VScroll->GetPosition(),
```

```
                    10, LIGHTRED, BLACK, "Exit" );
do

{

   Position = tmouse.Mpressed( ButtonL );

   if( Position.button_count )

   {

      Exit = ExitButton.BoxHit( Position.xaxis,

                                 Position.yaxis );

      if( !Exit )  do

      {

         ThumbMove = FALSE;

         switch( HScroll->ScrollHit() )

         {

            case LEFT:

            case HBAR:

            case RIGHT: ThumbMove = TRUE;

         }

         switch( VScroll->ScrollHit() )

         {

            case UP:

            case VBAR:

            case DOWN:  ThumbMove = TRUE;

         }

         if( ThumbMove )
```

```
                    ExitButton.Move( HScroll->GetPosition(),

                                        VScroll->GetPosition() );

                Position = tmouse.Mreleased( ButtonL );

            }

            while( !Position.button_count );

        }   }

    while( !Exit );

    VScroll->TScrollBar::~TScrollBar();    delay( 500 );

    HScroll->TScrollBar::~TScrollBar();    delay( 500 );

    tmouse.Mreset();

}
```

CHAPTER 10

DYNAMIC OBJECTS AND LINKED LISTS

While a simple example of dynamic object instances appeared in Chapter 9 using the ScrollBar object type, there was nothing in this example which could not be accomplished as well using static instances. In this chapter, dynamic objects will be used in circumstances where static objects are impractical or inappropriate and, in order to show the uses of dynamic objects, two demo programs will be created: PHONE1.CPP and PHONE2.CPP.

Both of the demo programs read a data file titled PHONE.LST, sort and store the contents as pointer-linked dynamic objects, and display the listings as shown in Figure 10-1. The PHONE.LST data file can be created using the MAKELIST program at the end of this chapter. Both the MAKELIST source code and a prepared PHONE.LST data file are provided on the program disk accompanying this book. Turbo C's coreleft() function is used to show the available memory before the list is created, after the list is allocated, and again after the dynamic objects are disposed.

The index item appearing in Figure 10-1 is not a part of the data file, but is provided to show the order in which the records were read from the file.

In PHONE1.CPP, sorting is accomplished by a conventional simple or bubble sort algorithm after the data file is read. In PHONE2.CPP, an entry sort algorithm is used to sort the data as it is being read from the file—a process which is somewhat more efficient than the bubble sort.

Figure 10-1: Text Display Generated By PHONE1 or PHONE2 Demos

Addison Wesley Publishing Co.	6	(617) 944-3700
Borland International	5	(408) 438 5300
Compuserve	7	(800) 848-8990
Computer Language	1	(415) 397-1881
Dr. Dobb's Journal	13	(415) 366-3600
... portions omitted ...		
PC Techniques	4	(602) 483-0192
Peter Norton Computing	15	(213) 453-2361
TurboGeometry	16	(800) 636-7760

```
Free memory before list allocated: (Mem1) 60944
               ... after list created: (Mem2) 59152    1792
          ...after list deallocated: (Mem3) 60944
```

A Brief Explanation of Pointers

Before going into how a linked list of objects is created, a brief explanation of pointers and pointer operations is in order. When dynamic objects or dynamic variables are created, memory is dynamically allocated according to the size of the object or variable. At the same time, the allocation process returns the address of the memory that has been set aside for the object or variable (and also prevents the allocated memory from being used for any other purpose).

The returned address value is stored in a special type of variable known as a *pointer variable* or simply as a *pointer*. These pointer variables provide the handles to access and manipulate dynamic objects or dynamic variables. Without a pointer to an object, the object exists only in never-never land; it's somewhere in the system's memory but it's also beyond recovery.

A pointer does not always have to point to a memory address. If a pointer has not yet been assigned to a dynamic object or variable, the pointer is called a *null pointer*, indicating that its value is undefined. Also, the NULL value can be explicitly assigned to a pointer, indicating that the pointer address is undefined or a pointer can be tested for a NULL value to determine if an address is undefined.

Using Pointers with Linked and Sorted Lists

Pointers and dynamic objects are a natural combination for much more than simply finding or accessing the object and one of the primary applications of pointer variables is their use in sorting lists.

When a list of static objects (or variables or records) is sorted, the task is accomplished as a series of swap operations and, for each swap, two complete objects must be moved. This usually requires copying the first object to a temporary object variable, copying the second object variable to the first and finally, copying the temporary object to the second for a total of three moves. Depending on the size of the object (or record), this can require quite a few CPU cycles to accomplish.

With dynamic objects or dynamic variables, however, the same swap operations are simpler to accomplish because the objects or variable records are not moved at all. Instead, only the pointers to the objects' memory addresses are swapped and the CPU time required becomes constant, irrespective of the size of the individual list entries sorted.

At the same time, objects or records can contain pointers. In this fashion, a linked list of objects can be created—as shown in Figure 10-2—in which each object in the list contains a pair of pointers to the objects preceding and following. Note also that the first and last objects in the list each have a NULL or undefined pointer.

Static pointers could also be used here; for example, to maintain pointers to the first and last entries in the list. For long lists, this may be advantageous. However, for present purposes, it's convenient to look for entries with NULL Prior or Next links to find the first and final links.

But one static pointer, NPtr (not shown), used in the sort routine is provided as a movable pointer to trace through the list.

For more information on pointers and pointer applications, refer to Chapter 7 of *Programming The IBM User Interface*, available from Addison-Wesley Publishing Company.

Sorting Lists

The data file used in both the PHONE1 and PHONE2 demonstrations has been deliberately disordered to show how the application can sort the list (in the first demo, through a Sort method and, in the second, at the same time the data is read from the disk file).

Figure 10-2: A Linked-List Structure

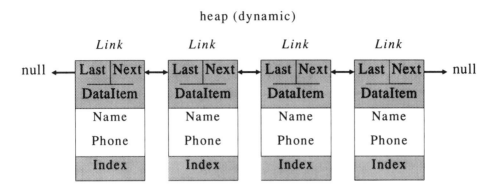

heap (dynamic)

In the PHONE1 demo, both the disk read and sort operation are accomplished in a relatively conventional manner, but in the PHONE2 demo both of these operations become object methods; thus the object is able not only to open and read its own data file, but to sort itself at the same time.

In the first case, the sort routine used is a simple or *bubble sort* —a sorting algorithm which works but which is also recognized as the least efficient sorting method.

The second sort routine is called an *entry sort*. While this is not the fastest sort algorithm in existence, it is certainly faster than the bubble sort and offers adequate performance while using simple coding. For applications that require sorting large quantities of data, you may prefer to use an *indexed entry sort* or to rewrite the object method to use a *quick sort* algorithm or the *binary tree sort* demonstrated in Chapter 11.

Sorting algorithms, implementations and a comparison of performance speeds using different algorithms (both theoretical and practical), will not be covered here in any detail.

The Entry Sort Algorithm

Rather than leave you entirely in the dark, however, I will describe how the entry sort algorithm used in PHONE2 works.

Since this is an Entry Sort, each item is sorted as it is read from the disk file source. Each item read from the data file is written to a newly created dynamic object, N, which has both its Prior and Next pointers set as NULL.

```
void List::Add( DataItem *NewItem, int ItemIndex )
{
   Node* N;

   N = new Node;
```

The node pointer, N, is strictly a local pointer and has no scope beyond the List::Add procedure. Therefore, each time the Add method is called, N requires the new operator to allocate memory for the object instance.

After this, the data passed in the NewItem argument is copied to N's data elements and null characters are appended to the string fields to comply with C's requirements for ASCIIZ strings. (If you wonder why this is necessary, simply comment out the first of these null assignments and run the program.)

```
strcpy( N->Name,  NewItem->ItemName );
N->Name[sizeof(N->Name)-1] = 0;
strcpy( N->Phone, NewItem->ItemPhone );
N->Phone[sizeof(N->Phone)-1] = 0;
N->Index = ItemIndex;
N->Prior = NULL;
```

The Index field is provided to show the order in which records have been read.

Last, N->Prior is assigned a NULL value as default to ensure that it does not point to anything at all. The N->Next pointer will be taken care of in a moment.

Naturally, the first item read is always a special case and is used to initialize the sorting algorithm:

```
if( NPtr == NULL ) N->Next = NPtr;
```

If NPtr itself equals NULL (an assignment made when List is initialized), this must be a new list with nothing in it. Therefore, N->Next is pointed to NPtr and NPtr will be set to N.

In any other case—if NPtr is not NULL—the NPtr pointer has already been moved to the end of the list by stepping down until NPtr->Next equals NULL. The next step is to find where the new entry belongs in the list, which is accomplished by stepping back up the list until either the Precede function returns a non-zero result or the top is found (NPtr->Prior is not NULL).

```
else
{
    while( ( Precede( N->Name, NPtr->Name ) ) &&
            ( NPtr->Prior != NULL ) )
        NPtr = NPtr->Prior;
```

The Precede function returns non-zero (TRUE) if the first string argument precedes the second alphabetically and returns zero (FALSE) for all other conditions.

If NPtr is at the top of the list, then the new entry is linked up as the new first entry.

```
if( NPtr->Prior == NULL )
{
    N->Next  = NPtr;
    N->Next->Prior = N;
}
else
```

Again, after all position tests are completed and N is linked, NPtr —whose scope extends beyond the List::Add procedure—will receive N's address.

If N belongs somewhere within the list, then not only do both N's Prior and Next pointers need to be assigned, but NPtr's currently indicated Next's Prior and NPtr's Next must be assigned back to N.

```
    {
        N->Prior = NPtr;
        N->Next  = NPtr->Next;
        NPtr->Next->Prior = N;
        NPtr->Next = N;
    }   }
```

These last two steps cannot be executed in reversed order because the current value of NPtr is needed to find NPtr->Next in order to assign its Prior before reassigning NPtr->Next to N.

```
    NPtr = N;
}
```

Finally, NPtr is assigned to N before N is lost when the Add method finishes.

While the operations are a bit complex to explain, execution of the operation is quite simple and relatively fast, with the slowest part of the whole process writing the final list to the screen. See Table 10-1 for operation times.

Table 10-1: Disk Read, Sort and Display Times (PHONE2.CPP)

OPERATION	TIME
File access time (16 items):	0.02060 seconds
Sort operations (16 items):	0.00955 seconds
Screen write (21 lines):	0.03680 seconds
Total:	0.06695 seconds

Operation times derived by averaging elapsed time for loop = 1..1000.

The Precede Utility

The Precede utility deserves a brief explanation and a recommendation. Too often, sort comparisons on lists containing alphabetical characters are made by the simple expedient of comparing the two entries directly. This results in *du Bois* following *Engles* and *MORSE* preceding *Miller*. For mixed alphanumerical entries such as *345-F-2469* and *345-a-2380*, ordering is not correct when the sort algorithm depends on the entry being made consistently using only upper- or lowercase characters.

Some programs attempt to avoid this problem by having all entries converted to uppercase as: *DU BOIS*, *ENGLES*, *MORSE,* and *MILLER*. This is fine for a stock number, but inconvenient for a name and address file. The ideal for all sort routines is to make the ordering comparisons independent of the UPPERCASE/lowercase format of the entries (unless the entries are actually intended to be case sensitive). For this reason, the Precede function uses C's stricmp function which executes comparisons ignoring case.

```
int Precede( char* Str1, char* Str2 )
{
   if( stricmp( Str1, Str2 ) < 0 ) return( 1 );
   return( 0 );
}
```

The stricmp function itself returns either -1, 0, or 1 depending on whether Str1 precedes Str2, is equal to Str2, or follows Str2. The Precede function, however, returns a true value for only one condition.

Having displayed the details of some of the mechanisms, I'll return to the demo programs themselves.

The PHONE1 Demo Program

The PHONE1 demo begins by defining two record types: DataItem, which conforms to the PHONE.LST data record file and a second record type, Node, which contains a pointer to the object, Data, as well as Next and Prior pointers to allow nodes to be linked together:

```
struct   DataItem   {  char ItemName[40];
                       char ItemPhone[14];  };

struct   Node       {  Data*   Item;
                       Node*   Prior;
                       Node*   Next;   };
```

The Data object class is defined with one integer field to index the items and two character fields to match the file data. Notice that the Name and Phone fields are each one byte larger than the corresponding fields in DataItem—a provision allowing room to append terminating null characters to each string.

```
class Data
{
   protected:
      int   Index;
      char Name[41];
      char Phone[15];
   public:
      Data( int       ThisIndex,
```

```
                    DataItem  *ThisItem );
        ~Data();
        void Print();
        char* GetName();
};
```

Four methods are also defined for the Data object, beginning with a constructor, Data::Data which is called with two arguments; a destructor, ~Data; the Print method; and the method GetName, which returns a string value. Implementation for these methods will be provided later.

A second object class is defined as List and contains only one record element, NPtr, which is a pointer to a Node record.

```
class List
{
    Node*  NPtr;
public:
    List();
    ~List();
    void Add( Data *NewItem );
    void Sort();
    void Report();
};
```

List also begins with constructor and destructor methods before declaring the Add, Sort, and Report methods. These will be implemented in a moment.

The Data Object Methods

Data's constructor method Data::Data is called with two parameters: ThisItem, which contains the information read from the disk file and ThisIndex, which is simply an integer value indicating the order in which each record was read and is used to show the sorting action:

```
Data::Data( int       ThisIndex,
            DataItem *ThisItem )
{
    Index = ThisIndex;
    strcpy( Name,  ThisItem->ItemName );
```

```
Name[ sizeof(Name)-1 ] = 0;          // add null character //
strcpy( Phone, ThisItem->ItemPhone );
Phone[ sizeof(Phone)-1 ] = 0;        // add null character //
}
```

After the string information is copied, both the Name and Phone object fields have null terminators added to comply with C's ASCIIZ string standards. In the data records no provisions are made to indicate the size of each file, nor to identify the end of a field; instead, the calling process is expected to know the extent (size) of each and to separate the data accordingly.

The destructor method, ~Data, is also implemented, without any explicit tasks to perform:

```
Data::~Data()   {      }
```

The Print method lists the contents of the Data record name, index, and phone number fields:

```
void Data::Print()
{
   printf( "%s  %3d  %s\n", Name, Index, Phone );
}
```

One last method, GetName, is provided to return the Name field from an object instance.

```
char* Data::GetName()
{
    return( Name );
}
```

At this time, the Data and List objects are pretty simple, containing only the methods needed to demonstrate basic handling because the bulk of this demonstration is not accomplished by object methods, but by conventional programming procedures.

The List Object Methods

The List constructor method (List::List) has only one task: to initialize the NPtr pointer to NULL because the list is currently empty.

```
List::List ()
{
    NPtr    = NULL;
}
```

The List::Add method is called with the address of another object instance of class Data, which contains the last set of data read from the record file.

```
void List::Add( Data *NewItem )
{
    Node* N;

    N = new Node;
```

The Add method declares a local Node pointer, N, and begins by calling new to allocate memory for the node. Next, N's data fields are pointed to the address of the Data object, the current address of NPtr and, for the Next field, to NULL.

```
    N->Item  = NewItem;
    N->Prior = NPtr;
    N->Next  = NULL;
```

In the following step, since the NPtr = N assignment hasn't been made yet, the preceding assignment could be made directly as: NPtr->Next = N rather than indirectly through N->Prior->Next = N, but the results are the same in either case.

```
    N->Prior->Next = N;
    NPtr = N;
}
```

Lastly, NPtr takes the address of N before N disappears as the Add method's scope terminates. This is another example of an implicit destructor call initiated by scope.

Once the data is read from the file, the data exists in memory and organized by a series of pointer objects, but it is not in any type of order. Therefore, the List::Sort method is provided to reorder the data. This task begins—using a simple or bubble sort—with three local pointers:

```
void List::Sort()
{
    Node*   T1;
    Node*   T2;
    Node*   T3;
```

Before sorting the list, NPtr is moved back to the start of the list.

```
    while( NPtr->Prior != NULL )
        NPtr = NPtr->Prior;
```

Now, starting at the top of the list, a double loop is executed to compare the name fields of the Data objects indicated by the Item pointer.

```
    for( T1=NPtr; T1->Next->Next!=NULL; T1=T1->Next )
        for( T2=T1->Next; T2->Next!=NULL; T2=T2->Next )
            if( Precede( T1->Item->GetName(),
                         T2->Item->GetName() ) )
```

Reordering is accomplished by swapping pointer addresses—a process which requires a minimum of CPU time.

```
            {
                T3->Item = T1->Item;
                T1->Item = T2->Item;
                T2->Item = T3->Item;
}           }
```

Even though address swapping is simpler and faster than swapping the data itself, this sort algorithm is still slow because of the number of swaps involved, and grows rapidly as the number of items sorted increases. Better sorting alternatives will be shown later.

The List::Report method—like the Add method—begins with a local Node pointer, N, which is initialized with NPtr's address and then moved to the top of the list.

```
void List::Report()
{
   Node* N = NPtr;

   while( N->Prior != NULL )
      N = N->Prior;
```

A simpler Report method could be created by using NPtr instead of the local pointer, N, but this form provides better general compatibility by using a separate pointer with local scope rather than using the global pointer.

After *N* is moved back to the top of the list, a loop executes—until N->Next points to NULL, indicating that the end of the list has been reached—calling the Data object's Print method for each instance.

```
   while( N->Next != NULL )
   {
      N->Item->Print();
      N = N->Next;
}   }
```

The destructor method, List::~List, has a relatively complex task and begins, again, by retracing NPtr to find the top of the list.

```
List::~List()
{
   while( NPtr->Prior != NULL )
      NPtr = NPtr->Prior;
```

After finding the proper start point (at the top), the destructor traces through the list, first deleting all of the Data object instances indicated by N->Item, then moving NPtr down the list to the next link and finally, deleting N.

```
   while( NPtr != NULL )
   {
      Node *N = NPtr;
```

A local pointer is used and is essential. Rather than being created global to the method, is declared and initialized within the loop because it will also be deleted each time the loop cycles.

Before N is deleted, however, it is used to pass an address to the Data object indicated by N->Item so that each of these object instances are disposed of correctly.

```
        delete( N->Item );
        NPtr = N->Next;
        delete N;
}   }
```

After doing so, NPtr takes the address of N->Next before N is deleted. The List object is deleted automatically when the destructor method is completed.

The ReadList() Procedure

In PHONE1.CPP, the ReadList procedure does more than simply open and read a data file including a couple of important tasks that will require a bit of explanation.

First, ReadList declares AList as an instance of the object List. When AList is declared, the List constructor (List::List) is invoked implicitly to initialize the object.

```
void ReadList()
{
    List      AList;
    FILE      *ReadFile;
    DataItem  NewItem;
    int       j = 0;
```

The remainder of the declarations are perfectly standard but you should recognize (and remember) that all of these are limited in scope to the ReadList procedure. Once ReadList is finished, each of these are terminated by scope, a factor whose importance will be explained in a momentarily.

The file NameFile is opened for read only. If it does not exist (if a NULL file handle is returned), an error message is written to the screen and the program terminates.

```
    if( ( ReadFile = fopen( NameFile, "r" ) ) == NULL )
    {
        cerr << "Cannot open " << NameFile
```

```
              << " as input file\n";
       getch();
       exit(-1);
   }
```

Otherwise, a loop executes until the end of the file is reached.

```
   while( !feof( ReadFile ) )
   {
       j++;
       fread( &NewItem, sizeof( NewItem ), 1, ReadFile );
       AList.Add( new Data( j, &NewItem ) );
   }
```

After each file record is accessed, AList.Add is called with the address of a new instance of the object Data which has been initialized with the information read from the file.

```
   fclose( ReadFile );
   Mem2 = coreleft();
```

After the file is completed and closed, Mem2 stores the current free memory value for later use. Mem1, Mem2 and Mem3 are global variables, declared as unsigned long and are used to track free memory at different points in the program.

Since the data read from the file is not in order (the file was deliberately disordered when it was created), the AList.Sort method is called to order the data.

```
   AList.Sort();
```

Next, the *AList.Report* method is called to list the sorted data on the screen.

```
   AList.Report();
}
```

But there is another event taking place here—even though it is both hidden and important.

The Destructor Method Is Called

Before the ReadFile procedure (preceding) terminates (or when it terminates—because AList's scope is limited to the ReadFile procedure) the List::~List destructor method is called implicitly to deallocate the AList object instance.

When the ReadFile procedure ends the List destructor method is called and all instances of the Data object linked by the List object are deallocated (by the *~List* method). Finally, *AList* is deallocated.

The remainder of the program, including the procedure main(), should be relatively self-explanatory. Provisions have been included to show the memory used by the objects in creating and organizing the list but none of these are specifically object-oriented and simply follow conventional C programming practices.

The PHONE2 Demo Program

The PHONE2 demo accomplishes the same task as PHONE1, but does so in a much more elegant manner by creating the object class, LinkObj, which takes over the task of both reading the data file and sorting the entries as they are read from the file. Before introducing LinkObj, however, there are a couple of other changes from Phone1.

In this application, the linking pointers used to create the data list are not contained in the DataObj objects. Instead, the object List has an element, Node, which contains both the data and the pointers linking the list together.

The record type, appearing in Phone1 DataItem, is still the same but the associated object type, DataObj, has been lost. Instead, the List::ReadFile method has a local element, NewItem, of type DataItem which is static and limited in scope to the ReadFile method.

The Node Definition

The Node definition from PHONE1 is revised here, losing the Data pointer and adding the actual data elements which will be read and stored. Several other forms could be used, including separate data record object., This is simply one variation convenient for the current task:

```
struct  Node
{
   Node* Prior;
```

```
    Node* Next;
    int   Index;
    char  Name[41];
    char  Phone[15];
}
```

This time, Prior and Next are not DataPtr pointers, but are Node pointers—pointers to other Node records that will create a chain of Node links instead of Data links.

The Link Class

The Link class definition consists of a private element, Node, constructor and destructor methods, and four additional handling methods: Add, ReadFile, Report, and Print.

```
class List
{
    private:
        Node *NPtr;
    public:
        List();
        ~List();
        void Add( DataItem *NewItem,
                  int ItemIndex  );
        void ReadFile();
        void Report();
        void Print( Node* N );
};
```

The List object consists of the single Node's data record and a series of methods that replace virtually all of the conventional programming used in PHONE1 demo program.

The List Methods

The List methods begin with the constructor method, List::List, which establishes the link object instance and initializes NPtr to NULL.

```
List::List()
{
   NPtr = NULL;
}
```

List's destructor method, List::~List(), is similar to the destructor method in PHONE1, but no longer needs the instruction: delete(N->Item).

```
List::~List()
{
   while( NPtr->Prior != NULL )
      NPtr = NPtr->Prior;
   while( NPtr != NULL )
   {
      Node *N = NPtr;
      NPtr = N->Next;
      delete N;
   } }
```

List's ReadFile method replaces the ReadFile procedure used in PHONE1. When called, the ReadFile method opens the specified filename, reading the contents and calling the Add method with each entry:

```
void List::ReadFile()
{
   FILE     *ReadFile;
   DataItem NewItem;
   int      j = 0;

   if( ( ReadFile = fopen( NameFile, "r" ) ) == NULL )
   {
      cerr << "Cannot open " << NameFile
           << " as input file\n";
      getch();
      exit(-1);
   }
```

```
   while( !feof( ReadFile ) )
   {
      j++;
      fread( &NewItem, sizeof( NewItem ), 1, ReadFile );
      if( !feof( ReadFile ) ) Add( &NewItem, j );
   }
   fclose( ReadFile );
}
```

The handling is very similar to the ReadList procedure in PHONE1. The primary difference is that this ReadFile is a method belonging to the List object instead of a procedure belonging to the application.

One enhancement could be made here. Passing the readfile name as an argument instead of accessing a global variable would make this object more versatile and could be used—as will be shown later—to read several files.

LinkObj's Add method accepts a pointer to each data item read from the file as a calling parameter, then uses the new operator to dynamically allocate a new Node N and then copies the information from NewItem to N.

```
void List::Add( DataItem *NewItem, int ItemIndex )
{
   Node* N;

   N = new Node;
   strcpy( N->Name,  NewItem->ItemName );
   N->Name[ sizeof(N->Name)-1 ] = 0;
   strcpy( N->Phone, NewItem->ItemPhone );
   N->Phone[ sizeof(N->Phone)-1 ] = 0;
   N->Index = ItemIndex;
   N->Prior = NULL;
```

After the data has been copied to the memory locations provided by N, N's pointers still need to be linked. The first task, however, is to decide where the current item belongs.

```
   while( NPtr->Next != NULL )
      NPtr = NPtr->Next;
```

Since many disk files will already be sorted and will be read top down, the Entry-Sort algorithm moves to the end of the list before asking if the list is empty, that is if NPtr is NULL. If this is an empty list then the current entry goes at the end of the list.

```
if( NPtr == NULL ) N->Next = NPtr;
else
```

Otherwise, the sort is starting at the end and the preceding entry is checked to see if the new entry precedes the NPtr entry. If so and if a preceding entry also exists then NPtr moves up the list until the proper location is found.

```
{
    while( ( Precede( N->Name, NPtr->Name ) ) &&
           ( NPtr->Prior != NULL ) )
        NPtr = NPtr->Prior;
```

If the top of the list is reached, the new entry is inserted at the top:

```
    if( NPtr->Prior == NULL )
    {
        N->Next  = NPtr;
        N->Next->Prior = N;
    }
```

Otherwise, the new entry is linked into the list at the location found:

```
    else
    {
        N->Prior = NPtr;
        N->Next  = NPtr->Next;
        NPtr->Next->Prior = N;
        NPtr->Next = N;
    }  }
```

Since N has only local scope and will be lost when the current procedure is finished, NPtr takes the address of N.

```
    NPtr = N;
}
```

When N's scope terminates only the address contained in N is lost. The memory at that address is not released and the information stored at that address is not lost. Instead, the address information has been passed to NPtr, which is not lost.

The Report method in this version is almost the same as in PHONE1 except that N->Item->Print() has now become simply Print(N).

```
void List::Report()
{
   Node *N = NPtr;

   while( N->Prior != NULL )
      N = N->Prior;
   while( N->Next != NULL )
   {
      Print( N );
      N = N->Next;
   }   }
```

List's Print method now accepts a Node pointer as an argument which wasn't required by Data's Print method.

```
void List::Print( Node* N )
{
   printf( "%3d   %s   %s\n",
           N->Index, N->Name, N->Phone );
}
```

Summary

In this chapter, we have shown how objects can be linked and sorted using pointers and; how a single object can manipulate a linked list and exercise methods controlling a series of other objects.

In Chapter 12 a different type of sorted listing, also using pointers but employing a binary tree organization, will be demonstrated. Also in Chapter 12, we will look at search methods for binary trees.

The MakeList program at the end of the listings will create a data file for use with both PHONE1 and PHONE2.

```
//====================================//
//                PHONE1.CPP          //
//   Demonstrates dynamic objects     //
//====================================//
```

```cpp
#include <alloc.h>          // for coreleft()           //

#include <conio.h>          // for getch()              //

#include <iostream.h>       // for cerr                 //

#include <stdio.h>          // for printf, file i/o, etc //

#include <stdlib.h>         // for itoa()               //

#include <string.h>         // for strcpy()             //


#define   NameFile   "PHONE.LST"


struct   DataItem  {   char ItemName[40];

                       char ItemPhone[14];  };


unsigned long  Mem0, Mem1, Mem2, Mem3;


class Data

{

   protected:
      int   Index;
      char Name[41];           // ItemName + null terminator  //
      char Phone[15];          // ItemPhone + null terminator //
   public:
      Data( int        ThisIndex,

            DataItem   *ThisItem );
```

```cpp
      ~Data();

      void Print();

      char* GetName();

};

struct Node

{

   Data   *Item;

   Node   *Prior;                  // point to last Node object //

   Node   *Next;                   // point to next Node object //

};

class List          // the list of objects pointed to by nodes //

{

   Node *NPtr;                     // points to a node //

public:

   List();                         // constructor         //

   ~List();                        // destructor          //

   void Add( Data *NewItem );      // add item to list //

   void Sort();                            // sort list  //

   void Report();                          // list items //

};
```

```
                //=========================================//
                //  definitions for standalone functions  //
                //=========================================//

int Precede( char* Str1, char* Str2 )

{

   if( stricmp( Str1, Str2 ) > 0 ) return( 1 );

   return( 0 );

}


unsigned long Status( char *Msg )

{

   char  MemStr[12];

   ltoa( coreleft(), MemStr, 10 );

   printf( "%s  %s\n\n", Msg, MemStr );

   return( coreleft() );

}


void Status( char *Msg, unsigned long Mem,

                        unsigned long Used )

{

   char  MemStr[12];

   ltoa( Mem, MemStr, 10 );

   printf( "%s  %s   ", Msg, MemStr );

   ltoa( Used, MemStr, 10 );

   if( Used ) printf( "%s", MemStr );
```

```
     printf( "\n" );

}

            // member functions for List class //

List::List ()

{

   NPtr    = NULL;         // sets node pointer to "empty" //

}                          // because nothing in list yet  //

List::~List()                              // destructor //

{

   while( NPtr->Prior != NULL )     // move ptr to first //

      NPtr = NPtr->Prior;

   while( NPtr != NULL )         // repeat to end of list   //

   {

      Node *N = NPtr;           // get node pointed to      //

      delete( N->Item );        // delete item's memory     //

      NPtr = N->Next;           // point to next node       //

      delete N;                 // delete pointer's memory  //

}  }

void List::Add( Data *NewItem )

{

   Node* N;                  // N is pointer to a node     //

   N = new Node;             // create a new node          //
```

```
   N->Item  = NewItem;           // store pointer in node      //

   N->Prior = NPtr;              // point new last to current //

   N->Next  = NULL;              // point new next to null     //

   N->Prior->Next = N;           // point current next to new //

   NPtr = N;                     // set new node current node //

}

void List::Sort()

{

   Node*   T1;

   Node*   T2;

   Node*   T3;

   while( NPtr->Prior != NULL )

      NPtr = NPtr->Prior;                     // move NPtr to top //

   for( T1=NPtr; T1->Next->Next!=NULL; T1=T1->Next )

      for( T2=T1->Next; T2->Next!=NULL; T2=T2->Next )

         if( Precede( T1->Item->GetName(),

                      T2->Item->GetName() ) )

            {

               T3->Item = T1->Item;

               T1->Item = T2->Item;

               T2->Item = T3->Item;

   }            }

void List::Report()
```

```
{
   Node *N = NPtr;

   while( N->Prior != NULL )

      N = N->Prior;                    // move to top of list //

   while (N->Next != NULL)

   {
      N->Item->Print();               // print current data //

      N = N->Next;                    // point to next node //
}    }

                 // Data implementation //
Data::Data( int      ThisIndex,
            DataItem *ThisItem )

{
   Index = ThisIndex;
   strcpy( Name,  ThisItem->ItemName );
   Name[sizeof(Name)-1] = 0;         // add null terminator //
   strcpy( Phone, ThisItem->ItemPhone );
   Phone[sizeof(Phone)-1] = 0;       // add null terminator //
}

Data::~Data()  {  }

void Data::Print()

{
```

```
    printf( "%s  %3d  %s\n", Name, Index, Phone );
}

char* Data::GetName()
{
    return( Name );
}

              //=================================//

void ReadList()
{
    List      AList;          // declare list, call constructor //
    FILE      *ReadFile;              // file of data items //
    DataItem NewItem;
    int       j = 0;

    if( ( ReadFile = fopen( NameFile, "r" ) ) == NULL )
    {
        cerr << "Cannot open " << NameFile
            << " as input file\n";
        getch();
        exit(-1);
    }
    while( !feof( ReadFile ) )
    {
        j++;
```

```
        fread( &NewItem, sizeof( NewItem ), 1, ReadFile );

        AList.Add( new Data( j, &NewItem ) );

    }

    fclose( ReadFile );

    Mem2 = coreleft();

    AList.Sort();

    AList.Report();

    return;

}

main()

{

    clrscr();

    Mem1 = Status( "    Free memory at start: " );

    ReadList();

    Mem3 = coreleft();

    printf( "\n" );

    Status( "Free memory before list is allocated: ",
            Mem1, 0 );

    Status( "             ... after list created:     ",
            Mem2, Mem1-Mem2 );

    Status( "             ... after list deallocated: ",
            Mem3, Mem1-Mem3 );

    getch();

}
```

```
//=====================================//
//              PHONE2.CPP             //
//  Demonstrates self-sorting object   //
//=====================================//
#include <alloc.h>              // for coreleft()          //

#include <conio.h>              // for getch()             //

#include <iostream.h>           // for cerr                //

#include <stdio.h>              // for printf, file i/o, etc //

#include <stdlib.h>             // for itoa()              //

#include <string.h>             // for strcpy()            //


#include <dos.h>


#define   NameFile   "PHONE.LST"


struct    DataItem
          {  char ItemName[40];

             char ItemPhone[14];  };


struct    Node
          {   Node   *Prior;            // point to last Node //

              Node   *Next;             // point to next Node //

              int    Index;

              char   Name[41];              // ItemName + null  //

              char   Phone[15];     };      // ItemPhone + null //

class List                            // list of data objects //

{
```

```
   private:

      Node *NPtr;                          // pointer to node  //

   public:

      List();                              // constructor      //

      ~List();                             // destructor       //

      void Add( DataItem *NewItem,
                int ItemIndex  );          // add item to list //

      void ReadFile();                     // read data file   //

      void Report();                       // list items       //

      void Print( Node* N );               // print item       //

};


           //=======================================//
           //  definitions for standalone functions  //
           //=======================================//

int Precede( char* Str1, char* Str2 )

{

   if( stricmp( Str1, Str2 ) < 0 ) return( 1 );

   return( 0 );

}


void Status( char *Msg )

{

   char  MemStr[12];


   ltoa( coreleft(), MemStr, 10 );
```

```
   printf( "%s  %s\n", Msg, MemStr );

}

void Status( char *Msg, unsigned long Mem,

                          unsigned long Used )

{

   char  MemStr[12];

   ltoa( Mem, MemStr, 10 );

   printf( "%s  %s   ", Msg, MemStr );

   ltoa( Used, MemStr, 10 );

   if( Used ) printf( "%s", MemStr );

   printf( "\n" );

}


            // member functions for List class //

List::List ()

{

   NPtr    = NULL;            // sets node pointer to "empty" //
}                             // because nothing in list yet  //


List::~List()                             // destructor //

{

   while( NPtr->Prior != NULL )     // move ptr to first   //

      NPtr = NPtr->Prior;

   while( NPtr != NULL )                // repeat until end    //
```

```
   {

      Node *N = NPtr;                  // get node pointed to //

      NPtr = N->Next;                  // point to next node  //

      delete N;                        // delete pointer      //

}  }

void List::Add( DataItem *NewItem, int ItemIndex )

{

   Node* N;                                    // node pointer //

   N = new Node;                           // create new node //
   strcpy( N->Name,  NewItem->ItemName );
   N->Name[sizeof(N->Name)-1] = 0;
   strcpy( N->Phone, NewItem->ItemPhone );
   N->Phone[sizeof(N->Phone)-1] = 0;
   N->Index = ItemIndex;
   N->Prior = NULL;
   while( NPtr->Next != NULL )      // start at end of list //
      NPtr = NPtr->Next;
   if( NPtr == NULL ) N->Next = NPtr;
   else                             // first entry ... else //
   {                                // find proper location //
      while( ( Precede( N->Name, NPtr->Name ) ) &&
             ( NPtr->Prior != NULL ) )
         NPtr = NPtr->Prior;
```

```
    if( NPtr->Prior == NULL )              // insert at top //

    {

      N->Next   = NPtr;

      N->Next->Prior = N;

    }

    else                                   // insert within list //

    {

      N->Prior = NPtr;

      N->Next   = NPtr->Next;

      NPtr->Next->Prior = N;

      NPtr->Next = N;

  }   }

  NPtr = N;                          // make new node current node //

}


void List::ReadFile()

{

   FILE      *ReadFile;                    // file of data items //

   DataItem NewItem;

   int      j = 0;

   if( ( ReadFile = fopen( NameFile, "r" ) ) == NULL )

   {

      cerr << "Cannot open " << NameFile

          << " as input file\n";
```

```
        getch();

        exit(-1);

    }

    while( !feof( ReadFile ) )

    {

        j++;

        fread( &NewItem, sizeof( NewItem ), 1, ReadFile );

        if( !feof( ReadFile ) ) Add( &NewItem, j );

    }

    fclose( ReadFile );

}

void List::Report()

{

    Node *N = NPtr;

    while( N->Prior != NULL )

        N = N->Prior;                        // move to top of list //

    while (N->Next != NULL)

    {

        Print( N );                // print the current data   //

        N = N->Next;               // point to the next node   //

}   }

void List::Print( Node* N )

{
```

```
    printf( "%3d  %s  %s\n",

            N->Index, N->Name, N->Phone );

}


            //================================//

unsigned long Mem1, Mem2, Mem3;

void ConstructList()

{

    List     AList;          // declare list, call constructor //

    AList.ReadFile();

    Mem2 = coreleft();

    AList.Report();

}                     // AList is implicitly deallocated by  //
                      // scope when ConstructList terminates //

main()

{

    clrscr();

    Mem1 = coreleft();

    ConstructList();

    Mem3 = coreleft();

    printf("\n");

    Status( "Free memory before list is allocated: ",

            Mem1, 0 );
```

```
   Status( "                ... after list created: ",

        Mem2, Mem1-Mem2 );

   Status( "              ... after list deallocated: ",

        Mem3, Mem1-Mem3 );

   getch();

}



        //===========================================//
        //  Create_Demo_Phone_List ==  MakeList.CPP  //
        //===========================================//

#include <conio.h>

#include <stdio.h>

#include <stdlib.h>

#include <string.h>


#define   NameFile  "PHONE.LST"

#define   NullStr   "                            "

struct  DataItem  {  char Name[40];

                     char Phone[14];  };


char* Read_Name()

{

   char* TempStr = "";

   printf( "Enter name: " );

   gets( TempStr );
```

```
   return( TempStr );

}

char* Read_Number()

{

   char*    TempStr = "";

   printf( "Enter phone number: " );

   gets( TempStr );

   return( TempStr );

}

main()

{

   FILE       *WriteFile;                    // file of DataItem //

   DataItem  FileEntry;

   int        Finish;

   clrscr();

   while( !Finish )

   {

      Finish = 0;

      clrscr();

      printf( "Enter names and phone numbers"

              " for demo program file\n" );

      printf( "Enter blank line to exit: \n" );
```

```
        WriteFile = fopen( NameFile, "a" );

        strcpy( FileEntry.Name, Read_Name() );

        strncat( FileEntry.Name, NullStr,
                40-strlen( FileEntry.Name ) );

        Finish = (strcmp(FileEntry.Name,NullStr)==0);

        strcpy( FileEntry.Phone, Read_Number() );

        strncat( FileEntry.Phone, NullStr,
                14-strlen( FileEntry.Phone ) );

        if( !Finish )

            fwrite( &FileEntry, sizeof(FileEntry),
                    1, WriteFile );

    }

    fclose( WriteFile );

    printf( "Done\n" );

}
```

CHAPTER 11

BINARY TREE OBJECTS

In previous examples, data was handled using pointer structures in linearly-linked lists. In the example in this chapter, the linear list is replaced by a binary-tree structure where the organization of the data is faster both to sort and to access than in a linear structure.

For additional information on the theory of tree structures in general, see *Algorithms & Data Structures* by Niklaus Wirth.

Binary-tree structures (aka B-Trees or Tree structures) are generally recognized as the most efficient data structures possible for general applications. In some specialized cases, where the structure and arrangement of the data itself is highly predictable and ordered, other organizational structures may be more efficient but these are exceptions rather than rules.

Also, binary-sorts are more efficient when the source of the data is disordered than if the data source is already ordered or alphabetized though, in either case, the binary sort is usually more efficient than a linear sort routine.

Binary Tree Structures

A binary tree structure is simply a data structure in which each element has two links to other elements and the elements are linked together in specific relationships. As an example, Figure 11-1 shows a binary-tree created from the integer list: 6, 3, 4, 2, 8, 12, 11, 5, 1, 9, 7, 10.

Figure 11-1: A Binary Tree of Integers

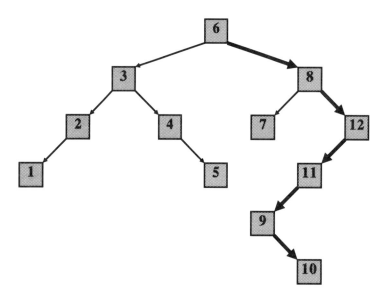

The rule ordering this binary tree is very simple—smaller to the left, greater to the right—and the tree grows according to the order in which the data elements were added to the tree. Starting with 6 which forms the root of the tree, 3 is added to the left (smaller) and then 4 begins by taking the lesser (left) branch from 6 and then the greater (right) branch from 3.

Binary trees are customarily illustrated upside down, beginning with the root at the top. Each subsequent integer entry searches for its own position within the growing structure.

Notice that, when the tree is built, at no time is any established link changed to favor a newer entry. Therefore, 10 begins at the root (bold path), is greater than 6, is greater than 8, is less than 12, is less than 11, and finally finds its place as greater than 9.

If the resulting tree appears confusing, consider how easy it is to locate any element in the tree. To locate the highest entry in the tree, for example, begin at the root, follow the greater (right) path, and, after the third step, the entry 12 is located and identified as the greatest element in the tree. In a linear arrangement, the same result would require four times longer to accomplish.

Any element in the tree can be found in the same fashion.

Binary trees are not limited to numerical or alphabetical data lists. Instead, a binary tree can be created for any type of data for which a relationship or relationships can be described. For a second example, consider the formula (a + b / c) - (d * e + f) and the binary tree representing the values and operations involved (Figure 11-2).

In this structure, all variables (numerical values) are found at the ends of branches and all non-terminal nodes indicate operations. Notice also that the parentheses in the written formula do not appear in the binary tree. Instead, the groupings are implicit in the structure of the tree.

Figure 11-2: A Binary Tree for a Formula

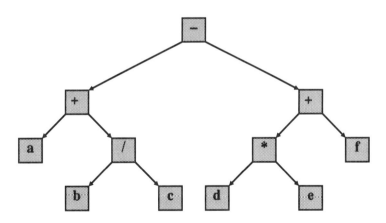

One simple application for a tree of this type might be a program to solve algebraic equations that were entered by the user in the text form similar to the preceding example.

Since the entered formula could take many different forms, any predefined structure would have to be unnecessarily complex to accept all of the possibilities. Using a binary tree structure similar to the one illustrated, any formula can be represented as a series of binary relationships. A program using this structure would begin by finding the extremities of the tree; for example, beginning with the d and e elements, executing the * operation indicated by their mutual root, then replacing the operation with the resulting value and discarding the two terminal nodes.

By operating recursively on each branch until no subnodes remain, the root contains the final result of the formula. (This is essentially how most programming languages handle formula processing in the first place.)

Naturally, if the formula is to be solved repeatedly for different values, instead of discarding nodes, the application would simply examine each node to see if it contained a value or only an operator, searching farther if the node does not contain a solution.

Other, more familiar, examples of binary tree structures would include family genealogies, basketball or tennis tournaments, or race horse pedigrees.

A Binary Tree Application

In Figure 11-3, the same data list used in previous examples is shown in a binary tree using an alphabetical relationship. In this case, the tree is turned sideways (root element at left) and the numbers by each entry show the order in which the elements are read from the data file.

This is essentially the binary tree structure which will be created by the PHONTREE program demonstrated in this chapter.

Before going into the intricacies of programming a binary tree, in Chapter 10 (Table 10-1) disk read, sort and display times were shown for a linearly-linked list. In Table 11-1, a time comparison is made between the linear sort used in Chapter 10 and the binary sort demonstrated here.

Table 11-1: Comparing Disk Read, Sort and Display Times

OPERATION	LINEAR SORT	BINARY TREE
File access time (16 items):	0.02060 seconds	0.02060 seconds
Sort operations (16 items):	0.00955 seconds	0.01071 seconds
Screen write (21 lines):	0.03680 seconds	0.01220 seconds
Total:	0.06695 seconds	0.04351 seconds

Operation times derived by averaging elapsed time for loop = 1..1000.

For the relatively short data list used for this example, the binary sort operations required a bit more time than the linear sort operations. For longer lists—when time becomes a real factor—the time requirements of the binary sort will be considerably shorter than for a linear sort, with the discrepancy increasing as the number of handled entries grows.

Figure 11-3: An Alphabetical Tree

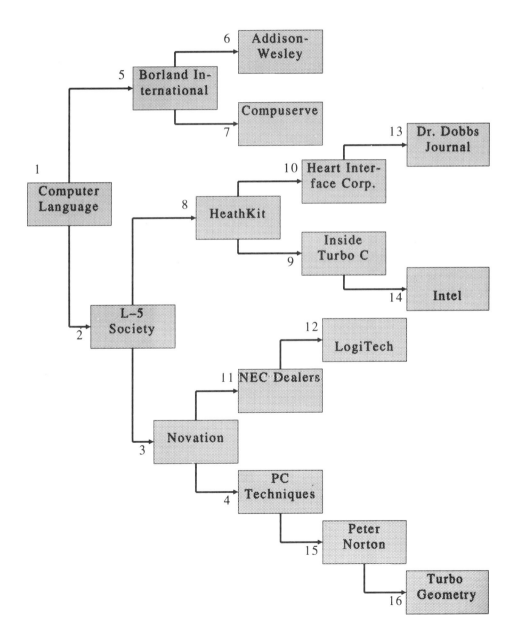

The discrepancy is produced in part by the fact that both sort times include the time required to dispose of the data elements. For the linear sort, the dispose time is relatively short compared to the time required to build the list because, for disposal, the linear list simply begins at the top and works down without regard to the order of the list. In this example it requires approximately $1/20$ of the time for disposal as was required to build the tree.

But the binary tree, to accomplish disposal of the elements, has to execute essentially the same operations as were required to build the tree, retracing each branch in turn and requiring equal time for both tasks.

The difference in execution speeds may be more obvious by looking at the *Screen write* times. Here, even though the linear sort is already ordered and has accomplished the screen write by stepping down an alphabetical list, the binary tree is still faster even while using a recursive process to search the tree for the proper order in which to write the data out to the screen.

In large part, the times are a product of how each version of the program has compiled and, to some degree, reflects the strengths of the Turbo C compiler. But, the bottom line for application programming is not the theoretical speed of a system but the actual real-time/real-world speed with which an application operates.

In the real world, data lists are not necessarily disordered. Therefore, what happens when the data set is already in alphabetical order?

A third set of operation times appear in Table 11-2 using the same data list contents, but with the data entries prearranged in alphabetical order.

Table 11-2: A Binary Sort with Ordered and Disordered Sources

OPERATION	DISORDERED SOURCE	ORDERED SOURCE
File access time (16 items):	0.02060 seconds	0.02060 seconds
Sort operations (16 items):	0.01071 seconds	0.01895 seconds
Screen write (21 lines):	0.01220 seconds	0.01219 seconds
Total:	0.04351 seconds	0.05174 seconds

Operation times derived by averaging elapsed time for loop = 1..1000.

Interestingly, the sort operations for the preordered list have actually taken longer than for the randomly ordered list.

In this case, this is not an unexpected outcome because the binary tree result is the analog of a linear list and each subsequent element sorted has to step farther down the tree to find its proper place than it did with a randomly ordered data set. The results are still faster than for the linear sort procedure.

You may also notice that the screen display time for the ordered list is faster—^{1}/10,000 of a second—than for the disordered list, reflecting the difference in the number of recursive steps required to display the list in proper order. Most of the time required for the screen display is the time required to write the data to the video memory. However, with either an ordered or disordered source, the handling time for the binary tree is significantly faster than for a linear listing.

Implementing a Binary Tree Object

The PHONTREE program is similar to the PHONE1 demo in Chapter 10, using an instance of LinkObj to create a tree of DataObj. But there are also a few differences. PHONTREE will use recursive handling and the Node structure changes to accommodate binary rather than linear linking.

```
struct Node
{
    Node  *Root;              // pointer to root node    //
    Node  *Prior;             // pointer to prior node   //
    Node  *Next;              // pointer to next node    //
    char  Name[41];
    char  Phone[15];
};
```

In the PHONE1 and PHONE2 demos, each Node had two pointers, Prior and Next which were used to create a chain. In this case, Prior and Next no longer point up and down the list but point to elements that precede or follow the current element, while the Root pointer points back to the root element of the current node or toward the root of the tree.

Also, where the original list could have been constructed with a single pointer linking the list only one way, for the binary tree, at least two links are essential. And the third link, Root, will be necessary later before an item can be deleted from the tree without destroying the tree.

The definition of List is similar—though several methods are now given overloaded definitions for convenience in recursive implementations.

```
class List                          // list of node objects //
{
    private:
        Node *NRoot;
    public:
        List();
        ~List();
        void   Add( DataItem *NewItem  );
        void   ReadFile( char *FileName);
        Node*  Find( char *SearchStr );
        Node*  FindPartial( char *PartialStr );
        void   PrintList();
        void   Print( Node* N );
        void   RemoveLink( Node *N );
    private:
        void   Add( Node *NRef, Node *NNew );
        Node*  Find( Node *NRef, char *SearchStr );
        Node*  FindPartial( Node *NRef, char *PartialStr );
        void   PrintList( Node* N );
        void   DeleteLink( Node *N );
};
```

In PHONTREE.CPP, several object methods, including the overloaded method versions, are declared private since these are intended only for use by other object methods and not intended to be called by an application.

Building the Tree

List's ReadFile method accesses the data file (or files), calling the Add method with each entry. But the Add method has changed slightly.

```
void List::Add( DataItem *NewItem )
{
```

```
Node* N = new Node;              // create new node //

N->Root = NULL;

N->Next = NULL;

N->Prior = NULL;
```

The Add method begins by declaring an instance of Node, using the new operator to allocate memory, then setting all pointers to initial NULL values. Since these pointers will not all receive immediate assignments to valid memory locations (only the Root pointer will be set immediately), failure to provide default assignments for these pointers can clobber the stack the first time the program executes. Even if the program does execute correctly, a system reset may be required afterwards before this program (or some other program) can operate subsequently.

```
strzcpy( N->Name,  NewItem->Name,
         sizeof( NewItem->Name ) );

strzcpy( N->Phone, NewItem->Phone,
         sizeof( NewItem->Phone ) );

if( NRoot ) Add( NRoot, N );

else         NRoot = N;
}
```

After copying the string values to object records, the Add method asks if this is the first entry read from the file (for example, is NRoot still NULL) and, if so, simply assigns NRoot to N.

If this is not the first entry, then the static pointer to the root entry (NRoot) and the dynamic pointer to the current entry (N) are passed to the recursive Add method for more handling.

Remember, the Add method is overloaded, appearing in two definitions. In the first case it is called with a data record, but in the second case it is called with two pointer values to initiate a recursive operation which will eventually result in the new instance reaching its proper location in the tree.

```
void List::Add( Node *NRef, Node *NNew )
{
  if( Precede( NNew->Name, NRef->Name ) )
```

Add begins by calling the Precede function to determine the order of the current and reference entries.

```
if( NRef->Prior )
    Add( NRef->Prior, NNew );
else
{
    NRef->Prior = NNew;
    NNew->Root  = NRef;
};
```

If the current entry precedes the reference entry, the next question is to ask whether the reference node's Prior is already linked or if it is NULL (empty).

If the latter is true, then the new entry can be linked directly, linking the reference node's Prior to the new item and the new item's Root pointer to the reference node. If not, Add is now called recursively using the reference node's Prior pointer to step down the tree structure.

If the current entry does not precede the reference entry, the same determination is made for the reference node's Next pointer and the current item is either linked here or a recursive call is made to step down the tree until the appropriate location is found.

```
else
    if( NRef->Next )
        Add( NRef->Next, NNew );
    else
    {
        NRef->Next = NNew;
        NNew->Root = NRef;
    };
}
```

Disposing of the Tree

After building the tree, the second most important task is being able to dispose of the tree. Remember, memory is being dynamically allocated for each item in the tree and, unless provisions are made to properly dispose of this memory, a lot of the available RAM can wind up allocated for defunct purposes and not available to other applications—even after the current program has terminated.

Naturally, this task falls to the destructor method, List::~List.

```
List::~List()
{
   while( NRoot->Root )
      NRoot = NRoot->Root;
```

Before anything else is done, a simple loop ensures that the static pointer NRoot is, indeed, pointed at the root of the tree.

```
   DeleteLink( NRoot );
}
```

In the PHONE1 demo (Chapter 10), the destructor method, ~List, provided a while loop to dispose of the linear list. For the binary tree, recursive handling is required and; therefore, ~List calls a recursive method, DeleteLink, with the static pointer, NRoot.

The DeleteLink procedure is multiply recursive, but begins with a test to determine if the current entry is NULL and, if so, does nothing since nothing remains to be done (the end of a branch has been reached).

```
void List::DeleteLink( Node *N )
{
   if( N )
   {
```

If N is not empty, before disposing of this link, the first step is to test the Prior pointer. If this link points anywhere, then DeleteLink is called recursively to travel down this branch.

```
      if( N->Prior ) DeleteLink( N->Prior );
```

The same test is executed for the Next pointer, again calling Delete-Link recursively if necessary.

```
      if( N->Next )  DeleteLink( N->Next );
```

After disposing of the Next and Prior branches, the node itself can now be disposed of:

```
    delete N;
}   }
```

If the delete operator were called for a node without first recursively handling the links descending from this node, these other links could no longer be reached and could not be released.

Printing the Tree

While building the tree and disposing of the contents after use are important, it also helps to be able to do something with the records in between. Even though the structure of the data is very different from the previous linear examples, the data will be displayed in essentially the same fashion: in alphabetical order.

In PHONE1, the PrintList method was called without arguments and handled printing the entire list by itself. In this case, however, the overloaded PrintList method is called initially in one form with no argument, but subsequently calls its overloaded counterpart to continue a recursive process writing the entire list to the screen.

```
void List::PrintList()
{
    PrintList( NRoot );
}

void List::PrintList( Node* N )
{
    if( N )
    {
```

As with the DeleteLink method, PrintList begins by checking the current entry to see if it is empty—if it is not NULL.

Assuming the entry is not empty, PrintList checks to see if there are any items that preceded the current item. This is not done by calling the Precede function but simply by checking the Prior pointer and calling itself recursively to handle any prior entries.

```
        if( N->Prior ) PrintList( N->Prior );
```

Only after checking the Prior pointer is the current entry listed by calling the Print method.

```
        Print( N );
```

And, after handling any prior items and the current item, the *Next* pointer is tested, again, calling PrintList recursively.

```
        if( N->Next )  PrintList( N->Next );
}   }
```

Binary Searches, Insertions, and Deletions

While previous demo programs did not execute searches nor make any provision for inserting and deleting items from the lists, using a tree organization requires slightly more sophisticated provisions for searching entries and for deleting individual entries.

For inserting new items in the tree however, no special provisions are required because the same method used to build the tree is used to add new items, and new entries are always made at an existing free node instead of attempting to insert the new element within the existing structure.

The current demonstration includes two search routines and, after locating the appropriate entries, deletes these nodes from the tree and restores the tree structure with minimal revisions.

Searching a Binary Tree

Searching a binary tree is different than searching a linear list and, for this reason, two methods—Find and FindPartial—are provided.

Both the Find and FindPartial methods are overloaded methods, each appearing in two forms. The first method form is called with a string to search for and is used to initialize the second method which operates recursively. Both versions of the Find and FindPartial methods return pointers to the located entry or, if no match is found, return a NULL pointer. Both execute searches without respect to the string case (both ignore upper- and lowercase differences).

The difference between the two method types, however, is that the Find method looks for a match beginning with the first character in a field and seeking an exact match for the length of the search string. The FindPartial method also seeks an exact match, but looks for a match anywhere within the target string field. In either case, the search string can be any length up to the length of the target entry but does not have to equal the complete field.

There is one more difference. The Find method, since it can traverse the tree directly to where the search entry should be located (if a matching entry occurs) is considerably faster than the FindPartial method which has to search the entire tree recursively, testing every entry until a match is found. While Find is faster, FindPartial is more flexible.

Both methods have a shortcoming in that only the first matching occurrence will be found.

The Find Method

The Find method searches recursively, looking for an exact match for the search string and beginning at the first of the Name field. Remember, the Find method is an overloaded function, with one public method version and one private.

The public version of the Find method is called with a search string argument and begins by ensuring that the NRoot pointer is actually pointed at the tree root before calling the private method version to initiate a recursive search.

```
Node* List::Find( char *SearchStr )
{
    while( NRoot->Root ) NRoot = NRoot->Root;
    return( Find( NRoot, SearchStr ) );
}
```

The second Find method, private, requires two parameters: the search string and a node pointer for the location to immediately be searched.

```
Node* List::Find( Node *NRef, char *SearchStr )
{
    Node *Result = NULL;
    int  Comp;

    if( !NRef ) return( Result );
```

Before anything is done, a NULL node pointer is created. Then the reference pointer (NRef) is checked to be certain that the current node is valid.

Next, Turbo C's strnicmp function is called to execute a case-independent string comparison for the length of the search string, storing the result of the test as Comp.

```
Comp = strnicmp( SearchStr, NRef->Name,
                       strlen( SearchStr ) );
```

If SearchStr precedes NRef->Name, strnicmp returns a negative result, zero if the two strings match or a positive result if SearchStr follows NRef->Name.

Depending on the value in Comp, Find is called to return the results of a recursive search on the Prior link, to return the current node or to return the results on the Next link.

```
if( Comp <  0 )
    return( Find( NRef->Prior, SearchStr ) );
if( Comp == 0 ) return( NRef );
if( Comp >  0 )
    return( Find( NRef->Next,  SearchStr ) );
}
```

In this fashion, Find can call itself recursively until either a match is found or the end of the branch is reached. It then passes the final result back up through the recursions until returning to the calling application. Of course, if no match is found a NULL result is returned.

The FindPartial Method

Unlike the Find method which optimizes its search pattern, the Find-Partial method searches the entire binary tree until it identifies a match for the search string somewhere within the Name field, returning a pointer to the first matching entry found.

As with the Find method, FindPartial is also overloaded with public and private versions.

```
Node* List::FindPartial( char* PartialStr )
{
    while( NRoot->Root ) NRoot = NRoot->Root;
    return( FindPartial( NRoot, PartialStr ) );
}
```

The public method is again used to initiate a recursive search by calling the private method version with a pointer to the tree root. And the second method version operates in essentially the same fashion as the second Find method.

```
Node* List::FindPartial( Node *NRef, char* PartialStr )
{
   Node   *Result = NULL;

   if( NRef )
   {
      if( strstr( NRef->Name, PartialStr ) )
         return( NRef );
      if( NRef->Prior )
         Result = FindPartial( NRef->Prior, PartialStr );
      if( Result ) return( Result );
      if( NRef->Next )
         Result = FindPartial( NRef->Next, PartialStr );
   }
   return( Result );
}
```

The only real difference between the two methods is that Turbo C's strstr function is used to determine if a partial match is found. Unlike strnicmp, strstr is case-sensitive.

Removing an Item from the Tree

The RemoveLink method is used to remove a specific entry from the binary tree. Before an item can be deleted from the tree, provisions to locate a specific entry are needed and have been supplied by the Find and FindPartial methods.

The real trick is deleting an entry from the binary tree structure without losing other elements which were linked to the deleted item—like cutting out the center of a tree branch without cutting off the limb.

One method that could be used is to delete the data element while leaving node element in place. This will work but is hardly an elegant solution and could leave a lot of useless, empty nodes within the tree. A better method is to remove both the data and node elements, relinking the affected portions of the tree.

Figure 11-4 shows an entry being deleted from the tree with the affected links shown as heavy lines.

After deleting the Novation entry, the L-5 entry has one free pointer but both the NEC and PC Techniques entries are left dangling with no connections to the rest of the tree. Obviously, only one of these can be linked back to the L-5 node. The question becomes which branch takes the immediate link and where does the other branch reconnect? But the choices are not completely arbitrary because there are restrictions that need to be observed to preserve the ordering of the tree.

Figure 11-4: Deleting An Element

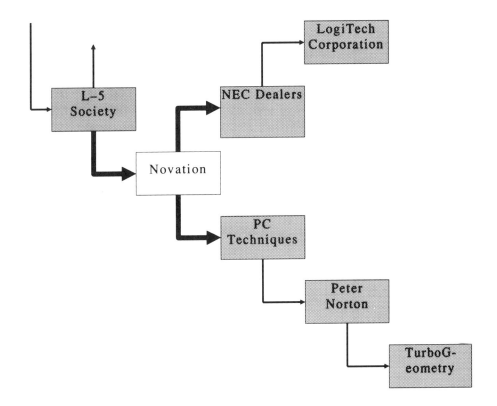

In the illustrated example, since the L-5 node's free link is a Next pointer, the obvious choice is to reconnect the Novation node's Next link, PC Techniques, thus maintaining the correct ordering.

This leaves the NEC node which was connected to a Prior link. A new Prior link is needed to reconnect and this is done simply by stepping down the restored branch of the tree until a free Prior pointer is found.

The results for this branch of the binary tree are shown in Figure 11-5, again with the new links appearing as heavy lines.

Figure 11-5: Relinking AfterDeletion

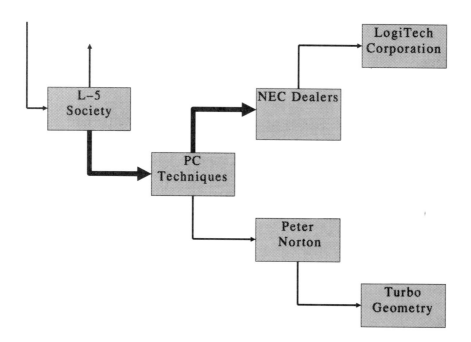

If the broken link to the main body of the tree had been a Prior pointer, then the descendant Prior link, if any, would have been reconnected first and the remaining branch stepped down until an empty Next pointer was found.

The fact that this will always result in a correct ordering is not entirely obvious but will become clear if you consider for a moment how entries were added to the tree in the first place.

Any entry that followed the L-5 entry but preceded the Novation entry would have originally connected to the tree either at the NEC entry or somewhere further along this branch and could not have been found on the PC Techniques branch. Therefore, everything on the NEC branch must precede all entries descended from PC Techniques, and all entries descended from the PC Techniques node must be lower than entries on the NEC branch.

There still remain special cases where the preceding handling is not sufficient.

First, if the deleted item is linked to only one subbranch—which can be either a Prior or Next link—this single link is reconnected to the deleted item's root node.

Second, if the deleted item is the end of a branch and has no dependent links the deleted item's root must be set to nil.

Last, if the deleted item is the root of the binary tree, the static pointer NRoot must be updated to point to the new root element.

The RemoveLink Method

The requirements and conditions discussed make the RemoveLink method a relatively complex if..else decision tree, at least, compared to the other methods used here.

The RemoveLink method uses two static pointers, imaginatively named ANode and BNode, to track positions through the binary tree. ANode begins by taking the pointer links of the item which will be deleted and then handles the first special case: is the current pointer the root of the entire tree?

```
void List::RemoveLink( Node *N )
{
   Node   *ANode = N, *BNode;

   if( ANode == NRoot )
   {
```

If this is the root, then a special case is executed to move NRoot to either the Prior link, if one exists, and then, if a Next link exists, reconnecting the Next branch.

```
      ANode = NRoot->Prior;
      if( ANode )
      {
         BNode = NRoot->Next;
         NRoot = ANode;
         if( BNode )
         {
            while( ANode->Next ) ANode = ANode->Next;
```

```
        ANode->Next = BNode;
        BNode->Root = ANode;
  }   }
```

If there is no Prior link then the Next link becomes the new root.

```
    else NRoot = NRoot->Next;
    NRoot->Root = NULL;
```

The new root's Root pointer is explicitly set as NULL. Remember, this Root pointer was previously pointing at the node about to be deleted. In a moment it will be pointing somewhere in never-never-land.

Last, N is deleted and an explicit return executed to complete this special case.

```
    delete N;
    return;
  }
```

Of course, if the tree is empty except for this root item, then there is neither a Prior nor a Next link. What happens then? Is this another special case? And is more special handling required?

While the case is special, additional handling shouldn't be necessary because, if the deleted item is the only remaining item in the tree, NRoot will now be pointing to a NULL pointer and nothing else needs to be done. In this instance, the special case has taken care of itself.

If the situation does not involve a root node, the next decision is to determine if the item to be deleted, indicated by ANode, was connected to a Prior or Next link. This is accomplished by calling the Precede function with the Name fields of the current item and its root.

```
  if( Precede( ANode->Name, ANode->Root->Name ) )
  {
```

If the current entry is determined to be descended from its root entry by a Prior link, this branch begins by deciding if the current entry has a Next link which will require handling.

```
    if( ANode->Next )
    {
      BNode = ANode->Next;
```

If there is a descendant Next link, BNode is assigned the address of the descendant node. The next question becomes is there a descendant Prior link or is this the end of the branch?

```
if( ANode->Prior )
{
    ANode->Root->Prior = ANode->Prior;
    ANode->Prior->Root = ANode->Root;
    ANode = ANode->Prior;
    while( ANode->Next ) ANode = ANode->Next;
    BNode->Root = ANode;
    ANode->Next = BNode;
}
```

In the event there is a descendant Prior link, this linkage is conveniently restored first, and the restored branch traversed until an appropriate Next node (a NULL link) is found where the remaining branch, presently addressed by BNode, can be restored. Otherwise, only the Prior link need be restored:

```
else
{
    ANode->Root->Prior = ANode->Prior;
    ANode->Next->Root  = ANode->Root;
}  }
```

If there is no Next node involved, then only the Prior link needs to be restored

```
else
{
    if( ANode->Prior )
    {
        ANode->Root->Prior = ANode->Prior;
        ANode->Prior->Root = ANode->Root;
    }
    else ANode->Root->Prior = NULL;
}  }
```

If the current entry is the end of the branch then the Root node is automatically set to NULL and that is all to be done. The current entry has been cut free (though not yet deleted).

If the link to be removed is descended as a Next link, then essentially the same events take place.

```
else
{
   if( ANode-Prior )
   {
      BNode = ANode->Prior;
      if( ANode->Next )
      {
         ANode->Root->Next = ANode->Next;
         ANode->Prior->Root = ANode->Root;
         ANode = ANode->Next;
         while( ANode->Prior ) ANode = ANode->Prior;
         BNode->Root = ANode;
         ANode->Prior = BNode;
      }
      else
      {
         ANode->Root->Next = ANode->Prior;
         ANode->Prior->Root = ANode->Root
   }  }
   else
   {
      if( ANode->Next )
      {
         ANode->Root->Next = N->Next;
         ANode->Next->Root = N->Root;
      }
      else ANode->Root->Next = NULL;
}  }
```

At this point, new links have been established for any and all descendant elements in the tree and all that remains is to dispose of the memory allocated to the current item and its node pointers:

```
delete N;
}
```

The static local pointers, ANode and BNode, were used so that these could be manipulated freely without losing track of the essential pointer, N, which is needed in the final step to call delete.

One feature worth comment: deletions within the binary tree tend to produce linear branches while new additions will tend to sprout subbranches. But, as the tree evolves, assuming a balance between additions and deletions, the structure of the tree will tend to simplify, approaching a linear structure (as demanded by the overriding laws of entropy).

However, even in a linear format the binary tree tends to be faster to transit than the equivalent, purely linear structure and this will remain true regardless of size. (Actually, binary tree efficiency increases with size compared with the equivalent linear structures.)

Other Methods

A variety of other methods could be created for use with the binary structure. For example, the Find and FindPartial methods could both be improved to meet probable application requirements. (See Chapter 12 for a different algorithm for locating multiple items.)

Taking the FindPartial method as a sample, an enhancement might be to include provisions, when a partial match is found, to inquire if this is the desired element or if a further search should be executed, continuing from the present, recursive location rather than beginning again at the root.

The same could be applied, though in a more limited fashion, to the Find method to provide for the circumstances where several entries might begin identically, as is the case with Jones, Bill, Jones, Sarah and Jones, John J..

Search methods do not need to be limited specifically to the Name field of an entry. With complex data fields they might well be designed to execute partial searches on several fields within an entry, or to execute different searches on different fields within a single trip though the tree.

For complex data, multiple binary trees can be constructed, each linking through a different field or through different rules (or both). Figure 11-6 shows the same tree organization as illustrated in Figure 11-3 and adds a second binary tree, using the same data, but linked through the Phone field instead of the Name field. For simplicity, the data entries have been replaced by integers showing the order in which each record was added to the tree and these are, of course, consistent for both trees.

Both trees have the same root entry since the root entry is simply the first record read from the file and, purely by coincidence, the second and fifth entries have the same relationship in both tree. Beyond this, however, the two trees are distinctly different.

Of course, in many cases, stored data files are already ordered—at least to some greater or lesser degree—and do not need elaborate sorting when read into memory. Even if the data source is ordered for one data field, it will most certainly be disordered for the second and third fields but, with binary trees, this disorder is an advantage rather than a liability.

When working with multiple tree indexes, it may help to work out and test the rules for each tree organization separately. But, once two or more trees are combined in an application, complex searches can be made very quickly by comparing the pointer addresses returned by separate search methods. Remember, even though the organization used by different tree structures will be different, the addresses of the data elements indicated by the separate link nodes will be the same, assuming that both trees' nodes are pointing to the same data element.

For an example, suppose the data consisted of thousands of entries and multiple data fields identifying name, occupation, and addresses and I wish to find an entry for a Dr. John Watson who lives in London. With multiple trees, instead of searching through hundreds of Watsons and then asking where each one lives and what his occupation might be, multiple searches can be executed to extract an array of addresses for Watsons, a second array of doctors, and a third array of Londoners. Then, given these subsets of pointer addresses, the addresses can be compared to find an element (or elements) which are common to all sets.

Which search process will be fastest depends on several factors, including the size of the data sets and how the searches are implemented. There are many circumstances where precisely this type of search is implemented not only for speed but also to overcome memory limitations when data sets are too large for available RAM.

Figure 11-6: Two Binary Trees

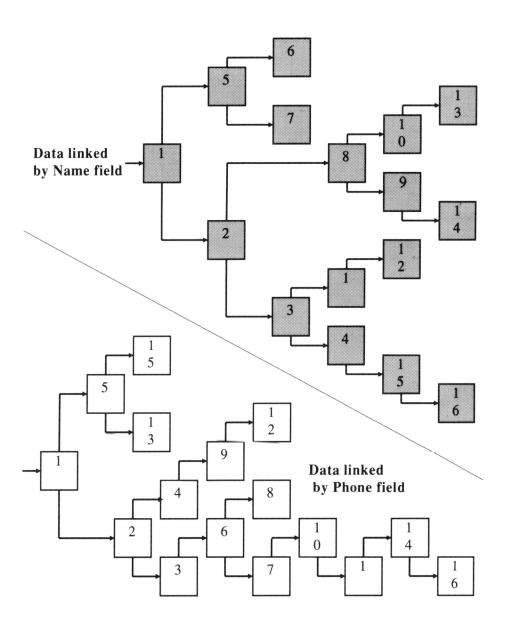

Data linked
by Name field

Data linked
by Phone field

All is not roses, however, because multiple trees will also require additional handling in the RemoveLink method to insure that all trees are correctly updated before an item is actually deleted. Since the data items do not have pointers to their nodes—only the nodes have pointers to the data, not vice versa—each tree's nodes would need to be searched independently and some care taken to assure that each tree's node was indeed pointing to the same data element.

With multiple trees a pointer for each tree could be added to the data element, pointing back to the data element's node for each separate tree. This could simplify several processes.

There are no simple answers for multiple trees but the results can be very powerful and very fast, especially when large data bases and complex data fields are used. Keep these possibilities in mind.

Summary

Binary tree structures are fast, powerful and compatible with object methods.

The PhonTree demo not only creates a binary tree organization but provides methods by which the tree object manipulates itself, adding, arranging, searching, and deleting data elements, even deleting the tree itself, all without requiring intervention by the application.

This is the heart and soul of object-oriented programming: once an object has been created and supplied with the appropriate methods, it is capable of acting by itself, exercising considerable powers of decision and, in general, carrying out complex tasks without requiring supplemental programing.

Some of the objects demonstrated have been static objects, declared by the program and remaining in memory until the program exits. Others have been dynamic objects capable of requesting their own memory allocation when created and, when no longer wanted, erasing themselves and releasing the memory for other tasks. Some have appeared both as static and as dynamic objects in different instances.

You've seen objects as graphic control elements, not only controlling their own presentation but querying the mouse object to find out if a mouse hit has occurred and reacting accordingly.

These are only a few of the ways objects can be created and only a very few of the tasks objects can undertake. An object can be anything from a simple scrollbar in a graphics program to a complex binary tree organizing data to an entire editor utility called on by an application as needed and released when no longer required.

The choices are yours—use simple objects for simple tasks or create complex objects for complex tasks, and anything in between. Anything can be programmed as an object or using objects. The only real limits are those of your imagination.

Unshackle your familiar fetters and habits and let yourself have fun!

```cpp
//===============================//
//          PHONTREE.CPP         //
//  self-sorting, -indexing list //
//===============================//

#include <alloc.h>          // for coreleft()              //

#include <conio.h>          // for getch()                 //

#include <iostream.h>       // for cerr                    //

#include <stdio.h>          // for printf, file i/o, etc   //

#include <stdlib.h>         // for itoa()                  //

#include <string.h>         // for strcpy()                //

struct DataItem

{

    char Name[40];

    char Phone[14];

};

struct Node

{

    Node  *Root;            // pointer to root node         //

    Node  *Prior;           // pointer to prior node        //

    Node  *Next;            // pointer to next node         //
```

```
      char   Name[41];                   // size of ItemName + null  //

      char   Phone[15];                  // size of ItemPhone + null //
};

class List                              // list of node objects //
{
   private:
      Node *NRoot;                              // pointer to node  //
   public:
      List();                               // constructor      //
      ~List();                              // destructor       //
      void  Add( DataItem *NewItem  );
      void  ReadFile( char *FileName);
      Node* Find( char *SearchStr );
      Node* FindPartial( char *PartialStr );
      void  PrintList();
      void  Print( Node *N );
      void  RemoveLink( Node *N );
   private:
      void  Add( Node *NRef, Node *NNew );
      Node* Find( Node *NRef, char *SearchStr );
      Node* FindPartial( Node *NRef, char *PartialStr );
      void  PrintList( Node *N );
      void  DeleteLink( Node *N );
```

```
};


        //=======================================//
        //  definitions for stand-alone functions  //
        //=======================================//

int Precede( char* Str1, char* Str2 )

{

   if( stricmp( Str1, Str2 ) < 0 ) return( 1 );

   return( 0 );

}

void strzcpy( char *str1, char *str2, int Size )

{

   strcpy( str1, str2 );

   str1[ Size ] = 0;                    // add null terminator //

}



        //===================================//
        // member functions for List class //
        //===================================//

List::List()                              // constructor //

{

   NRoot = NULL;         // sets node pointer to "empty" //

}                         // because nothing in list yet  //

List::~List()                             // destructor  //

{
```

```
    while( NRoot->Root )

        NRoot = NRoot->Root;        // move pointer to root    //

    DeleteLink( NRoot );            // begin recursive delete //

}


void List::DeleteLink( Node *N )

{

    if( N )

    {

        if( N->Prior ) DeleteLink( N->Prior );

        if( N->Next  ) DeleteLink( N->Next );

        delete N;

}   }


void List::Add( DataItem *NewItem )

{

    Node* N = new Node;                     // create new node //

    N->Root = NULL;

    N->Next = NULL;

    N->Prior = NULL;

    strzcpy( N->Name,  NewItem->Name,
             sizeof( NewItem->Name ) );

    strzcpy( N->Phone, NewItem->Phone,
             sizeof( NewItem->Phone ) );

    if( NRoot ) Add( NRoot, N ); else NRoot = N;
```

```
}

void List::Add( Node *NRef, Node *NNew )

{

   if( Precede( NNew->Name, NRef->Name ) )

   {

      if( !NRef->Prior )

      {

         NRef->Prior = NNew;

         NNew->Root  = NRef;

      }

      else Add( NRef->Prior, NNew );

   }

   else

   {

      if( !NRef->Next )

      {

         NRef->Next = NNew;

         NNew->Root = NRef;

      }

      else Add( NRef->Next, NNew );

} }

void List::ReadFile( char *NameFile )

{
```

```
    FILE      *ReadFile;                    // file of data items //

    DataItem NewItem;

    if( ( ReadFile = fopen( NameFile, "r" ) ) == NULL )

    {

        cerr << "Cannot open " << NameFile

            << " as input file\n";

        getch();

        exit(-1);

    }

    while( !feof( ReadFile ) )

    {

        fread( &NewItem, sizeof( NewItem ), 1, ReadFile );

        if( !feof( ReadFile ) ) Add( &NewItem );

    }

    fclose( ReadFile );

}

void List::PrintList()

{

    PrintList( NRoot );

}

void List::PrintList( Node* N )

{

    if( N )
```

```
    {
        if( N->Prior ) PrintList( N->Prior );

        Print( N );

        if( N->Next  ) PrintList( N->Next );
}   }

void List::Print( Node* N )

{
    printf( "%s  %s\n", N->Name, N->Phone );
}

Node* List::Find( char *SearchStr )

{
    while( NRoot->Root ) NRoot = NRoot->Root;

    return( Find( NRoot, SearchStr ) );
}

Node* List::Find( Node *NRef, char *SearchStr )

{
    Node *Result = NULL;

    int  Comp;

    if( !NRef ) return( Result );

    Comp = strnicmp( SearchStr, NRef->Name,

                        strlen( SearchStr ) );

    if( Comp <  0 )
```

```
        return( Find( NRef->Prior, SearchStr ) );

   if( Comp == 0 ) return( NRef );

   if( Comp >  0 )

      return( Find( NRef->Next,  SearchStr ) );

}


Node* List::FindPartial( char* PartialStr )

{

   while( NRoot->Root ) NRoot = NRoot->Root;

   return( FindPartial( NRoot, PartialStr ) );

}


Node* List::FindPartial( Node *NRef, char* PartialStr )

{

   Node   *Result = NULL;

   if( NRef )

   {

      if( strstr( NRef->Name, PartialStr ) )

         return( NRef );

      if( NRef->Prior )

         Result = FindPartial( NRef->Prior, PartialStr );

      if( Result ) return( Result );

      if( NRef->Next )

         Result = FindPartial( NRef->Next, PartialStr );

   }
```

```
      return( Result );

}

void List::RemoveLink( Node *N )

{

   Node   *ANode = N, *BNode;

   if( ANode == NRoot )

   {

      ANode = NRoot->Prior;

      if( ANode )

      {

         BNode = NRoot->Next;

         NRoot = ANode;

         if( BNode )

         {

            while( ANode->Next ) ANode = ANode->Next;

            ANode->Next = BNode;

            BNode->Root = ANode;

      }  }

      else NRoot = NRoot->Next;

      NRoot->Root = NULL;

      delete N;

      return;

   }
```

```
if( Precede( ANode->Name, ANode->Root->Name ) )

{

   if( ANode->Next )

   {

      BNode = ANode->Next;

      if( ANode->Prior )

      {

         ANode->Root->Prior = ANode->Prior;

         ANode->Prior->Root = ANode->Root;

         ANode = ANode->Prior;

         while( ANode->Next ) ANode = ANode->Next;

         BNode->Root = ANode;

         ANode->Next = BNode;

      }

      else

      {

         ANode->Root->Prior = ANode->Prior;

         ANode->Next->Root  = ANode->Root;

   }  }

   else

   {

      if( ANode->Prior )

      {

         ANode->Root->Prior = ANode->Prior;
```

```
            ANode->Prior->Root = ANode->Root;

      }

      else ANode->Root->Prior = NULL;

}   }

else

{

   if( ANode->Prior )

   {

      BNode = ANode->Prior;

      if( ANode->Next )

      {

         ANode->Root->Next = ANode->Next;

         ANode->Prior->Root = ANode->Root;

         ANode = ANode->Next;

         while( ANode->Prior ) ANode = ANode->Prior;

         BNode->Root = ANode;

         ANode->Prior = BNode;

      }

      else

      {

         ANode->Root->Next = ANode->Prior;

         ANode->Prior->Root = ANode->Root

   }   }

   else
```

```
      {

          if( ANode->Next )

          {

              ANode->Root->Next = N->Next;

              ANode->Next->Root = N->Root;

          }

          else ANode->Root->Next = NULL;

    }  }

    delete N;

}


                //===============================//
                //   end of object implementation   //
                //===============================//

unsigned long Mem1, Mem2, Mem3;

char   Str1[20] = "Borland";

char   Str2[20] = "Turbo C";

void Status( char *Msg, unsigned long Mem )
{

    char   MemStr[12];

    ltoa( Mem, MemStr, 10 );

    printf( "%s   %s\n", Msg, MemStr );

}
```

```
void ConstructList( char *ListName )

{

   List  AList;              // declare list, call constructor //

   Node *ANode;

   AList.ReadFile( ListName );

   Mem2 = coreleft();

   AList.PrintList();

   printf( "\nList constructed, \
           press Enter to continue\n" );

   getch();

   printf( "\nSearching for \"%s\" ...\n", Str1 );

   ANode = AList.Find( Str1 );

   if( ANode )

   {

      printf( "FOUND ... " );

      AList.Print( ANode );

      printf( "Removing this entry, \
              press Enter to continue\n" );

      getch(); printf( "\n" );

      AList.RemoveLink( ANode );

      AList.PrintList();

   }

   else printf( "Not found!\n" );
```

```
        printf( "\nPartial search for \"%s\" ...\n", Str2 );

        ANode = AList.FindPartial( Str2 );

        if( ANode )

        {

            printf( "FOUND ... " );

            AList.Print( ANode );

            printf( "Removing this entry, \

                    press Enter to continue\n" );

            getch(); printf( "\n" );

            AList.RemoveLink( ANode );

            AList.PrintList();

        }

        else printf( "Not found!\n" );

        printf( "\nPress Enter for final report\n\n" );

        getch();            // AList is implicitly deallocated by  //
                            // scope when ConstructList terminates //
}

main()

{

    clrscr();

    printf("   Name and Phone List\n");

    Mem1 = coreleft();

    ConstructList( "PHONE.LST" );

    Mem3 = coreleft();
```

```
    printf( "\n" );

    Status( "Free memory before list allocated: (Mem1) ",

            Mem1 );

    Status( "               ... after list created: (Mem2) ",

            Mem2 );

    Status( "          ... after list deallocated: (Mem3) ",

            Mem3 );

    getch();

}
```

CHAPTER 12

MULTIPLE SEARCHES ON BINARY TREES

Finding multiple entries with linear lists is relatively simple; search until a match is found, then continue the search until the next match is found or the end of the list is reached. Simple and efficient.

For a binary tree structure the task of multiple entry searches is not quite as simple.

To understand why there are problems, consider the execution of a binary-tree search analogous to a multiple linear search. Finding the first matching entry is simple, just use the same technique demonstrated in the PartialFind method or call the PartialFind method itself. Figure 12-1 shows an initial search finding a match at the node labeled 1. Other theoretical matches are located at nodes 2, 3, and 4.

Now, after a match occurs, you have one node pointer indicating an entry, but this is where things get hairy. The current node can be used as a starting point for another search, but this second search will only cover nodes descended from the starting node (1), as shown in Figure 12-2. While it is essential to continue the search down both descendant branches from 1, it isn't very productive. Even acting recursively, the search cannot go back up the tree beyond the starting point.

Figure 12-1: Multiple Search—Step 1

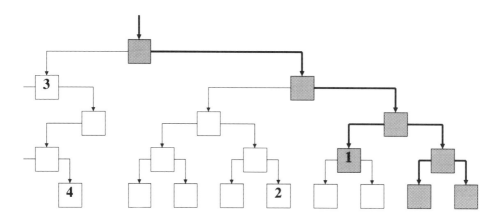

Provisions can be added to climb back up the tree looking for a Next branch (all Prior branches can be assumed covered). Several steps back, a Next branch is found and the descent can begin again. Figure 12-3 shows that eventually the next match will be found at node 2.

Starting at node 2, multiple retraces are required. Remember, with recursion, retracing is automatic. But with each successive search beginning at a new node, the special provisions to retrace the tree looking for new branches to explore quickly become quite cumbersome.

What about taking a different approach?

Creating a Search Index

The most efficient means of searching an entire binary tree is to begin at the root and traverse the entire structure recursively—in precisely the same fashion as the PrintList method employs. Once an entry is located, how can this information be returned to the application without disrupting the recursive search?

The PartialSearch method terminates once a match is found and retraces itself to the root to return the match location. But, in doing so, the recursive structure that defines the progress of the search is lost and, as discussed previously, attempting to resume the search, even from a known location within the structure, is not very practical.

Figure 12-2: Multiple Search—Step 2

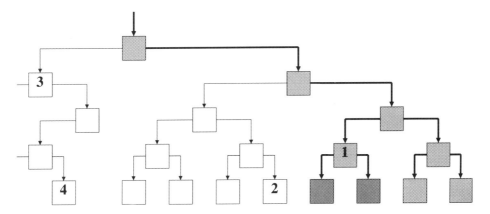

One alternative might be to resume each new search recursively from the root but not to report a match until the last match location has been reached and passed. This approach can become horrendously slow, particularly as the size of a tree increases.

Instead, in order to keep the advantages inherent in the tree structure and still minimize search time for multiple matches, a different method is selected using a search index to store the results of a tree search—an algorithm which is demonstrated, in a basic form, in PHONTRE2.CPP and illustrated in Figure 12-4.

Figure 12-3: Multiple Search—Step 3

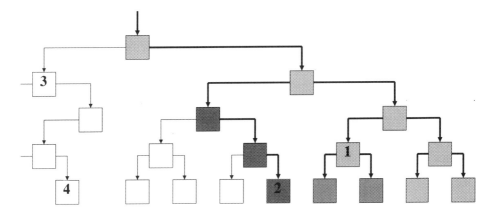

Figure 12-4: A Search Index

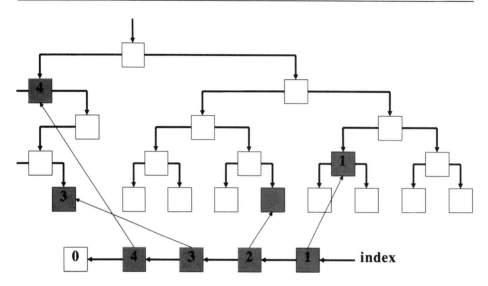

The search index is quite simple, consisting of a linear arrangement of nodes which contain only two links, a Next link joining this chain together and a Data link which points to the node locations where each match was found. To build this simply-linked list, the FindPartial method is modified slightly so that, instead of terminating a search when a match is found, a new method, AddIndex, is called with the match node and then the search continues recursively until the entire tree has been examined.

As before, FindPartial is an overloaded method, but this time, neither version returns a value and the first implementation is provided simply as a convenience in initializing the second, recursive version.

```
void List::FindPartial( char* PartialStr )
{
    while( NRoot->Root ) NRoot = NRoot->Root;
    FindPartial( NRoot, PartialStr );
}
```

The second FindPartial method shows two changes. The order of recursion has been changed to search the tree in an ordered fashion, working down the Prior links first, then testing the current node and traversing the Next links.

```
void List::FindPartial( Node *NRef, char* PartialStr )
{
   if( NRef )
   {
      if( NRef->Prior )
         FindPartial( NRef->Prior, PartialStr );
      if( strstr( NRef->Name, PartialStr ) )
         AddIndex( NRef );
      if( NRef->Next )
         FindPartial( NRef->Next, PartialStr );
}  }
```

The second change is the action taken when a match is found. In the previous version, a return instruction was executed—terminating the search—when a match occurred. Now, instead of a return instruction, the AddIndex method is called to store the node location, but the search is not interrupted.

Building the Index

The AddIndex method is quite simple. Called with a single argument, a node address, AddIndex begins by using the new operator to create a new index node, NIndex, and assigns the node address to the Data field and the Next field as NULL.

```
void List::AddIndex( Node *N )
{
   INode *NIndex = new INode, *TIndex;

   NIndex->Data = N;
   NIndex->Next = NULL;
```

Beyond this point, the index list is treated as a simple chain of nodes with a provision to make this item the root of the chain if the chain is empty or, if not, to place it at the end of the chain.

```
   if( IRoot )
   {
      TIndex = IRoot;
      while( TIndex->Next ) TIndex = TIndex->Next;
```

```
      TIndex->Next = NIndex;
   }
   else IRoot = NIndex;
}
```

No provisions are made here for any form of ordering this list of links because, first, the source list is already ordered and, second, the general expectation here is that this list will be relatively short.

If necessary, however, this index list could also be implemented as a binary tree or could be embellished with any additional provisions an application requires.

Listing The Search Index

Reporting the index list is also simple, as you can see in the ListIndex method.

```
void List::ListIndex()
{
   INode *IIndex = IRoot;

   if( IRoot )
   {
      while( IIndex )
      {
         Print( IIndex->Data );
         IIndex = IIndex->Next;
}  }  }
```

The ListIndex method asks if an index exists (for example, if IRoot is not NULL) and then proceeds down the list. If the index is implemented as a tree, some revisions would be required here as well but the report process is still simple.

Remember, the index nodes do not contain the located list data, only addresses for the nodes in the main list. Therefore, the Print method is called as Print(IIndex->Data) instead of Print(IIndex).

Disposing of the Index

Obviously, since the index list is dynamically constructed, provisions are necessary for deallocating the entire index, as well as removing a specific entry from the index list.

This first consideration—deleting the entire index—is handled by the ClearIndex method:

```
void List::ClearIndex()
{
   INode   *TIndex;

   while( IRoot )
   {
      TIndex = IRoot->Next;
      delete IRoot;
      IRoot = TIndex;
   } }
```

The ClearIndex method may be explicitly called by an application in preparation for another search, but it is also used by the ~List (destructor method) to free memory before the List object instance is terminated.

The second consideration is a method to remove a single item from the index and is supplied by the RemoveIndex method. Where the RemoveLink method was relatively complex (as required by the tree structure) for a linear list, the task is comparatively simple.

```
void List::RemoveIndex( Node *N )
{
   INode *Index1 = IRoot, *Index2;

   if( IRoot->Data == N )
   {
      IRoot = IRoot->Next;
      delete Index1;
      return;
   }
   while( Index1->Data != N )
   {
      Index2 = Index1;
```

```
        Index1 = Index1->Next;
    }
    if( Index1->Data == N )
    {
        Index2->Next = Index1->Next;
        delete Index1;
}   }
```

While the RemoveIndex method is public and directly accessible to the application, RemoveIndex is also used by the RemoveLink method because, when a link is removed from the tree, it is also necessary to ensure that the index does not potentially hold an address that will no longer be valid.

If a node passed by RemoveLink is not in the index list, then the RemoveIndex method will not find a match and, appropriately, will do nothing.

Other Considerations

A variety of possibilities exist for utilizing the index list but have not been implemented here, in part because precise implementations would be application specific.

For one, the search index would be greatly enhanced if it were provided with a selection mechanism rather than simply listing the match entries, but this consideration is also true of the List object itself.

Precisely how such a selection mechanism should be implemented, however, is entirely dependent on your application and purposes, aside from requiring a lengthy block of code to provide even in a sketchy format.

For an application, list display would also need to be enhanced, but precisely how it is done would be dependent on the application and the material being handled.

And what about preselection before display—displaying only a subset of a large data array? The selection methods are application dependent, but this is another area where the search index method will be quite useful.

Tree lists and indexes are hardly limited to alpha/numeric data but could arrange mathematic operations or other processes.

Keep in mind, methods which are ideal for one application may be terrible in another. Always keep an open mind about what needs manipulation and how it can best be handled because new methods can be customized for anything.

Since the PHONTRE2.CPP program differs from PHONTREE.CPP only in a few areas, the entire listing is not repeated here—only an outline of the overall program, together with the new methods and any changes required to existing methods.

```
//===============================//
//          PHONTRE2.CPP         //
//   self-sorting, -indexing list  //
//===============================//

#include ...                          // no change //

struct DataItem                       // no change //

struct Node                           // no change //

struct INode                      // new - index nodes //
{
    INode *Next;

    Node  *Data;
};

class List              // list of node objects - revised //
{
    private:
        Node  *NRoot;                 // pointer to node   //

        INode *IRoot;                 // pointer to index  //
    public:
        List();                   // constructor - revised //
```

```
    ~List();                              // destructor  - revised //

    void  Add( ... );                        // no change //

    void  ReadFile( ... );                   // no change //

    Node* Find( ... );                       // no change //

    void  FindPartial( char *PartialStr );    // revised //

    void  PrintList();                       // no change //

    void  Print( ... );                      // no change //

    void  RemoveLink( Node *N );              // revised //

    void  ListIndex();               // new - list index  //

    void  ClearIndex();              // new - clear index //

  private:
    void  Add( ... );                        // no change //

    void  AddIndex( Node *N );       // new - add index   //

    Node* Find( ... );                       // no change //

    void  FindPartial( Node *NRef, char *PartialStr );

                                             // revised   //
    void  PrintList( ... );          // no changes //

    void  DeleteLink( ... );         // no changes //

    void  RemoveIndex( Node *N );    // new - remove index //
};


        //=====================================//
        //  definitions for stand-alone functions  //
        //=====================================//

int Precede( ... )                           // no changes //
```

```
void strzcpy( ... )                          // no changes //


         //===================================//
         // member functions for List class //
         //===================================//

List::List()                          // constructor - revised //
{
   NRoot = NULL;                 // set node and index pointers //
   IRoot = NULL;                 // to empty - nothing in list  //
}

List::~List()                         // destructor - revised   //
{
   ClearIndex();                 // delete index entries   //
   while( NRoot->Root )
      NRoot = NRoot->Root;       // move pointer to root   //
   DeleteLink( NRoot );          // begin recursive delete //
}

void List::DeleteLink( ... )                  // no changes //

void List::Add( ... )                         // no changes //

void List::Add( ... )                         // no changes //

void List::ReadFile( ... )                    // no changes //

void List::PrintList()                        // no changes //
```

```
void List::PrintList( ... )                    // no changes //

void List::Print( ... )                        // no changes //

Node* List::Find( ... )                        // no changes //

Node* List::Find( ... )                        // no changes //

void List::FindPartial( char* PartialStr )        // revised //
{
   while( NRoot->Root ) NRoot = NRoot->Root;

   FindPartial( NRoot, PartialStr );
}

void List::FindPartial( Node *NRef, char* PartialStr )
{                                                 // revised //
   if( NRef )
   {
      if( NRef->Prior )
         FindPartial( NRef->Prior, PartialStr );
      if( strstr( NRef->Name, PartialStr ) )
         AddIndex( NRef );
      if( NRef->Next )
         FindPartial( NRef->Next, PartialStr );
} }

void List::RemoveLink( Node *N )                  // revised //
```

```
{

   Node  *ANode = N, *BNode;

   if( IRoot )

      RemoveIndex( N );              // check index for deletion //

   if( ANode == NRoot )

   {

      ... no further changes ...

   }

   if( Precede( ANode->Name, ANode->Root->Name ) )

   {

      ... no further changes ...

   }

   delete N;

}

void List::AddIndex( Node *N )                          // new //

{

   INode *NIndex = new INode, *TIndex;

   NIndex->Data = N;

   NIndex->Next = NULL;

   if( IRoot )

   {

      TIndex = IRoot;
```

```
      while( TIndex->Next ) TIndex = TIndex->Next;

      TIndex->Next = NIndex;

   }

   else IRoot = NIndex;

}

void List::RemoveIndex( Node *N )                    // new //

{

   INode *Index1 = IRoot, *Index2;

   if( IRoot->Data == N )

   {

      IRoot = IRoot->Next;

      delete Index1;

      return;

   }

   while( Index1->Data != N )

   {

      Index2 = Index1;

      Index1 = Index1->Next;

   }

   if( Index1->Data == N )

   {

      Index2->Next = Index1->Next;

      delete Index1;
```

```
}   }

void List::ListIndex()                              // new //

{

   INode *IIndex = IRoot;

   if( IRoot )

   {

      while( IIndex )

      {

         Print( IIndex->Data );

         IIndex = IIndex->Next;

}   }   }

void List::ClearIndex()                             // new //

{

   INode  *TIndex;

   while( IRoot )

   {

      TIndex = IRoot->Next;

      delete IRoot;

      IRoot = TIndex;

}   }
```

```
//===============================//
//      end of object methods    //
//===============================//

unsigned long Mem1, Mem2, Mem3;

char  Str1[20] = "N";

void Status( ... )                          // no changes //

void ConstructList( char *ListName )        // revised //
{
    List    AList;

    Node    *ANode;

    AList.ReadFile( ListName );

    Mem2 = coreleft();

    AList.PrintList();

    printf( "\nList constructed, \

            press Enter to continue\n" );

    getch();

    printf( "\nPartial search for \"%s\" ...\n", Str1 );

    AList.FindPartial( Str1 );

    printf( "Search results are:\n" );

    AList.ListIndex();

    AList.ClearIndex();

    printf( "\nSearch index complete, \
```

```
          press Enter for final report\n" );

   getch();

}

main()

{
                                    // ... no changes ... //

}
```

APPENDIX A

LINKED LISTS AND MIXED OBJECTS

In Chapter 10, a simple linked-list was created with pointers to objects. Since all pointers are the same and consist of segment and offset addresses, why not have the link Item pointers pointing to different object types and create a linked-list with mixed objects? In this manner, a single list could contain several different types of records while, at the same time, still treat each record in a different fashion. Sound useful? Unfortunately, what sounds useful isn't always practical or possible.

How Not To Do It

Normally, the subject of a book like this is "things that work". If something doesn't work, it isn't covered. But there are exceptions. This particular experiment is one which seems practical and an obvious extension to object-oriented programming. It is presented so you can avoid similar problems.

Two approaches suggest themselves in creating a link list with pointer to a mixed list of objects: either using a null (void) pointer or using a pointer of a base object type. Both are severely flawed.

375

Null Pointer Limitations

Null pointers are valid both in C and in C++, but—and here's the sting—these also have limitations on how they can be used.

The principal limitation is simply that null pointers cannot be used in the controlling expression of for, if, or while statements, on the right side of an assignment, or as the argument of a function anywhere that an actual value is required. Also, in many circumstances, it may not be possible to use a void pointer within the body of a loop expression.

Because of these limitations alone, it simply isn't practical to use a null pointer to reference a list of mixed object instances.

Base Object-Class Pointers

The second approach is to limit the mixed list to a base object class and its descendant object classes. This is also a valid approach because pointers of a base class type are perfectly validly assigned to descendant object class instances.

While all pointers, in their internal structure, essentially the same, there do remain a few restrictions: pointers to object types are assignment compatible with pointers to ancestor object types. This means a pointer to an object may point to an instance of the object or to any descendant of the object type (see Figure A-1). Pointers to unrelated object types, however, are not assignment compatible.

But, there's a catch here also.

In this case, the catch is something which you need to watch for in other circumstances as well. While it is quite simple to address a descendant object instance with a pointer of the base (ancestor) type class, as demonstrated in the POINTBAD.CPP program, methods belonging to the descendant object classes cannot be called via the pointer reference. This is because the pointer always references the base object method even though the instance data is a different type. The referenced method is the method belonging to the pointer's defined object type, not the object instance type which the pointer actually references.

For an example of how this happens, run the POINTBAD demo program and observe that only the base type Print() method is called, regardless of the instance type.

Figure A-1: Linked-List With Mixed Object Types

The desired intention in POINTBAD.CPP is to create a linked list of objects following the structural organization demonstrated below. But, unfortunately, this just doesn't work.

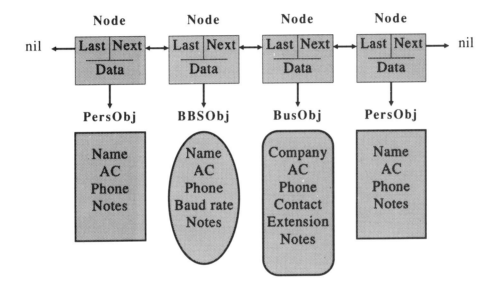

What About Virtual Methods

Again, the POINTBAD program is provided as an example of the problem faced by a mixed object list. If you will add the keyword virtual to the base class declaration, void Print(); and recompile and run POINTBAD, the answer should be obvious. (Be prepared to reset at this point.)

Solutions and Suggestions

I hate to say there is a problem and then not have a solution to offer in response, but I don't have an answer for the root problem here except to say that this attempt violates C++ structures.

For the simpler question of mixed data types, however, a solution does exist, but it is found in C rather than being specific to C++. Several different data structures can be combined as a union and then used as a data element within an object type. Separate handling methods, such as several different PrintXXX() methods, or a single handling method with provisions to adapt handling to the data structure type can be used. This is simply a conventional programming answer, not an object-oriented programming solution.

A Trio of Demo Programs

The POINTBAD.CPP demo program is provided to show how the discussed approach fails to operate as desired, while the MAKELSTS.C program creates a trilogy of data files for POINTBAD to read. The MIXLIST.C program is provided simply to show how a union of structures can be created but an object-oriented program to read this type of file is left as an exercise for the reader—a sort of final exam if you wish.

The POINTBAD.CPP, MAKELSTS.C, and MIXLIST.C programs are included in the listings below, and are included on the program disk accompanying this volume.

```
//===================================//
//            POINTBAD.CPP           //
// Demonstrates a pointer problem    //
//===================================//

#include <alloc.h>

#include <conio.h>

#include <iostream.h>

#include <stdio.h>

#include <stdlib.h>

#include <string.h>


#include <dos.h>
```

```
#define   PerFile  "PHONEPER.DAT"

struct    PerItem { char Name[40];

                    char AC[3];

                    char Phone[14];

                    char Notes[60];   };


#define   BusFile  "PHONEBUS.DAT"

struct    BusItem { char Name[40];

                    char AC[3];

                    char Phone[14];

                    char Contact[20];

                    char Ext[5];

                    char Notes[60];   };


#define   BBSFile  "PHONEBBS.DAT"

struct    BBSItem { char Name[40];

                    char AC[3];

                    char Phone[14];

                    char Baud[4];

                    char Notes[60];   };


unsigned long  Mem1, Mem2, Mem3;

class PerData

{

   protected:
```

```
        int   Index;

        char Name[41];                    // Name + null terminator //

        char AC[4];                         // AC + null terminator //

        char Phone[15];                 // Phone + null terminator //

        char Notes[61];                 // Notes + null terminator //

    public:

        PerData() {   }

        PerData( PerItem  *Item, int ThisIndex );

        ~PerData();

        char* GetName();

    // virtual void Print();       // alternate form of Print //

        void Print();

};


class BusData : public PerData

{

    protected:

        char Contact[21];

        char Ext[6];

    public:

        BusData( BusItem  *Item, int ThisIndex );

        ~BusData();

        void Print();

};
```

```
class BBSData : public PerData

{

   protected:

      char Baud[5];

   public:

      BBSData( BBSItem  *Item, int ThisIndex );

      ~BBSData();

      void Print();

};

struct Node

{

   PerData   *Item;

   Node      *Prior;                  // point to prior Node //

   Node      *Next;                   // point to next Node  //

};

class List

{

   public:

      Node *Nodes;                          // pointer to node //

   public:

      List();                               // constructor  //

      ~List();                              // destructor   //

      void Add( PerData *NewItem );   // add item to list //
```

```
   void Sort();                          // sort list      //

   void Report();                        // list items     //
};


             //=======================//
             //  stand-alone functions  //
             //=======================//

int Precede( char* Str1, char* Str2 )

{

   if( stricmp( Str1, Str2 ) > 0 ) return( 1 );

   return( 0 );

}


void strzcpy( char *str1, char *str2, int Size )

{

   strcpy( str1, str2 );

   str1[ Size-1 ] = 0;                   // add null terminator //

}


             //=======================//
             // PerData implementation //
             //=======================//

PerData::PerData( PerItem *Item, int ThisIndex )

{

   Index = ThisIndex;

   strzcpy( Name,  Item->Name,  sizeof(Name)  );

   strzcpy( AC,    Item->AC,    sizeof(AC)    );
```

```
   strzcpy( Phone, Item->Phone, sizeof(Phone) );

   strzcpy( Notes, Item->Notes, sizeof(Notes) );

}

PerData::~PerData()  {  }

void PerData::Print()

{

   printf( "PER: %s (%s) %s  %3d\n",

           Name, AC, Phone, Index );

   printf( "      %s\n", Notes );

}

char* PerData::GetName()

{

   return( Name );

}


               //=======================//
               // BusData implementation //
               //=======================//

BusData::BusData( BusItem *Item, int ThisIndex )

{

   Index = ThisIndex;

   strzcpy( Name,   Item->Name,   sizeof(Name)   );

   strzcpy( AC,     Item->AC,     sizeof(AC)     );

   strzcpy( Phone,  Item->Phone,  sizeof(Phone)  );
```

```
    strzcpy( Contact, Item->Contact, sizeof(Contact) );

    strzcpy( Ext,     Item->Ext,     sizeof(Ext)     );

    strzcpy( Notes,   Item->Notes,   sizeof(Notes)   );

}


BusData::~BusData()   {   }

void BusData::Print()

{

    printf( "Bus: %s (%s) %s   %3d\n",

            Name, AC, Phone, Index );

    printf( "    contact: %s   ext: %s\n", Contact, Ext );

    printf( "    %s\n", Notes );

}


                    //=======================//
                    // BBSData implementation //
                    //=======================//

BBSData::BBSData( BBSItem *Item, int ThisIndex )

{

    Index = ThisIndex;

    strzcpy( Name,  Item->Name,  sizeof(Name)  );

    strzcpy( AC,    Item->AC,    sizeof(AC)    );

    strzcpy( Phone, Item->Phone, sizeof(Phone) );

    strzcpy( Baud,  Item->Baud,  sizeof(Baud)  );

    strzcpy( Notes, Item->Notes, sizeof(Notes) );
```

```
}

BBSData::~BBSData()   {   }

void BBSData::Print()
{
    printf( "BBS: %s (%s) %s  %3d\n",
            Name, AC, Phone, Index );
    printf( "      baud rate: %s\n", Baud );
    printf( "      %s\n", Notes );
}


            //=================================//
            // member functions for List class //
            //=================================//

List::List()
{
    Nodes = NULL;                // sets node pointer to "empty" //
}                                // because nothing in list yet //

List::~List()
{
    while( Nodes->Prior != NULL ) Nodes = Nodes->Prior;

    while( Nodes != NULL )                   // until end of list //
    {
        Node *N = Nodes;                     // get node pointed to //
        delete( N->Item );                   // delete item's memory //
```

```
        Nodes = N->Next;                    // point to next node //

        delete N;                      // delete pointer's memory //
}   }


void List::Add( PerData *NewItem )

{

   Node *N = new Node;          // N is pointer to a new node //

   N->Item  = NewItem;

   N->Prior = Nodes;

   N->Next  = NULL;

   N->Prior->Next = N;

   Nodes = N;

}


void List::Sort()                     // bubble sort - slow //

{

   Node  *T1, *T2, *T3;

   while( Nodes->Prior != NULL ) Nodes = Nodes->Prior;

   for( T1 = Nodes; T1->Next->Next != NULL;

        T1 = T1->Next )

      for( T2 = T1->Next; T2->Next != NULL;

           T2 = T2->Next )

         if( Precede( T1->Item->GetName(),

                     T2->Item->GetName() ) )
```

```
          {

              T3->Item = T1->Item;

              T1->Item = T2->Item;

              T2->Item = T3->Item;

}          }


void List::Report()

{

   Node *Current = Nodes;

   while( Current->Prior != NULL )

      Current = Current->Prior;

   while (Current->Next != NULL)

   {

      Current->Item->Print();          // print current data //

      Current = Current->Next;         // point to next node //

}   }


          //=======================================//
          //  definitions for stand-alone functions  //
          //=======================================//

void Status( char *Msg, unsigned long Mem )

{

   char  MemStr[12];

   ltoa( Mem, MemStr, 10 );

   printf( "%s  %s   \n", Msg, MemStr );
```

```
}

void ExitError( char* FileName )

{

    cout << "Cannot open " << FileName

        << " as input file\n";

    getch();

    exit(-1);

}

void ReadList()

{

    List     AList;

    FILE     *ReadFile;

    PerItem  NPerItem;

    BusItem  NBusItem;

    BBSItem  NBBSItem;

    int      j = 1;

    if( ( ReadFile = fopen( BBSFile, "r" ) ) == NULL )

        ExitError( BBSFile );

    else

    {

        while( !feof( ReadFile ) )

        {

            fread( &NBBSItem, sizeof( NBBSItem ),
```

```
                    1, ReadFile );

        if( !feof( ReadFile ) )

            AList.Add( new BBSData( &NBBSItem, j++ ) );

    }

    fclose( ReadFile );

}

if( ( ReadFile = fopen( BusFile, "r" ) ) == NULL )

    ExitError( BusFile );

else

{

    while( !feof( ReadFile ) )

    {

        fread( &NBusItem, sizeof( NBusItem ),

                1, ReadFile );

        if( !feof( ReadFile ) )

            AList.Add( new BusData( &NBusItem, j++ ) );

    }

    fclose( ReadFile );

}

if( ( ReadFile = fopen( PerFile, "r" ) ) == NULL )

    ExitError( PerFile );

else

{

    while( !feof( ReadFile ) )
```

```
        {
            fread( &NPerItem, sizeof( NPerItem ),
                    1, ReadFile );
            if( !feof( ReadFile ) )
                AList.Add( new PerData( &NPerItem, j++ ) );
        }
        fclose( ReadFile );
    }
    Mem2 = coreleft();
    AList.Sort();
    AList.Report();
}

        //=========================================//
main()
{
    clrscr();
    printf("   Name and Phone List\n");
    Mem1 = coreleft();
    ReadList();
    Mem3 = coreleft();
    printf( "\n" );
    Status( "Free memory before list allocated: (Mem1) ",
            Mem1 );
```

```
    Status ( "           ... after list created: (Mem2) ",

          Mem2 );

    Status ( "        ... after list deallocated: (Mem3) ",

          Mem3 );

    getch();

}




          //=======================================//
          //                MakeLsts.C             //
          //  creates three separate data lists for //
          //    use with POINTBAD.CPP demo program   //
          //=======================================//

#include <conio.h>

#include <stdio.h>

#include <stdlib.h>

#include <string.h>

#include <dos.h>


#define  NullStr   "                                        "

enum    RecType { NONE, PER, BUS, BBS };

struct  PerItem { char Name[40];

                  char AC[3];

                  char Phone[14];

                  char Notes[60];   };
```

```
struct    BusItem { char Name[40];

                    char AC[3];

                    char Phone[14];

                    char Contact[20];

                    char Ext[5];

                    char Notes[60];    };

struct    BBSItem { char Name[40];

                    char AC[3];

                    char Phone[14];

                    char Baud[4];

                    char Notes[60];    };

char* ReadData( char* Prompt, int Size )

{

   char TempStr[80] = "";

   cprintf( Prompt );

   gets( TempStr );

   strncat( TempStr, NullStr, Size - strlen( TempStr ) );

   return( TempStr );

}

RecType ReadType()

{

   char Ch;
```

```
    cprintf( "Select 1) personal 2) business \
             3) bulletin board 0) EXIT: " );

    Ch = getche();

    cprintf("\r\n");

    switch( Ch )

    {

       case '1' : cprintf("Personal\r\n"); return( PER );

       case '2' : cprintf("Business\r\n"); return( BUS );

       case '3' : cprintf("Bulletin\r\n"); return( BBS );

       default  : cprintf("Done\r\n\b");   return( NONE );

} }


main()

{

    FILE      *WriteFile;

    PerItem  FPer;

    BusItem  FBus;

    BBSItem  FBbs;

    RecType  Finish = 0;

    clrscr();

    cprintf( "Enter names and phone numbers \
             for demo program file\r\n" );

    do

    {
```

```
Finish = ReadType();

switch( Finish )

{

   case PER:

   {

      strcpy( FPer.Name,

              ReadData( "        Name: ", 40 ) );

      strcpy( FPer.AC,

              ReadData( " Area code: ", 3  ) );

      strcpy( FPer.Phone,

              ReadData( "       Phone: ", 14 ) );

      strcpy( FPer.Notes,

              ReadData( "       Notes: ", 60 ) );

      WriteFile = fopen( "PHONEPER.DAT", "a" );

      fwrite( &FPer, sizeof(FPer), 1, WriteFile );

      fclose( WriteFile );

   } break;

   case BUS:

   {

      strcpy( FBus.Name,

              ReadData( "        Name: ", 40 ) );

      strcpy( FBus.AC,

              ReadData( " Area code: ", 3  ) );

      strcpy( FBus.Phone,
```

```
                ReadData( "        Phone: ", 14 ) );
        strcpy( FBus.Contact,
                ReadData( "      Contact: ", 20 ) );
        strcpy( FBus.Ext,
                ReadData( " Extension: ", 5  ) );
        strcpy( FBus.Notes,
                ReadData( "        Notes: ", 60 ) );
        WriteFile = fopen( "PHONEBUS.DAT", "a" );
        fwrite( &FBus, sizeof(FBus), 1, WriteFile );
        fclose( WriteFile );
    } break;
    case BBS:
    {
        strcpy( FBbs.Name,
                ReadData( "        Name: ", 40 ) );
        strcpy( FBbs.AC,
                ReadData( " Area code: ",  3 ) );
        strcpy( FBbs.Phone,
                ReadData( "        Phone: ", 14 ) );
        strcpy( FBbs.Baud,
                ReadData( " Baud Rate: ",  4 ) );
        strcpy( FBbs.Notes,
                ReadData( "        Notes: ", 60 ) );
        WriteFile = fopen( "PHONEBBS.DAT", "a" );
```

```
                fwrite( &FBbs, sizeof(FBbs), 1, WriteFile );

                fclose( WriteFile );

            }

            printf("\n");

    }   }

    while( Finish );

    delay( 500 );

}




        //=======================================//
        //                MIXLIST.C              //
        //   demonstrates a union of structures  //
        //   and creates a file of mixed entries //
        //=======================================//

#include <conio.h>

#include <stdio.h>

#include <stdlib.h>

#include <string.h>

#include <dos.h>


#define  FileName  "MIXPHONE.LST"

#define  NullStr  "                                      "


enum    RecType { NONE, PER, BUS, BBS };


struct  DataItem  {  RecType ThisRec;

                     char Name[40];
```

```
                              char AC[3];

                              char Phone[14];

                              char Notes[60];   };

struct    BusItem    {  DataItem   Data;

                              char Contact[20];

                              char Ext[5];        };

struct    BBSItem    {  DataItem   Data;

                              char Baud[4];       };

union     MixRec     {  DataItem   Data;

                              BusItem    Bus;

                              BBSItem    BBS;    } UnionRec;

char* ReadData( char* Prompt, int Size )

{

   char TempStr[80] = "";

   cprintf( Prompt );

   gets( TempStr );

   strncat( TempStr, NullStr, Size - strlen( TempStr ) );

   return( TempStr );

}

RecType ReadType()

{
```

```
      char Ch;

      cprintf( "Select 1) personal 2) business \
                3) bulletin board: " );

      Ch = getche();

      cprintf("\r\n");

      switch( Ch )

      {

         case '1' : return( PER );

         case '2' : return( BUS );

         case '3' : return( BBS );

         default  : return( NONE );

}   }


main()

{

   FILE     *WriteFile;

   MixRec   FE;

   int      Finish = 0;

   clrscr();

   cprintf( "Enter names and phone numbers \
             for demo program file\r\n" );

   cprintf( "Enter blank line to exit: \r\n" );

   WriteFile = fopen( FileName, "a" );

   while( !Finish )
```

```
{
    strcpy( FE.Data.Name,
            ReadData( "        Name: ",  40 ) );
    Finish = ( strcmp( FE.Data.Name, NullStr ) == 0 );
    if( !Finish )
    {
        strcpy( FE.Data.AC,
                ReadData( " Area code: ", 3  ) );
        strcpy( FE.Data.Phone,
                ReadData( "       Phone: ", 14 ) );
        strcpy( FE.Data.Notes,
                ReadData( "       Notes: ", 60 ) );
        FE.Data.ThisRec = ReadType();
        switch( FE.Data.ThisRec )
        {
            case PER: break;
            case BUS: strcpy( FE.Bus.Contact,
                         ReadData( "   Contact: ", 20 ) );
                      strcpy( FE.Bus.Ext,
                         ReadData( " Extension: ", 5  ) );
                      break;
            case BBS: strcpy( FE.BBS.Baud,
                         ReadData( " Baud rate: "  4 ) );
        }
```

```
        fwrite( &FE, sizeof(FE), 1, WriteFile );

   }  }

   fclose( WriteFile );

   cprintf( "Done\r\n" );

   delay( 500 );

}
```

OOP TERMINOLOGY

Abstract Data Types   A set of data structures (data types) defined in terms of structure's features and the operations executed on these structures. In OOP, **object types** are abstract data types.

Ancestor Type   Any type from which another object type inherits. *See also* **Immediate Ancestor**.

Binding   The process by which the address of a procedure is given to the caller. This may be **early binding** occurring at compile/link time or **late binding** occurring at run time when the procedure is called. Traditional compilers such as C and Pascal support early binding only, while C++ and OS/2 (.DLL libraries) compilers support both early and late binding. *See also* **Early Binding** and **Late Binding**.

C++   An object-oriented superset extension to the C compiler language originally developed by Bjarne Stroustrup.

Classes   A term used by C++, Smalltalk, and others to identify object definitions. Synonymous with **object types**.

Client Relationship   *See* **friend**.

Concurrency   Not implemented by DOS languages at present, concurrency is a potential implementation of object-oriented programming for systems employing concurrent or parallel processors or multitasking systems such as OS/2. The capability of object-oriented programs to communicate by messages removes some of the difficulty of synchronization between concurrent or parallel processes.

Constructor   A special type of **method** initializing any instance object. If no explicit constructor method is defined, the C++ compiler will create an implicit constructor method.

Descendant Type   Any type that inherits from an **object** type. *See also* **Inheritance**.

Destructor   A special type of **method** used to deallocate dynamic objects. Destructor methods may be explicitly defined and may include provisions to deallocate other data elements or to execute other exit procedures. If no destructor method(s) are declared, the C++ compiler will create an implicit destructor method. Destructors also allow **polymorphic** objects to be correctly deallocated even though their exact type and exact size, is not known at compile time.

Dynamic Binding   Late or delayed binding. *See* **Late Binding**.

Dynamic Instance   Any object instance created by dynamic memory allocation. *See also* **Static Instance**.

Early Binding   The traditional method of compiling in which the addresses of procedures or functions are determined at compile/link time. Object-oriented language compilers, however, may use **late binding** in which the procedures' address codes are not known at compile/link time, but are only determined at run time when the procedure is actually called. *See also* **Virtual Methods**.

Encapsulation   The wedding of code to data within an **object** unit. This is modularity applied to data—combining records with procedures and functions that manipulate data to form a new data type which is called an object. Encapsulation renders an object's data invisible to the user of the object, while the methods for manipulating the data remain visible.

Extensibility A feature allowing the user of object-oriented code to extend the code without having the source code. Descendant object types can be made to inherit the ancestor object type's properties even though the ancestor object type belongs to an externally compiled module. Extensibility allows sharing or selling object libraries without revealing trade secrets or algorithms. Also, extensibility allows existing objects to be customized for new applications by extending these as new object types.

Friend Object classes or procedures may be declared as **friend** to another class, allowing data elements to be shared by the friend. Class friendship is neither transitive nor reciprocal.

Hybrid Paradigms Some systems such as Smalltalk (and OS/2) are pure object-oriented programming systems, operating solely by message passing. Others such as Object-Oriented Pascal, Object C, or C++ are hybrids that provide both OOP and non-OOP programming features. Hybrids are popular largely for ease of development, the presence of familiar capabilities, and speed in execution and creation.

Immediate Ancestor An object type may have several ancestors, but the ancestor named in the object's type definition is the type's immediate ancestor. *See also* **Ancestor Type**.

Information Hiding Information hiding is a feature of modular programming in which the information within a module is private to the module except as made public through an interface definition (method). *See* **Encapsulation**.

Inheritance The property of all object types that allows a type to be defined which "inherits" all data and method definitions that were contained in a previously defined type. It does so without restating these definitions. Any type inheriting from another type is called a **descendant type**. Inheritance is a property of objects, allowing creation of a hierarchy of objects with descendants of objects implicitly inheriting access to their ancestors' code and data structures. See also **Private**, **Protected,** and **Public**.

Instance A variable of type object or an instance of a specific object type. Also, in conventional usage, the term **object** refers to an instance of an object type.

Late Binding   A method of calling procedures in which the address of the procedure (the address to which control is passed when the procedure is called) is not known at compile/link time and is only determined at run time when the procedure is actually called. Late binding is characteristic of object-oriented language compilers and, in conjunction with **inheritance**, late binding makes **polymorphism** possible. *See also* **Early Binding** and **Virtual Methods**.

Messages   Action parameters or orders passed to object calls, instructing the object to execute specific capabilities or features.

Method   A procedure or function that is defined as belonging to an **object type**. Methods may be **static** or **virtual**.

Modularity   Program construction in modules, blocks or units that are combined to build complete programs. Ideally, the redesign or reimplementation of a unit or module can be accomplished without affecting the operation of the rest of the program or system. The DOS, CRT, and GRAPH units in Turbo Pascal and Turbo C are good examples of modularity.

Multiple Inheritance   C++ permits multiple inheritance, allowing an object to inherit features and data from two or more ancestor objects. With single inheritance, the inheritance structure is a tree. With multiple inheritance, the inheritance structure is a web or maze with multiple ancestors contributing separate data and methods. They may contribute identical or entirely different versions of the same method, the latter case generally leading to confusion. Not implemented in Object Pascal.

Object Hierarchy   A group of object types related through **inheritance**. The Turbo Debugger, executing an object-oriented module, can be used to display a graphic representation of an object hierarchy by selecting Views, Hierarchy from the menu.

Object Type   A special structure that may contain procedure and function definitions called **methods**. The **object type** structure is similar to the Pascal **record** structure or C **struct** structure. Object types may be defined as including all data and method definitions that were defined within a previous object type. *See* **Ancestor Type**, **Descendant Type**, and **Inheritance**.

Object-Oriented Term for programming practices or compilers that collect individual programming elements into hierarchies of classes, allowing program objects to share access to data and procedures without redefinition.

Polymorphic Object An instance of an object with a descendant object is a polymorphic object because the descendant object inherits the shape of any of the ancestor types, but can polymorph into a new shape.

Polymorphism The property of sharing a single action (and action name) throughout an object hierarchy, but with each object in the hierarchy implementing the action in a manner appropriate to its specific requirements.

Private Data and methods belonging to a class (object) are private by default. Private data elements can be accessed by methods belonging to the class but not by methods belonging to a descendant class. Private methods can be accessed only by other methods belonging to the same object class but cannot be referenced by descendant object classes or by applications. *See also* **Protected** and **Public**.

Protected Methods belonging to a class (object) may be explicitly declared as protected and can be accessed by other member functions of the same class and by member functions of a descendant class but cannot be accessed directly by applications. Data elements can not be declared **protected**. *See also* **Private** and **Public**.

Public Methods belonging to an object class may be explicitly declared public, making them accessible both to descendant object classes and to applications. Data elements belonging to an object class may also be declared public, making them accessible to descendant classes but not accessible to applications. *See also* **Private** and **Protected**.

Redefinition The mechanism which allows the client programmer to employ the same name to refer to different things depending on the class to which each is applied. For example, both Point and Circle possess the property of location, but this property may be redefined from one object to the next. For Point, location would be a single pixel on the screen, but for Circle, location could be either the center of the circle or the corner of the screen rectangle in which the circle was created. *See also* **Selective Inheritance**.

Repeated Inheritance A special case of multiple inheritance in which an object *D* is the descendant of *A* by more than one path. Permitted in C++ bu not implemented in Object-Oriented Pascal.

Reusability A principal feature and objective of object-oriented programming, to allow software to be reused instead of reinvented. Libraries and include files are early examples of reusability, while the Turbo Pascal units (TPUs) are a later development.

Selective Inheritance Not currently implemented. Selective inheritance would allow objects to discard data or features belonging to their ancestor objects. Currently, redefinition is the only method of changing inheritance features, but selective inheritance may appear at a later time.

Simula-67 The original object-oriented language, Simula-67 was designed for writing test simulations of physical objects such as mechanical devices.

Smalltalk An early object-oriented language, Smalltalk is an interpreter language (like BASIC), not a compiler.

Static Instance Any instance of an object which is named in a **var** declaration and is statically allocated in the stack and data segment. *See also* **Dynamic Instance**.

Static Method A **method** implemented using **early binding**. The method's address is determined at compile/link time, just as the address of any conventional procedure or function is known at compile time. Static method calls require less overhead and should be used as optimization when the flexibility of virtual methods is not required.

Static Object Similar to static data definitions, static object definitions are allowed in C++, but not in Object-Oriented Pascal. *See also* **Static Instance**.

This An invisible identifier which is automatically declared within an object. May be used to resolve identifier conflicts by qualifying data fields belonging to an method's object. In Object-Oriented Pascal, the equivalent term is **Self**.

Types   Templates or definitions for creating **objects**.

Virtual Method   Any **method** implemented with **late binding** by using the reserved word **virtual**. In actual operation, a virtual method is usually a group of methods with identical procedure or function headers within an object hierarchy. When a virtual method is executed, a special mechanism determines which implementation of the virtual method is appropriate to the object type of the calling instance. The selection mechanism is installed by calling the object's **constructor**.

Virtual Method Table (VMT)   A table appearing in each virtual object type's data segment. The VMT contains the size of the object type (record size) and pointers to the procedures and functions implementing the object type's methods. Each object instance's **constructor** creates a link between the calling instance and the VMT, with the VMT used to call the method implementations.

THE OBJECT MOUSE UTILITY

The Object Mouse (MOUSE.I) is an object-oriented mouse unit for use with Turbo C++ application programs. It supplies two mouse types for general use: a graphics mouse and a text mouse. The following procedures are available in MOUSE.I:

General Mouse Object Procedures

Mpos   Reports mouse position and button status (all).

Mpressed   Reports requested button down event and position.

Mreleased   Reports requested button up event and position.

Mmotion   Reports mouse movement.

Mreset   Resets mouse to default status.

Mspeed   Sets acceleration point for enhanced mouse movement.

Mxlimit/Mylimit   Restricts mouse movement to selected screen area.

Mmoveto   Sets position of mouse cursor on screen.

Mmove_ratio   Sets ratio of physical mouse movement to screen movement.

Mshow   Shows or hides mouse cursor.

Text Mouse Object Procedures

Set_Cursor   Sets hardware or software text cursor.

Graphic Mouse Object Procedures

Mconceal   Selects screen area where graphic cursor is hidden.

Set_Cursor   Selects graphics mouse cursor.

Mlightpen   Enables or disables lightpen emulation for both text and graphics lightpen mouse objects.

The type definitions for each mouse are available to any application program including the statement *#include "mouse.i"* in the header.

General Mouse Procedures and Functions

Many of the procedure and functions supplied by the mouse unit are common to all of the object mouse types. Two record structures and seven constants are defined globally in the mouse unit and are available to the application using the mouse unit.

The first structure, defined as Mstatus, is used by all mouse object types to report mouse button events:

```
typedef struct { int button_status,
                     button_count,
                     xaxis,  yaxis;
               } Mstatus;
```

The second structure, defined as type g_cursor, is used by the GraphicMouse object type to set the graphics mouse cursor:

```
typedef struct { unsigned int
                    ScreenMask[16],
                    CursorMask[16],
                    xkey,  ykey;
           } g_cursor;
```

The seven constants shown in Table C-1 are globally defined by the mouse.

Table B-1: Constants

CONSTANT	VALUE	APPLICATION
ButtonL	0	Left button
ButtonR	1	Right button
ButtonM	2	Middle button
SOFTWARE	0	Used to set software text cursor
HARDWARE	1	Used to set hardware text cursor
FALSE	0	Boolean false
TRUE	1	Boolean true

Mreset

The Mreset procedure is used to reset the mouse driver to its default state. Two arguments are required, returning a Boolean status and the number of buttons supported by the physical mouse. The procedure is called as:

```
int  Status, BtnCount;

gmouse.Mreset( &Status, &BtnCount );
```

Status will return TRUE if the mouse and mouse driver are present and installed; FALSE if the mouse cannot be used. *BtnCount* will return with a value of 2 or 3 indicating the number of buttons supported by the physical mouse.

In graphics applications, the default mouse cursor is enabled by the Mreset function, but see also the Initialize procedure supplied by the GraphicMouse.

Mshow

The Mshow procedure is used to turn the mouse cursor on or off and is called with a single boolean argument specifying the desired state. The Mshow procedure is called as:

```
gmouse.Mshow( TRUE )                    { shows mouse cursor }
gmouse.Mshow( FALSE )                   { hides mouse cursor )
```

Initially, the mouse cursor is always hidden and must be explicitly rendered visible. The visible or invisible state of the mouse, however, does not affect tracking the mouse position or reporting on mouse button events.

Note: conventional mouse Show and Hide functions decrement or increment a cursor counter such that two or more calls to hide the mouse cursor will require two or more calls to make the mouse cursor visible again and vice versa. The object mouse avoids this potential problem and multiple calls to Mshow(TRUE) do not require multiple calls to Mshow(FALSE).

Mpos

The Mpos procedure is called with three integer arguments: BtnStatus, XPos, and YPos. These are returned with the current status of the mouse buttons and the x- and y-axis mouse pointer coordinates and are called as:

```
int  BtnStatus, XPos, YPos;

gmouse.Mpos( &BtnStatus, &XPos, &YPos )
```

The BtnStatus variable returns with the three least-significant-bits—beginning with bit 0—indicating the status of the left, right, and middle buttons respectively. If the button is down, the bit is set. If the button is up, the bit is cleared. The XPos and YPos variables return the current screen coordinates of the mouse cursor.

In text modes, the coordinates are always returned in incremental steps determined by the character cell width and height, but are still in pixel coordinates. For example, if the system is in text mode and the mouse cursor is in the third column, second row, the coordinates returned would be 24, 16 (assuming an 8x8 character cell).

In graphics modes, the coordinates returned are the pixel coordinates of the graphics cursor's hotspot. See also Mpressed, Mreleased, Mxlimit, and Mylimit.

Mmoveto

The Mmoveto procedure allows the application program to position the mouse cursor independent of the movement of the physical mouse. The Mmoveto function is called with two integer arguments establishing the x- and y-axis position for the mouse cursor:

```
gmouse.Mmoveto( 315, 200 );
```

In text modes, the x- and y-axis coordinates are rounded to the nearest character boundaries in pixel coordinates. Assuming an 8x8 character cell, the arguments shown would position the cursor at column 39, row 25. In graphics modes, the mouse cursor would be positioned with the cursor hotspot at the specified coordinates.

All subsequent movements generated by the physical mouse will begin at the location established by the Mmoveto function.

Mpressed and Mreleased

The Mpressed and Mreleased procedures require two arguments: a integer argument selecting the mouse button to be reported and a variable of type Position (globally defined by the mouse unit) which returns the button status, event count, and coordinates of the button event requested.

Mpressed reports button pressed events; Mreleased reports button released events.

```
mouse_event   BtnEvent;

BtnEvent = Mpressed( ButtonL );
BtnEvent = Mreleased( ButtonM );
```

The returned BtnEvent structure reports the number of times (if any) the queried button has been pressed (or released), the current status (up or down) of the queried button, and the screen coordinates of the mouse cursor when the most recent button event occurred.

The button event counter—for the specific button and type of event—is reset by this call.

Mmotion

The Mmotion procedure returns a structure with two integer arguments (x_count and y_count) containing the horizontal and vertical step counts. The values returned are always in the range -32768..32767 with positive counts indicating motion from left to right or from top to bottom:

```
Mmovement   MMove;

MMove = Mmotion();
```

The horizontal and vertical step counters are reset to zero by this call. See also Mspeed.

Mspeed

The Mspeed procedure is used to set a physical speed threshold (in mickeys/second) over which the mouse driver adds an acceleration component. With an acceleration threshold set, fast mouse movements move the cursor farther than slow movements over the same physical distance, allowing fine positioning by slow movements and broad changes with fast movements:

```
Mspeed( 300 );
```

Mouse acceleration can be disabled by setting an arbitrarily high threshold value (such as 7FFFh). See also Mmove_ratio.

Mxlimit/Mylimit

The Mxlimit and Mylimit procedures set minimum and maximum screen limits, restricting cursor movement to the selected area. If the cursor is outside the area set, the cursor is immediately moved just inside the new borders:

```
Mxlimit( 0, getmaxx() );
Mylimit( 0, getmaxy() );
```

The shown calls sets the mouse boundaries to cover the entire graphics screen. If either minimum value is greater than the corresponding maximum, the two values are swapped.

Mmove_ratio

The Mmove_ratio procedure uses two integer arguments to set the ratio of physical mouse motion to horizontal and vertical screen mouse motion:

```
Mmove_ratio( 16, 16 );
```

Default movement ratios are 8 mickeys (units of physical movement) to 8 pixels horizontal and 16 mickeys to 8 pixels vertical. Ratio values may be in the range 1..32767 mickeys. See also Mspeed.

Mconceal

The Mconceal procedure is called with four integer parameters: left, top, right, and bottom, in this order—establishing an area of the screen where the mouse cursor is automatically concealed:

```
int  left, top, right, bottom;

Mconceal( left, top, right, bottom );
```

The Mconceal procedure can be used to guard an area of the screen which is about to be repainted. If the mouse is in the area selected, the cursor visible counter is decremented just as if Mshow(FALSE) was called. Any subsequent call to Mshow(TRUE) reenables the cursor within the entire region established by the SetLimits procedure.

The Text Mouse Object

The Text Mouse object includes all of the general mouse procedures with one addition.

Set_Cursor

The Set_Cursor procedure is used to select either a SOFTWARE or HARDWARE text cursor and to set the cursor style. The SOFTWARE and HARDWARE constants are predefined by the mouse unit.

If the HARDWARE cursor is selected, the second and third parameters specify the start and stop scan lines for the cursor:

```
Set_Cursor( HARDWARE, 8, 7 );
```

If the SOFTWARE cursor is selected, the second and third parameters set the screen and cursor masks:

```
Set_Cursor( SOFTWARE, 0x0000, 0x8F18 );
```

The Graphic Mouse Object

For the graphics mouse, the Set_Cursor procedure is also implemented, but in a different form from the text mouse.

Set_Cursor

With the graphics mouse, the Set_Cursor procedure is slightly different than with the text mouse and is called with a single parameter that must be type g_cursor as defined in the mouse unit:

```
Set_Cursor( ARROW );
```

Five graphic cursors are predefined in the mouse unit, including ARROW, CHECK, CROSS, GLOVE, and IBEAM, the latter four appear in Figure C-1.

Figure C-1: Four Graphic Mouse Cursors

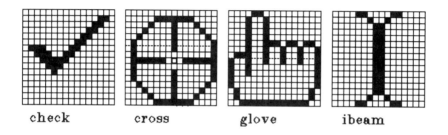

check   cross   glove   ibeam

Additional graphics cursors can be created using the MOUSEPTR utility and may be included directly in the application program or added to the mouse unit.

The Mlightpen Method

Both text and graphic versions of the Mlightpen method are provided by the mouse unit. The Mlightpen procedure is the same for both text and graphics versions and is called with a single Boolean parameter to either enable or disable lightpen emulation by the mouse:

```
Mlightpen( TRUE );                           { lightpen enabled  }
Mlightpen( FALSE );                          { lightpen disabled }
```

A

Access 8, 99
  public versus private 63
Ancestors 9
  and constructor/destructor methods 31
Arguments, 30

B

Base object class 376
  access to 63
Binary trees 315, 357
  searching 327
Binding 193
Bubble sort 276, 286
Button objects 141-142
Button Styles 153
Buttons 156

C

C programming
  conventions of 15
  and null pointers 376
  and overloading 69
  and the Precede function 281
C++ programming

conventions of 15
and destructor/constructor methods 30
and inheritance 7, 191
and MOUSEPTR program 90, 107
and multiple ancestors 66
and null pointers 376
and overloading 33, 69
and streams 45
and virtual methods 206, 377
Child methods 190
Child objects 184
cin 45
Circle 64
Circle::draw 42
Circle::erase 43
Clean-up methods 263
Color settings 149
Compatibility 184
Constructor calls 30, 207
  and button operations 146
  constructor method 29, 209
  cout 45
  cprintf 149
  explicit 219
  overloaded 262
  properties of 31

Cursors
    graphic 90
    hardware vs. software 103
    options 104

D

Data abstraction 183
Data elements 8
Data fields
    inheritance 191
    and Turbo C++ 11
Declarations 220
    record versus object 3
Delayed response 231
delete operator 265
    delete vs. destructor 266
Derived class
    access 63
    descendant 9
    and inheritance 64
Descendant objects 184, 215, 220, 376
Destructor calls 264
    and button operations 146
    implicit 285
Destructor method 29, 266
    calling 290
    properties of 31
Destructor tasks 266
Dispose 263
Dot-referencing
    to gain access to record fields 12
    in object-oriented Pascal 39
Drivers 98
Duplication 38
Dynamic binding 193
Dynamic instances 261
Dynamic objects 29, 276
    allocation and initialization 262
    instances 219
Dynamic variables. *See* Dynamic objects 276

E

Early binding 193
EGA resolution 107
Encapsulation 10
    defined 2
Endpads 220

Entry sort 276, 278
Erase 264
Exist flag 145
Extending objects 185
Extensibility 206, 215
    object 215
    programming for 216

F

Files
    include 88
Forward compatibility 184
Friends of classes 71
Function names 39

G

Global elements 31
Global pointers 287
Global variables 190
GMouse
    function 9, 100
gprintf 185
Graphics buttons 141, 156
    and true/false states 142

H

Hot-spot 104

I

Identifiers 65
    uppercase versus lowercase 39
Implicit destructor calls 285
Include declaration 88
    file 190
Inheritance 2
    and C++ 7
    and constructor/destructor methods 31
    defined 2
    multiple 66
    and objects 63, 216
Initialization parameters 219
Inline disadvantages 34

K

Keywords 63

L

Late binding 193, 216

Libraries 11
Linked lists 277, 375
Local pointers 286

M
Memory pointers 190
Methods 8, 11
   child 190
   constructor 29, 92
   declaration of 9
   destructor 29, 92, 264
   dummy 184
   implementation of 12
   properties of constructor/destruc-
      tor 30
   redundant 70
   static 201
   virtual 31, 42
Mickeys 97
Mouse 92-98, 101-102
   function 6, 16, 95, 98
   and Mmotion 97
   as graphics cursor 90
   button mouse selection 143
   coordinates 149, 228
   drivers 98
   GMouse Implementation 99
   mpos 94
   object 89, 92
Mconceal 98
Mlightpen 101
Mmotion 97
Mmove_ratio 97
Mmoveto 94
Mouse object 89
Mpressed 95
Mshow 93
Mspeed 98
Mxlimit 96
Mylimit 96
   Reset 92
   Set_Cursor (Graphics) 100
   Set_Cursor (Text) 102
   TMouse 101
Multiple trees 337

N
Names 66
New 207, 262

Nodes 290
Null characters 282
Null pointer 276, 375

O
Object inheritance 216
Object instances 219
Object methods 9
OO programming 8
   and reusability 38
Objects
   complex 263
   and data abstraction 183
   definitions 90
   and descendants 184, 220
   and inheritance 3, 5, 63
   pointers to 262
   as variables 6
Operators 45
   scope resolution 71
   the delete 31
Overloading 32, 221

P
Parameters 141
Pascal 30
Pixels 94
Point 64
Point::Create 42
Pointers 276, 376
   global 287
   memory 190
   null 276
Polymorphism
   defined 2, 16
   and early binding 193
   late binding 193
Precede function 280-281
printf 148, 185
Private 8, 63
Protected 8
Public 8, 10, 63

Q
Qualified names 66
Quotes 88

R
RAM 338

Recursive procedures 325, 328-329
Redeclaration
    of data fields 191
    of static method as virtual method
        206
Registers 92
Relationships 71-72
Relinking 332
Reserved words 63
Resolution operator 12
Reusability 38

S
Scope 285
    access operator 12
Scope resolution 188-189
ScrollBar
    constructor 221
    Draw 223
    EraseThumbPad 227
    methods 219
    RestoreViewPort 223
ScrollHit 228
SetLoc 223
SetThumbPad 226
Scrollbar control objects 218
Scrollbar object 217
Search index 360
Siblings 102
Simple sort 286
Smalltalk 10
Sort
    binary 315
    bubble 276, 278
    entry 278
    lists 277
Square object 44
    and duplication 38
Square::draw 43
Stack overload 66
Static instances 261, 275
Static methods 201
    compiler operations 191
    inheritance 185, 188
    redefinition 206
    versus virtual methods 193, 205
Static object instances 29, 219
Step count 97
Streams 45

T
TBoxes 143-144
Text button 156
    parameters 141
    using the Create method 146
This 267
Tilde character 30
Toolboxes 215, 217
Tracking operations 94
Tree structures 315, 337
Turbo C 185
    and ASCII conversion 105
    and the mouse object 90
Turbo C++ 10
    and clean-up 264
    and the malloc function 262
    Integrated Development Environ-
        ment 217
Turbo Pascal 10
    and virtual methods 206

U
Unions 31
Utilities 104

V
Variables
    as classes (objects) 6
    global 14
Viewport 152
Virtual Method Table 201, 205,
    216, 267
Virtual methods 42, 201
    and constructor/destructor meth-
        ods 31
    creation of 207
    descendants 206
    versus static methods 193